Teaching Reading with Words in Color

A Scientific Study of the Problems of Reading

Caleb Gattegno

Educational Solutions Worldwide Inc.

A New Dynamic Approach to the Teaching of Reading and Writing.

First published in 1967. Reprinted in 2010.

Copyright ©1967-2010 Educational Solutions Worldwide Inc.
Author: Caleb Gattegno
All rights reserved
ISBN 978-0-87825-258-9

Educational Solutions Worldwide Inc.
2nd Floor 99 University Place,
New York, N.Y. 10003-4555
www.EducationalSolutions.com

Foreword

Early in 1964, the United States publisher of Words in Color heard from various users that the existing Teacher's Guide (1962) was less explicit than they needed and asked for additional guidance. This book contains it.

A prepublication edition has been circulated for about two years and has been found to meet most of teachers' needs. The present edition coming almost six years after the first Guide (which had a number of reprints with minor alterations) has not been written to replace the previous one in all respects. For instance, a number of general considerations covering a chapter will be found only in the original Guide, but they are not necessary to understand the techniques of teaching in this program.

Some minor changes have been made in the pupil and classroom materials since they were first published. This book takes them into account.

Research in the field of reading is now taking a new turn because Words in Color has been made available. Rather than test people before and after participation in a program, Words in Color has built in a feedback procedure which informs student and teacher continuously of what is going on. This very new feature of the teaching—very different from the stimulus-response procedure, particularly since it accepts errors as the concomitant of lack of mastery and permits everyone to have as much individual initiative and independence as needed—could be taken to be the first cybernetic approach to reading.

In the preparation of this text, my friends and colleagues in the United States and in England have spent endless hours revising and advising. In particular, I owe Dorothea Hinman a debt of gratitude that no words can repay.

C. Gattegno

Table of Contents

Introduction 1

Chapter I The First Certificate of Reading 11

Section 1 Some Conventions of Writing and
Recording English 12

Section 2 First Use of the Pointer – Words and Sentences
Through Visual Dictation 1 17

Section 3 Second Use of the Pointer – Sentences Through
Visual Dictation 2. Study of Some Links-by-Transformation
Between Words 31

Section 4 Oral and Visual Dictation. Visual Dictation 3 :
The Worksheets and Testing 48

Chapter II Meeting the Sounds of English 69

Section 1 Word Charts 2 to 12. Visual Dictations 2 and 3.
Oral Dictation 72

Section 2 Book 2—Words, Sentences, Stories 98

Section 3 Worksheets—Control of Progress 104

Section 4 Word Building Book—Phonemes and Some of Their
Graphemes 121

Chapter III Meeting of Spellings 127

Section 1 Word Charts 13-21 — Visual Dictations 2 and 3 128

Section 2 Word Building Book, Phonic Code, Visual
Dictation 1: 142

Section 3 Oral Dictation 153

Section 4 Book 3 and the Worksheets 156

Section 5 The Book of Stories and Worksheet 13 169

Chapter IV A Study of Structures 179

Section 1 Dictation and Writing 180

Section 2 Games with Word Cards 183

Section 3 Worksheet 14 193

Section 4 Conclusion — Self and Speech 201

Appendix 1 ....**205**

Appendix 2 ....**209**
    A. Description of the Materials 209
    B. Alternative Sequences 210

Appendix 3 .... **213**
    Analysis of Links-by-Transformation Between Words on Word
        Charts 3, 4, 5, and 6.. 213
        for Word Chart 3..215
        for Word Chart 4.. 216
        for Word Chart 5 217
        for Word Chart 6 218

Appendix 4 .... **217**

Appendix 5 .... **219**

Appendix 6 .... **231**

Bibliography **239**

Index...**245**

Introduction

This text is a new publication and is designed to function as a reasonably adequate guide for teachers. The first guide for teachers (1962) can be used as a complement. Six years of progress (1961-1967) in the study of *Words in Color* in the classroom have led to the development of new ways of working and have crystallized outlooks only suspected earlier. These are presented here in print for the first time. While it was always known that the Pilot Edition of 1962 could not show the author's future experience, it was not clear then that life would offer the opportunities for making distinctive progress in a number of directions. The passage of time has actualized what could only be presumed at first, and luck has done the rest.

As a teacher, the author found a number of opportunities for further development of the approach while teaching very young children, other opportunities while working with some children who had encountered various reading difficulties, and still others in intensive work with adolescents and adults having differing backgrounds and who were nonreaders or in serious reading difficulty. This learning by the author-as-teacher on these occasions was often witnessed by observers and later discussed with them. Progressively, certain remarks became the focal points for further inquiry. This yielded, in the author's opinion, remarkable insights which in turn either provided the proper foundation for the existing techniques or proposed new techniques to serve some of the newly discovered purposes. During this time, the study of reading developed into the study of people engaged in activities yielding skill in reading as a by-product. This shift from the conventional view that reading is a separate activity to that of seeing it as a by-product of the extension of intellectual and linguistic powers is, perhaps, the most important single finding made so far. As a result, the researcher was faced with the question of what one must do, while being mentally active in certain ways in order that, finally, one discovers that one can read.

Indeed, reading is a skill. One does not know reading itself; one knows how to read, as one knows *how* to walk, talk, or drive an automobile. Practice, not rules or instructions, teaches us how to drive. The analogy between learning to read and learning to drive can serve us here, for the level of experience sufficient to obtain a driving license is far inferior to that reached by most drivers. The license indicates only that one has shown a degree of familiarity with some situations that are commonly encountered in the usual environment, and that one can cope with them. Driving in *all* sorts of circumstances follows; and it is this that provides the full-fledged skill of driving.

Beginners at school can be considered as having to qualify for a license to read, which we will call the "First Certificate of Reading." It is only *after* this that through practice the learner advances further and further into reading, meeting greater demands and some hazards. At what level, then, can we give this first certificate, and what comes after?

We shall see in Chapter I which activities lead with certainty to the successful passing of the test for the first reading certificate. These activities must cover, in a schematized but nevertheless natural manner, *all* the fundamental techniques that make reading as smooth and organic an activity as possible.

Just as the environment for a learner-driver cannot encompass all possible situations, so the language for which the first certificate is designed for the learner-reader will also be restricted, though the exercises using it will not.

The concept of a *restricted language* is an important one for teachers of reading and of languages. We use the term "restricted" for all those sectors of a language which permit the display of some, but not all, of the normal linguistic behaviors associated with the whole of the language.

This, of course, includes the language, spoken and written, which every individual uses. For there is so much of the mother tongue which is unknown to any one of us. A reference to the vast accumulation of words in our expanding technology makes this obvious. This does not, however, mean for one moment that our reading skills are of inferior quality.

So it will be with beginning readers. Their skill will develop through use of the selected restricted language we introduce in Chapter I. The first restricted languages will then be replaced by languages less and less restricted once the learners' skills are fully developed. For the learners, there will be a continual expansion of the field of experience and of what can be done as they develop greater facility and experience. After the first certificate has been obtained by the learners, the role of the teacher becomes one of presenting challenges extending students' powers, those newly acquired or those newly displayed. This leads to an awareness on the part of the students and teachers that more can be gained by practicing in situations and under conditions differing from the initial ones, although they still make use of what has been mastered earlier.

Another important concept is that of the *cumulative effect of learning*. This takes into account the fact that performances before and after the mastery of a skill are different. Practice develops a skill and, as the performance of the skill increases, more highly developed practice increases it still further.

Once, therefore, the student has obtained the first reading certificate, he can use these same skills to attack more difficult reading tasks and hence read more challenging texts. Thus, in Chapter II we describe how learners can be helped to meet, *in far less time than ever known before*, all the sounds of English.

In Chapter III we show a way of meeting rapidly the complete set of spellings for each of these sounds. Both stages—meeting all the sounds and then all the spellings—offer greater challenges than were met in the opening lessons.

It follows that learners can, early in their study, be made aware of grammar or of the structure of English which, as a language, presents additional challenges approached in Chapter IV. In this manner, we will have passed smoothly from the relatively simple activity of associating sound and sign to the very complex activity consisting of the study of texts to acquire linguistic and literary insights. Thus, this program provides a comprehensive introduction to the study of English.

However, as this program is concerned with introducing people to their language, we must ask ourselves questions that involve not only the language but people too.

Beginners bring with them to the first reading lesson a contribution in the form of spoken speech. This is, among other things, a flow of experiences concerned with the organization of parts of one's body to produce definite sounds in a definite sequence in order to convey a meaning. Beginning readers are thus already highly knowledgeable and skilled in a number of ways which they demonstrate by being capable of translating meanings into adequate sequences of sounds (words and sentences) which include such elements as stress, emphasis, intonation, timbre, structure, and a number of other dimensions unconsciously brought in to serve the end of communication. It is the intuition or awareness of meaning on the part of the speaker that calls up the adequate words to produce the proper flow of speech. In speaking, we translate meanings into words and into their accompanying supporting nonverbal forms of communication, such as head and face gestures, or pitch, stress, and intonation. We all know how to do this quite well, early in our lives.

To reach the meaning of any recorded speech—i.e. written language—we must in a sense "listen" to the sentences much as we do when we hear someone speaking. Underlying all written material there must be somewhere the spoken word, actually or potentially, with all of its characteristics. To read is to restore the voice to the printed page. This observation presents the teacher of reading with a number of problems, the most vital of which can be stated as: *helping the learner to understand the connection between the temporal aspect of spoken speech and the spatial arrangement of print.*

In order to read English we must (1) introduce an order in the movements of our eyes so that signs in each word are scanned from left to right just as they were put down in writing; (2) observe that the order of the words in the sentence is in the same direction; and (3) wait until the sentence is finished to extract the meaning that these words in their particular order were intended to convey.

The two-dimensional space of the page is not oriented in any specific direction. The straight line is so oriented but it is reversible, while *time* is ordered but not reversible. For this reason, in different languages, the direction in which speech is recorded or written down can be chosen arbitrarily, from the left or from the right. In some languages speech is recorded horizontally, in others, vertically. But in all languages the same respect for the temporal sequences is displayed when writing and reading.

In some languages writing is done above the line, in others below, and in still others both above and below. In some languages (the phonetic), each sound is represented by a single sign, and conversely in others (the non-phonetic—such as English), certain irregularities have evolved, while in still others some sounds are not recorded at all and must be added by the reader (e.g., Arabic). But all these modalities of recording the various languages do not seem to present major problems to vast numbers of learners, who manage to master the operation common to all languages—phonetic or non-phonetic—of translating speech into print (writing) and print into speech (reading).

Indeed, the problems are *not* in the correspondences between spoken and written forms—different in different languages—but rather in the relationship of teacher to learner, and in the techniques of teaching. If the teacher is aware of what a learner has to master in order to make the correspondence, and knows techniques to help the learner achieve this, all goes quickly and smoothly. But if the teacher forgets that what is to be communicated is meaning, through finding speech in print in a natural way, or if the teacher ignores the fact that learning requires concentration without distraction, then learners have trouble.

Let us list some aspects of language which learners must deal with to bridge the gap between spoken and written speech. Then let us order these findings to produce a learning plan based on the reality of the requirements of this process.

1   The conventions of the written code of each language, being arbitrary, cannot be justified on rational grounds and need to be introduced as purely arbitrary aspects of a game played without any relationship to the meaning or spelling of the spoken language of the pupil—in this case, English. And it is in this manner that we meet the left to right convention, the alignment of letters and words with respect to the horizontal, and see that certain designs or sets of designs are associated with certain sounds.

2   Some languages use single signs to represent their syllables, and such languages have been found the easiest to be acquired by native readers. English, on the other hand, uses vowels and consonants. In reality, vowels can be sounded alone while consonants only sound when linked with vowels to form syllables. So, though we do use different signs for writing both vowels and consonants, we sound vowel signs on their own but *never* sound by themselves the signs that stand for the consonants. When multiple consonants are part of the written words, we have techniques that make learners capable of sounding them blended—as they come naturally in speech—rather than in isolation.

3   To maintain *time* at the center of the activity of reading, we shall use a pointer as a linking instrument between the signs that form words or between the words that form sentences. The actual movements of the pointer reveal the temporal sequence that needs to be followed in order to generate the instructions necessary for the learner to determine for himself the corresponding spoken word or sentence.

4   In addition, when words are uttered, only the complete statement with *proper intonation and rhythm* can convey the full meaning. This aspect of time, obviously present in speech, can be lost if one reads orally from the printed line as if each word were isolated from the rest. Hence, the kind of reading in which the learner utters one word after another carefully, slowly, and mechanically is of no use if he can be instead induced from the start to hold in his mind a set of words he has scanned, and then to say them naturally in the manner of everyday speech. Reading-as-talking is of fundamental importance from the beginning.

5   Anyone who hears words does so by receiving them in the ear, a very sophisticated instrument which can perform a number of tasks at the same

time. It sorts out harmonics, ignores irrelevant noises, filters some of the sounds—and so on. A living ear does this all the time. The ability to analyze sounds is with us from the first few months of our lives and it guides us competently on many occasions all day long. But the ear cannot normally do away with temporal sequences; sounds are in time and so is the functioning of the ear. The eye also functions in time, as a scanning instrument, but in addition it photographs vast expanses. Space therefore *can* be taken in as a whole in one glance and when this happens time is not really consumed.

But when reading, the eye is not employed to take in the whole page at once. Indeed, all words save one, or one and its immediate neighbors on the right, are ignored. While scanning, the eye does not function panoramically. Indeed, we simply retain the words in our mind until meaning is conveyed, and then drop the image of the words scanned in the sentence once the eye has passed over them. Thus, the eye does not operate photographically on words when reading, any more than the mind retains words when we speak, write, or listen.

To use the eye when reading is a specialized exercise. This accounts for the multitude of slips of the pen, the typewriter, the typographic compositor, and the legion of unnoticed printing errors—all far more numerous than errors of the tongue. But if we wish to study words as designs, we *do* need to use the eye panoramically as a photographic instrument, particularly if no rational principle will generate the word from other elements that may be already in the mind. To achieve correct spelling, therefore, we have to "photograph" words, not simply scan them or utter them as in reading. Hence, special exercises are needed to induce learners to look at, take in, and evoke words as designs. *Color* can help to convey a *phonetic clue* to words like a relief map does to the spatial arrangement of an area, easing the task of the eye functioning panoramically, as a camera. Consequently, color will be used in the designs of letters and words in order to reduce the chances of overlooking correct spellings.

Reading demands the use of mental processes that are opposite in function to those used in spelling. Therefore, special exercises and materials must be devised to avoid the neutralizing effects of one use upon the other. Normally the eye is synthetic in its functioning, and the ear analytic. But both can function in the other way because the mind that rules them is both by nature.

6   If one becomes aware of words as aspects of reality and starts being interested in them as such, there is no end to the observations that can be made about their structure, and the relationship of sounds, forms, and meanings. This can be ex-tended to sets of words and to the analysis of sentences in order to observe which are general behaviors and which are particular ones. For example, the effect of reversing the order of words, particularly of verbs, can be noted. That is, can we say "is it" other than as a question?

To be concerned with such matters is an indication of the freeing of the mind from other preoccupations which earlier were deemed vital. At one time the mechanics of reading required all the energies of the learners for their performance. Now we may move from purely technical considerations on to a linguistic study, and later pass from a linguistic to a literary level, when decoding no longer spontaneously calls on all of the learner's available energy.

7   Imbedded in this early study of words and their individuality is the study of the order of their component signs. What would happen were the order to be reversed? a sign added? or both done? or another sign inserted? or all three operations performed in succession?

The *Game of Transformations* is based on links suggested by the phonetic structures of words, not their meanings. It results in an awakening of the learner to a reality which as a user of words he cannot stop to perceive. He realizes that signs in words are signs that may have a life of their own, that the creators of words may have chosen particular forms for reasons lost in the past, and that it is always possible to produce new words either arbitrarily or by fusion of others, and by other principles.

Linguistic awareness is the reward of progress in the use and observation of words. This in turn helps further progress to take place in one's linguistic education, which in turn permits the meeting of deeper and more demanding challenges.

8   Such linguistic awareness can take the form of analysis of sentences of which grammatical awareness is one side and sensitivity to ambiguity, precision, and rigor another. It must be understood that the possibility exists of meeting all the challenges within a restricted language, and that it is not necessary to wait until a certain age or a certain stage has been reached before attempting to make awareness more clearly present. As will be shown later, a change of intonation is as clear an indication of recognition of meaning as will later be the explicit statement of a rule.

Formalized grammar is the explicit stating of how language is used correctly and adequately.

Rejection of nonsensical or contradictory statements as useless is a sure sign of understanding that content, not only form, is carried by words.

9   In this whole approach, the education of the *linguistic powers* of the learners *in toto* is achieved. This includes the reading of books, preferably of books that bring valuable experience to the readers and make sense of the activity of reading, providing a channel for growth through *vicarious experience* or experience by proxy as contrasted with growth through direct experience. And it includes also expressing one's own inner experiencing of events and insights so that others may share in these by proxy.

Words in Color is successful if learners understand that the successive certificates of reading acquired through the program are merely stepping stones toward independent and critical reading and creative writing, and toward the use of a vocabulary which is continually expanding and increasingly sensitive and adequate to the meaning the writer intends to communicate.

Chapter I
The First Certificate of Reading

In this chapter we meet the first challenges of reading and writing and offer a solution which should be effective with all children except for a very small fraction requiring some other treatment.

As we proceed, both the classroom activities of the teacher and of the pupils will be outlined. It should be recognized that when a definite recommendation is made and stressed and the teacher neglects it, responsibility for any eventual trouble encountered must rest with her and not with the program. An author can convey his experiences only through words, diagrams, and pictures, leaving it to the reader to supply the understanding and the actual classroom performance. It will be an understanding in this text that the writer will not trespass and take upon himself what only teachers in their classrooms can do safely and knowingly. To work together in this context is to leave to each what each can do best in the circumstances.

The initial steps in the process of learning to read will be presented. They aim principally at providing an insight into the conventions of the recording of speech in English. This will be accompanied by a study that must not be by-passed even though it could be said that the material explored is not part of the English language. While the pointer and its uses will be met from the start, special sections will be devoted to this tool since its role increases constantly throughout most of the program. In explaining the uses of the pointer, material will be considered which when mastered permits the learners to earn their first reading certificate.

The early work with the pointer produces words that can be recorded and which appear in colored print on Word Chart 2, and on the pages of *Book 1* in black on white. With these words, sentences can be made. The book and the Chart are introduced and used in conjunction with the remaining materials for this phase—the *Word Building* Book and Worksheet 1. The chapter ends with a discussion of the testing of reading and of some of its specialized aspects.

It should be remembered that restricted languages (as defined in the Introduction) are the only ones involved, and that they make it possible that nothing learned need be unlearned and that nothing should absorb the learner's energies uselessly.

Section 1
Some Conventions of Writing and Recording English

1   English is written upon horizontal lines, with parts of some signs going beneath the line and parts of others rising above the other signs. Conventions of writing such as this can best be explained if we introduce as the very first step an *arbitrary* language having only *one* sound and *one* sign.

2   The sign we choose is *a*, which we produce on the board in the usual handwritten form rather than in the alternative shape a of Roman print. To *a* we associate the sound that readers find first in the left-hand letter in the English word *at*.

Every time this sign is drawn, the learners utter the associated sound. The teacher writes this sign in white chalk on the chalkboard a number of times and elicits the "same" sound on each occasion.

The teacher now writes on the board the white signs—some larger, some smaller, or alternately larger and smaller. Sometimes kindergarten pupils raise their voices when the sign is larger and whisper when it is very small.

Chapter I
The First Certificate of Reading

This spontaneous feedback from the class can be accepted without comment despite the fact that it is usually enjoyable. Pupils soon forget about this once the letters are written consistently in an acceptable average size.

Since there is only one letter and only one sound, there is neither danger of confusion nor reason to forget. Repetition of the sign, of its associated sound, or the cessation of such sound—these are the only activities possible. But as the game of repetition is played it is noticed that a new variable appears: the *time* taken between two successive utterances. One can act on this by reducing it or prolonging it. The variation in the lengths of time between two successive utterances can then be shown as a conventional spatial representation: two a signs are placed *contiguously* if the time is just sufficient to indicate that two separate *a*'s have been uttered instead of one

aa

and a *small distance* apart on the horizontal line when some perceptible time is left between the two utterances

a a

This is followed by:

- *Visual Dictation.* The pointer is used to touch one sign *a* as many times as seems fruitful. The pointer can be used increasingly rapidly, or its speed reduced, or it can be used with varying rhythms. Pupils reply according to the rules of the game. When the pointer taps out this rhythm for example,

    a aa a aa aa a a aaa aa

    the teacher can easily hear whether the replies correspond or not.[1]

---

[1] In working with remedial groups (elementary, high school, adult), the teacher may find that since they can work for longer, more intensive periods, and also need to feel rapid progress for self-confidence, it is often wise to use only Visual Dictation on the chalkboard until 5 vowels and 4 consonants (the scope of Word Chart 2) or sometimes 6 vowels and 6 consonants (the scope of Word Charts 2 and 3) have been introduced. With students

- Then the teacher writes several groupings of *a* on the board (one group at a time) in horizontal lines which might look something like these:

  aaa
  a aa aaa
  aa aaa a aaa
  a aaa aa aaa

  and asks pupils to respond to a whole grouping by a single gesture of the pointer.
  This gives practice in seeing that the amount of distance between signs indicates the time pattern for utterance and begins to make clear (1) that written "words" are separated from each other by a larger amount of space than the space which is conventionally left between letters in a word, and (2) that in reading, the decoding moves from left to right.

- *Reading.* Page 1 of *Book 1* is read silently by the students. After this, some of them may read it aloud to the others, while those not speaking watch the pointer to see if they agree.

- *Oral dictation.* "Sentences" like

  a aa   aaa aa
  aa a   a aaa aa
  aaa a

  are spoken by the teacher. The pupils may write them on paper or on the chalkboard (or perhaps find where the teacher has written them on the chalkboard or where they are printed in *Book 1*).

- Another exercise. The pupils may be given an opportunity to dictate their own sentences to the rest of the class. This may be done orally, or with the pointer, or each pupil may create his own distinctive "sentences" on his paper if writing comes easily.

3   In a similar way, the "language of *u*" (as in us) is introduced and the same game played. The sign *u* is written with a pale yellow chalk.

---

who have a small sight vocabulary or a little spelling or knowledge of the alphabet, this forces them to leave aside these inadequate guides and play an entirely "new game."

Chapter I
The First Certificate of Reading

Page 2 of *Book 1* is now to be read.

4   Up to this point we have been able to use repetition only as a procedure to follow in the case of "single-sound languages." Now, however, *a* and *u*, used together, enable us to imagine a "two-sound language," and we find that we have at our disposal a new tool: *combination*. Of the various ways in which one or more of each of these signs can be linked, the most valuable is reversal: we can distinguish *au* from *ua*.

These are first met in Visual Dictation when the pointer reverses *its* direction, touching *a* before *u* (*a, u*) and then *u* before *a* (*u, a*).[2] Then the reversals may be met in the spatial order, from left to right, of *au* and *ua*. (Many similar combinations using some *a*'s and some *u*'s can also be dealt with in this way.) It is thus made clear early in the program that "words" are read aloud by first sounding the sign at the left and then the signs that are contiguous. This will remain the rule in all subsequent reading. Page 3 of *Book 1* is used for such reading.

5   In like manner *i* (pink), *e* (pale blue), and *o* (orange)—sounding as in *it, pet*, and *lot* respectively—are introduced and practiced through the same sequence of activities already outlined.[3]

Pages 4 to 9 of *Book 1* give examples of "words" in the various successive restricted "languages" already presented, some words having one sound only, others employing as many as five vowel sounds. It is to be noted that when vowels follow each other rapidly, their sounds merge to form diphthongs and triphthongs, etc.

6   Word Chart 1 is the permanent record in color of what has been mastered so far. It goes on the wall *after* reading has been done either with the aid of (1) the pointer used on the chalkboard by the teacher (Visual Dictation), or (2) *Book 1,* in which the pupils "read" silently by sounding "words" to themselves or aloud by uttering them in turn to a small group.

---

[2] Again, with remedial cases, the teacher may choose to integrate the new sound with *a* through Visual Dictation only and move on to introduce the next sound, leaving until later writing combinations on the board, reading in the Book, and oral dictation. These aspects can be taken up when a less restricted language is in use when Word Charts 2 and 3, and Book 2 have been introduced (see footnote 15 on p.33).
[3] See above and also the schema on this page.

All this can be summed up in the following table[4] of alternative directions for Visual Dictation:

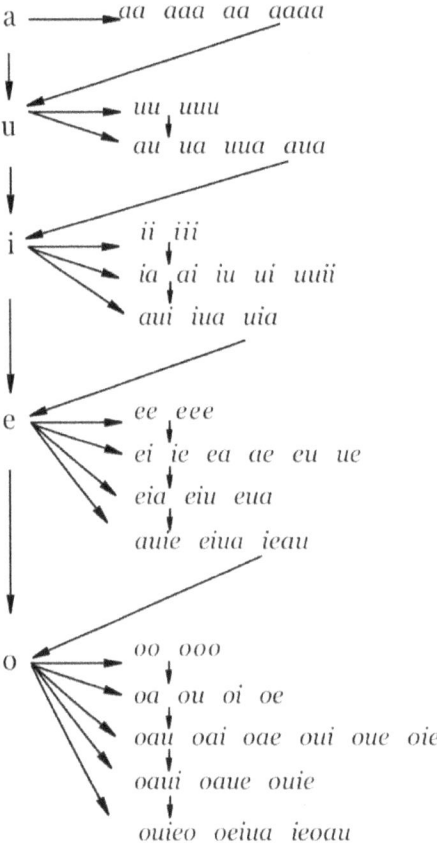

If, when introducing a new sign, teachers adopt the practice of uttering clearly and distinctly its corresponding sound *once and once only* for the pupils to hear, they will soon become convinced of the value of this practice. For it is the learner who must prove his mastery of the situation through his actions. It does not assist him if the teacher displays the teacher's mastery. Repetition of the sound is therefore to be avoided, no matter how hard it seems for teachers to break traditional habits. The teacher can best help her pupils by giving them a chance to sort out for *themselves* the problems that they confront, rather than by giving answers to their questions, or by asking them to chant responses after her. Allowed the opportunity to develop his *inner criteria* further and further regarding

---

4 Contributed by D. E. Hinman.

the reality he himself has met, the student learns to go to his own sources to find answers, and does not depend on outside authority. Often silence and patient waiting provide the best means of assistance. Sometimes a simple silent movement of the pointer will alert the student to a factor of reality not yet taken into account by him.

Section 2
First Use of the Pointer–Words and Sentences Through Visual Dictation 1

1   Teachers who have seen lessons of *Words in Color* know that the pointer is an extremely important instrument and they try to master its uses as early as possible. Indeed, teachers learn to help and not to interfere in the process of learning. Through it they become silent and hence very effective. Through the pointer, *time* is restored to its cardinal place in learning to read, and speed of reading is continuously increased.

We have already seen that a mastery of the five vowels (*a, u, i, e, o*, in their respective colors representing five distinctive sounds), and their repetition in combinations or permutations, is gained through Visual Dictation, i.e., through the use of the pointer.

2   In this program, *consonants are not sounded in isolation*; but syllables are formed and sounded. The first consonant met has the shape *p* (dark brown). Here is one possible arrangement on the chalkboard for all the signs introduced thus far:

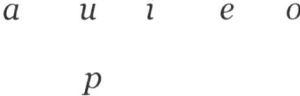

From the beginning, the brown sign is only sounded with one of the above vowels. With the first vowel, *ap* is produced (as heard in the beginning of the word *apple*). This combination is not written down. It is formed by moving (sliding) the pointer from *a* to *p*. The teacher says first, "Sound this," (showing *a*); then, while moving from *a* to *p* she says, "For the white immediately followed by the brown, we say *ap*." After forming this pair again rapidly with the pointer so that all the learners can see it, the teacher asks, "What is this, then?" asking for the sounding of *ap* once more in order to have it spoken and heard by the learners and not by herself. The teacher then switches with the pointer from the pair (*a, p*) to the pair (*u, p*) without sounding it, trying to find out whether some of the learners can make the transfer which blends the yellow sign with the brown in the same manner as they have done with the white and brown. If the answer is obtained and all pupils say *up*, a shift to the next pair (*i, p*) follows, and then to the remaining pairs (*e, p*) and (*o, p*).

It is most important to recognize that when the transfer is made to the combination of the consonant *p* with the other four vowels, a number of things have taken place:

1. memory has not been loaded, since the learner is not required to retain anything; rather, there is a reason which directs him to say what he now says;

2. initiative at a level not too demanding has been passed on to the learners;

3. judgment of correctness has been left to the learners;

4. reward has been the usual biological one—the recognition of the fact that ability to function leads to better functioning.

As to a reward for the learner, teachers who previously have found it necessary to provide adequate motivation by congratulating their students on each achievement will prove to themselves that in this approach—if they refrain from the usual reaction—the learners no longer need this praise, and that it even interferes with and distracts them from their learning. The excitement the pupils feel inwardly in meeting those challenges inherent in the intellectual game is more than sufficient motivation for continuing.

3   It is possible now to combine such syllables in differing orders, but it is not recommended. In English, unstressed vowels get distorted, and *apap* does not sound as *ap* repeated, any more than the beginning of *upon* sounds like the isolated word *up*.

4   So we move on to another exercise, that of reversal. Moving the pointer from the brown to the white, we form the syllable corresponding to the

pair *p* and *a*. When linking these two signs quickly with the pointer, some pupils may suggest the sound *pa* (as in *pad*). If they do not, the teacher says, "This is *pa*." And then she continues, "What do you say for . . ." leaving the syllable unsaid but indicating *pu, pe, pi,* and *po* with the pointer. The order of presentation is immaterial, but it is important that pupils who have already learned to reverse *a, u* into *u, a* and so on, see these new syllables as the reverses of those met earlier.

Note that if *pa* is the reverse of *ap*, the converse is true and should be requested in a number of ways:

1. how, for example, *ip* with the pointer, and after the learners read it, ask for its reverse;

2. immediately after, ask for the reverse of the sound just made by the pupils;

3. immediately after that, ask for the reverse of any one of the five syllables;

4. or ask for the reverse of the reverse of the reverse of them;

5. or ask a pupil to show (with the pointer) one of the syllables sounded;

6. or ask a pupil to point to its reverse.

This type of game should further establish that each syllable has a reverse which can be thought of and sounded.

To strengthen the imagination, this game can be played with the eyes shut, teacher and learners referring to the pairs by the colors found in the sequence of their signs. For instance, one could ask, "What is the reverse of the reverse of the sound for the pair *pink, brown* (or of any other pair)?"

5 Of all the syllables used so far, *up*, alone, is a word in the English language. It is *not* necessary to draw pupils' attention to this fact; there is no harm in their not noticing, in the midst of this game with sounds and signs, that they have produced a "word" they already know. The learners are concerned with other, more important, matters.

6   As explained above, in order to form words from the above syllables, we must avoid the distortion of sound due to stress. Hence, we must restrict ourselves to the *fusion, merging*, or *blending* of reverse syllables, beginning with the syllable which starts with the consonant (*pa*) and fusing it with the reverse which ends with the consonant (*ap*). In this way *pap, pup, pip, pep,* and *pop* are all generated, all of them English words and most of them used by young learners. To obtain the blending, yet without giving the answer, the teacher can adopt either of two techniques. Since it is mastery of the first example chosen that will lead to the rest, it is important to give the necessary attention and time to it, and to permit the learners to discover the answer. It is our experience that they always do the blending themselves if really helped by the teacher's *silence*. She may, however, talk to explain what must be done to produce this next step in the game.

- The pointer moves from *p* to *o*, forming *po*. It stops for a second at *o* so as to elicit from the pupils the now familiar *po*, and then returns from *o* to *p* to get the sound of the reverse, *op*. This is repeated a number of times in succession, the pointer moving only when the right sounds are produced.

  The rhythm is then speeded up as fast as is needed to make the one continuous movement from *p* to *o* and back to *p*. The teacher can then request a single sound from the two syllables that have been uttered in increasingly rapid succession. Someone usually offers *pop*.

  This is immediately followed by a transfer to these transformations:

  > (*pa, ap*) into *pap*
  > (*pu, up*) into *pup*
  > (*pi, ip*) into *pip,* and
  > (*pe, ep*) into *pep*

  When this has been achieved, the teacher may pause to inquire for the first time what meaning these sounds evoke. It is not yet the moment to give definitions for such words sounded or written, but it is reasonable, once so many have been obtained through the blending process, to spend a minute or so to make sure that the game is now going to produce English words and serve useful purposes.

Even a sentence, *pop up*, can be dictated visually by making two combinations follow each other rapidly; this usually evokes a delighted response from the learners, (*pep up* is also possible.)

- It may happen, however, that some learners are still unable to blend the sounds after the teacher has used the pointer as above. She can, in this case, ask the learners to play a new game, in which one pretends that a sound can be held in one's hand. Pointing at the syllable *pa*, for instance, the teacher obtains its sound from the class and suggests that they hold it in their closed left hands.

"What have you got in your hand?" is a serious question in this context and is answered seriously by all as *pa*. The teacher then asks for its reverse to be placed in the *right* hand, which is then closed. The teacher makes sure that the pupils understand by asking successively, but in any order, "What have you got in your left hand? your right hand? this hand? that hand?"

Pupils are now asked to do as the teacher does and put the sounds together, clapping the *right hand onto the left* as if holding *pa* and moving *ap* over onto it. At first the noise of the clapping may cover the resulting sound uttered, but a repeat will most probably yield *pap* from some. And they will be asked to say it loud or louder so that the whole class knows that this is the response the teacher was seeking. Reward for their efforts is in a transfer of their insight to the other pairs of reverses, not compliments or approval. This clapping technique can be used several times and may solve problems of blending on a number of occasions as the approach proceeds. All teachers will benefit from having mastered it.

7   The precise arrangement of the six signs on the chalkboard is not something the learners worry about, provided the teachers are convinced that in the game, so far, the order of the sounds in words as they are formed by the pointer are temporal. Any order which corresponds to the spatial order conventionally used in books is, as yet, a coincidence. A class could be given the signs in any one of the arrangements shown here, and teachers could test which suits their classes best. A new arrangement could, in fact, be used in each lesson, so that flexibility is emphasized as one of the essentials of the work.

a	p
	a u i e o
u	
	i
i	u e
	a p o
e p	u e
	a i o
o	p

In the experience of the author, any particular arrangement is more a convenience to the teacher at work than a problem to the learners. In any case, they have so far been working mentally and on sounds, rather than seeing words as complete designs, though visual imagery is being stimulated to some extent by the use of the individual signs.

8   Page 10 of *Book 1* can now be read. From among the many possibilities for producing syllables and words with the six signs available, a restricted selection has been made. Among those there are words in the English language, and these English words are distinguished on the pages of *Book 1* by underlining.

9   Let us complete this section on the use of the pointer by introducing the sign *t* (magenta). Since it is a consonant, it is not sounded alone, but the sound *at* is given when the pointer moves from the white sign to the magenta sign. The chalkboard may now look something like this:

a   u   i   e   o

p   t

Much of what has been established with the brown sign (*p*) can be transferred to the magenta one (*t*). The syllables

at, ut, it, et, ot

and their reverses

ta, tu, ti, te, to

can be formed. Thus, two more English words are found—*at* and *it*. (*to*, of course, has the sound as in *top*.)

The blending of these new syllables produces the English words

tat, tit, tot

and also

tut and tet

10   Page 11 of *Book 1* can now be read.

11   The merging of syllables to form words, now that two consonants are available for combining with the five vowels, can now produce further "words," some of which are part of the English language.

The pointer, used as above on (*p, a*) and (*a, t*) to form *pa* and *at*, will, with blending, produce *pat*, whose reverse is *tap*. The pointer, in a single sweeping movement, connects the brown, the white, and the magenta signs to elicit the sound *pat* and, in a movement in the opposite direction, creates *tap* in the minds of the pupils, and they can then say it. Passing on now to include the pink sign instead of the white in this sweeping movement of the pointer, we obtain two other words and their reverses:

pit and *tip*   or   *tip* and *pit*

depending on where the pointer has started.

Similarly, *top* and *pot* are generated.

Since *tep* is not an English word, we may decide not to generate it and limit ourselves to *pet*. But there is no harm in forming it, together with the "words" *tup* and *put*. The latter is not English with this sound of *u*, or with the single writing of the magenta. (Once the spelling of the double magenta sign is added on the board under the single writing of this sign, *putt* can be created to refer to a certain stroke or action in the game of golf.)

12 Having generated all this by the use of the pointer and the blending of syllables, we can do a number of things.

   1 Establish the convention that every time the pointer is moved away from the area of the seven signs on the chalkboard, it means that one word has been formed. We can then ask the pupils to hold in their minds the words formed by the pointer (either by touching particular signs individually or by sweeping over them). In this manner, sentences like these are produced:

tap it	*top it*
tip it	*pop it*
tip it up	*pot it*
pat it	*pet it*
tip it up pat	*pet it up*

   After each sentence, we may turn to the class and ask, "What have I shown?" showing it again, if need be, to elicit the sentence, and increasing the pointing speed so that the class is truly challenged. (If the teacher practices, she will become adept with the pointer.)

   Should the responses be poor, each word would be sounded in turn, and then two of them uttered together in the manner of speech. This could be followed by the whole sentence being recalled as the pointer indicates the remaining word or words, and the learners say the first two, now, clearly followed by the last part. The teacher may finally want to indicate the whole sentence again rapidly, so that it can be read as a whole when the pointer stops moving.

   2 A gradual speeding up of this reading from Visual Dictation is recommended. Pupils will thus know from the start that speed is one of the things that is to be achieved. Increases in speed are obtained by using the pointer with various

rhythms—at first on words or groups of words that have been well established. For example, if we consider *tip it up pat*, the sequence of quick alterations of the pattern of time could be:

1   *tip, it, up, pat*, shown separately and mastered as individual words;

2   *tip it*, shown as two words in quick succession;

3   *tip it up*, sounded as a sentence;

4   *tip it up*, quickly shown, followed a second later by *pat* to indicate the complete sentence, but with a slight pause to indicate there is to be a pause before *pat* and a special tone when it is uttered.

In the end, the only pattern acceptable is a well expressed sentence, uttered as in conversation, with its natural rhythm, pitch, and intonation.

No printed words have been shown so far. In the next section, we shall introduce Visual Dictation 2 which is a type of work where words are seen printed. Then pupils can easily see how to write words. In Visual Dictation 1, words and sentences are formed as time sequences by the pointer. This activity generates within the mind of the learner sequences of sounds which can be uttered since they have been heard and are known. The game involves auditory memory and, therefore, time and is more reminiscent of spoken words than evocative of printed words.

13   Page 12 of *Book 1* can now be read. On this page, another spelling of the magenta sign is given: *tt* as met in the word *putt* and the proper noun *pitt*. It is found in the arrangement of signs at the *top* of the page which corresponds to that on the chalkboard. Since *tt* has now been introduced in the same color as the t, identity in sound is indicated. The two words above can now be formed with the help of the pointer and sounded by the class.

14 At this stage, Table 1 of the *Word Building Book* is introduced.⁵ This is the first time this book is opened by the pupils.

Table 1 contains, in black and white and horizontally arranged, the vowels on one line and the two consonants on the lines underneath. These are equivalent to the first arrangement of the colored signs used by the teacher on the chalkboard, and to the arrangement met in black at the top of page 12 in *Book 1*.

$$a \quad u \quad i \quad e \quad o$$

$$p \quad t$$

$$tt$$

Table 1 in the *Word Building Book* is to be used by the pupils in the same way as the teacher has used the colored signs on the chalkboard—a pointer being used to link signs to form "words," some of which are part of the English language. The pupil's own pencil, the unsharpened or the eraser end, can serve as a pointer when the pupil is working in the *Word Building Book*.

Each pupil can now produce words with his "pointer" by touching the signs of the *Word Building Book* table. The teacher may first orally give a few "words" (some English, some not) and ask the class to move their pencil-pointers over the signs in the book in a way that produces in their minds what they have heard dictated, just as any of them might have done at the chalkboard by moving the pointer over the signs.

Pupils can now with their own *Word Building Book* point out their own combinations of signs, pointing to the signs and then uttering the "words" created just as they do when the teacher uses the pointer at the chalkboard.⁶

---

5 The numbers on the pages of the *Word Building Book* will be referred to as table numbers.
6 Later, on page 1 of Worksheet 1, there is an opportunity to keep a record of these discoveries (see p. 44).

Chapter I
The First Certificate of Reading

As vowels and syllables are the phonetic units, not all "words" formed can be sounded (for example, *pttptp*). But words such as *apt* or *opt* can be formed by substituting *ap* for *a* in *at*, or *op* for *i* in *it*. These two words are English and can be uttered, even if young children may not have consciously heard or used them before.[7]

15 The next step in progress toward the first reading certificate is the introduction of two sounds with the same shape. In this way, the learners know from the start that in written English, graphemes and phonemes are not related in a one-to-one correspondence. The shape of the sign introduced here is *s* (lilac). If the pointer moves from the pink sign (*i*) to the new sign (*s*) colored lilac, we have the word is. But if the yellow (*u*) is followed by a sign of the same shape (*s*) but colored lime green,[8] then we have us. The word sat is obtained when the lime s precedes the syllable at. Naturally, the teacher gives the class these or other examples to put the new sounds into circulation, and then continues with Visual Dictation 1, using an extended restricted language whose elements now are:

$$a \quad u \quad i \quad e \quad o$$

$$p \quad t \quad s \quad s$$

This arrangement, as has already been said, does not need to be made in two parallel and horizontal rows. Any arrangement would do, and teachers can find it challenging to try others. On Table 2 of the *Word Building Book*, and on pages 13, 14, and 15 of Book 1, they are horizontally arranged as here, but there is no reason for that other than typographical convenience. (Two more signs are also introduced in Table 2 because the

---

[7] Some teachers have found that they can assist those two or three pupils for whom there is still some barrier to full insight into how to combine signs to make words, by giving each child a piece of black paper. On it, there can be an arrangement in colored chalk (as has been done on the chalkboard) of the signs found on Table 1 of the *Word Building Book*—one of several different arrangements that have been suggested for the chalkboard on page 17. (Each child's sheet may have a different arrangement.) The teacher then dictates sounds, syllables, and words (and perhaps short sentences), while the pupils are asked to use their pencils as "pointers" and make the appropriate movements for what has been dictated (just as suggested above with the *Word Building Book* itself for students who have no problem). Since the arrangement of signs may be different for each pupil, the pupils must sort out by careful thinking where and when to move their "pointers." They cannot go by any memory of what they saw the teacher do with the pointer or what their neighbor is doing. The challenge of this new game is very great even with signs already met.

[8] In this *Guide*, names will be given to the colors to help teachers identify which sounds are being discussed, but the author strongly advises that these names *not* be used with the pupils except during the work in Chapter I—and even then, "curly purple" and "curly green" are suggested instead of "lilac" and "lime green".

lime *ss* and *'s* will soon be part of the lessons given in the classroom—see p. 23.)

16   Further practice of Visual Dictation 1 will permit us to extend the scope of word and sentence formation :

> *sat, sit, as, is, set, sap, sup,* as well as their reverses, are some of the words that can be generated now, while

> *is it, it is, it is us, it is pat, is pat up, pat sat up, sit up pat, set it up, set it up pat* are some sentences that can be generated now.

These sentences scarcely demand more of the learners than the work done when only two consonants were in use. Still, the sentence

> *is it as it is*

that is now possible represents a real boost to the pupils. They hardly expect such short and so-called "simple" words to give such an interesting result!

17   With very young beginners (4 or 5 years old), it may take a little time to get started on Visual Dictation 1, and they may not grasp the blending of syllables to form words in the manner we suggested earlier. These one-syllable words may provide the bridge to start them off. The two words *it* and *is*—the teacher's own examples given to introduce the magenta consonant *t* and the lilac consonant *s*—can immediately be used to form two different sentences with distinctively different pitch and intonation, if said naturally.

The pointer forms *it* and then *is* according to a rhythmic pattern that causes their sounds to be elicited one rapidly after the other, as in speech. If this does not help the students read *it is*, the teacher may tell the learners to hold *it* in one hand and *is* in the other, she herself doing it. When she holds out her clenched fist containing *it*, they do likewise and say *it*. She does *not* say *it*. When the other fist is thrust forward (and the original fist withdrawn) *is* is uttered. It is sufficient to present one hand after the other in increasingly accelerated movements to gain the speed giving the successive utterances of *it* and *is* the natural and customary intonation of speech when *it is* or *is it* are said. What is worth watching is that when *is it* is said rapidly, the learners are forced to raise their voices as happens when a question is spoken. They do it without prompting. The intonation forces the understanding and makes it possible to establish a stepping stone in their progress toward *functioning as readers.*

Next, the word *as* can be read by the pupils as they watch the teacher's pointer moving between the white sign (*a*) and the curly lilac sign (*s*). The phrase *as it is* can easily be found by them. Then *is it is* put in one hand and *as it is* in the other hand. The accelerated fist movements yield *is it as it is*. The speed of saying it introduces the proper intonation.

18 This sentence, and the ones used to form it, can provide the teacher with significant evidence about how the group of learners is entering into the game of Visual Dictation.[9]

Table 2 of the Word Building Book and the last pages of Book 1 provide us with additional opportunities for making words and sentences and for seeing them in print in black and white.

When Table 2 of the *Word Building Book* is studied, it is clear that we have not only met different sounds represented by the same sign (*s* and *s*), but also three signs in one of the columns corresponding to the same sound (*s*, *ss*, and *'s*). We must practice these signs through Visual Dictation 1, using first the chalkboard in the classroom and then the *Word Building Book* and a pencil.

Reproducing here the signs of Table 2, we have:

a	u	i	e	o
	p	t	s	s
		tt	ss	ss
				's

---

[9] A teacher may want to do a simple form of Visual Dictation 2 by writing words in colored chalk on the board—see footnote on p. 31.

Examples of the use of the sign on the bottom line (s) are:

> *pat's pet*
> *pat's pup's top*

Examples of the simultaneous use of two of the signs (*'s, s*) in the column of lime-colored signs are:

> *pat's pets*
> *pat's pots*

Examples of more complicated forms to show similarities and differences between the signs (*'s, s, ss*) of this column are:

> *It's tess's pass*
> *tess tests pitt's pups*

Other examples are left to the reader's imagination to devise. When names such as *tom* or *pam* appear on Word Chart 3, the lilac column of *s* will be used in a similar way as shown in Table 3 of the Word Building Book, since in *tom's* the last sign (*'s*) has the same sound as the last sign in is.

The significance of this set of signs lies in its preparation of the learners for the realistic encounter with the truth about the way English is written. Pupils will know from the start that for various words and meanings, different signs are used, even when these signs represent the same sound and, conversely, that like signs are sometimes used to represent quite different sounds. Although this is not explained explicitly, the observation alone of the routine pointing to this or that sign according to which word it is used in, or to which sound is heard, will indicate that attention must be paid to both sound *and* shape, and not only to one of these elements. Since the successive tables of the *Word Building Book* never contradict this rule, but only add more signs, the idea will be established that one must know in each case which sign to select from which column.

It seems that the creation of this degree of *awareness* of the true nature of written English is a much healthier state of affairs than the memorizing of rules and exceptions, particularly where exceptions will be numerous.

19 We have thus far met a number of techniques which make use of ideas not previously recognized as forming part of the exercise of reading. But clearly our beginners in these very early lessons will have acquired an

insight into sounds and their relationship to signs that will serve them well in work that follows which will seem to be more akin to reading.

The materials introduced so far comprise books for individual study and, for classroom group work, one colored Word Chart and the first suggestion of the Phonic Code drawn in color on the chalkboard. The true conveyor of insight in Visual Dictation is the pointer, but it is the books which give some body to this very flexible material.

So far, reading has meant producing proper sounds with the proper integrating rhythm when the pointer passes over the signs standing for those sounds. This is met again later, when *Book 1* is studied for recognition of spatial arrangements of signs that are in some way equivalent to the temporal sequences of signs which have already been produced by the pointer through Visual Dictation 1. These stand for temporal sequences of sounds found in English speech.

Section 3
Second Use of the Pointer – Sentences Through Visual Dictation 2
Study of Some Links-by-Transformation Between Words

1   The learners are now ready for an alternative course: the study of Word Chart 2. This shows in color some of the words that can be (or have been) formed from the set of signs introduced so far.[10] This chart is reproduced on the inside back cover of this teacher's guide.

2   The pointer will now be used again, this time moving from one word to another on the Chart to form sentences. This activity is an extension of the work on Word Chart 1 with only vowels and was begun before English words were met. However, this is only done after words have been recognized for what they are—a pattern in which the letters stand adjacent

---

[10] The teacher of *young* beginners may want to write a few of these words on the chalkboard in their colors after she has introduced the sounds through Visual Dictation 1, but before she has introduced enough sounds to bring out Word Chart 2—thus bridging the gap between the temporal and the spatial sequence more gradually, although it is done in *Book 1*. A very simple form of Visual Dictation 2 (making sentences) can then be used by moving her pointer between these words written in chalk.

one to the other, from left to right, on one level, to represent the time sequence of the pointer in Visual Dictation 1. It is neither necessary nor even useful to go over all the words of the Chart before making sentences. It is advisable to start Visual Dictation 2 with the small words *it, is, up, as,* and *us,* pointing to some of them in turn so as to form a few sentences: it is us, is it up, and so on, showing that now the pointer is linking words rather than merely linking signs to form words.

3   The reason for the choice of words and their position on the Chart needs some explanation. Reverses are placed near each other deliberately. But the placing of *pat* as the first word is arbitrary, although the aesthetic factor was considered in planning the Chart. Hence, teachers must know that the Charts are not to be scanned like a printed page. Indeed, each Chart has been produced so that it would *not* make any sense if this were done. A large number of sentences can be made by the pointer out of these few words by simply touching different words in turn. Some of those which can be formed on Word Chart 2 are found on pages 14 and 16 of *Book 1*. Among them are other possible words made with the signs introduced so far on the chalkboard.[11]

---

11 See also pp. 41 and 47.

If teachers spend considerable time forming sentences with the pointer on Word Chart 2, they will begin to understand the full power of what we have called Visual Dictation 2. The pointer, at first slowly, and when progress permits, more rapidly, indicates which words are wanted and in what order. The learners first say each word in turn so that they are sure of the particular words pointed to. But soon they are able to wait until all the words of the sentence have been touched by the pointer and then, as soon as the pointing stops, say this whole sentence in one quick utterance as they would in ordinary conversation. Thus, the relating of whole units of meaning to whole sentences is encouraged by the technique from the beginning and assures that reading is *never* separated from comprehension. Whether the movements of the pointer are slow or fast, this is the game called Visual Dictation 2; but naturally, as learners progress, the movements of the pointer remain as fast as speech or are even speeded up. In a short time, learners can even accept long and complicated sentences in the same way (once a few additional Word Charts are in use).

During any concentration on the speeding-up process, the same set of words should be used so that time and energy need not be spent on deciphering new words. A teacher would be advised to see this exercise in actual use to appreciate its great power. It is possible that part of a lesson might be concerned with (1) making sure that the words *step, it, up,* and *pat* are known; (2) making every learner say *step it up* faster and faster until it sounds like the instruction it is; and (3) adding *pat* at the end so that the instruction is addressed to a person.

A test of transfer of power can immediately be applied either (1) by pointing rapidly at *set* instead of *step* and forming the sentence *set it up pat,* obtaining immediately the correct rhythm and intonation without requiring the successive stages of speeding-up, or (2) by pointing at *pat steps it up* at a considerable speed.

This, it should be understood, is not a first exercise in Visual Dictation 2, but serves as well as any other example to describe how to use it.

4 Word Chart 2 does not include the most useful words, nor the most frequent, nor the simplest of those that could have been formed from the

signs available. The words were chosen to introduce a number of ideas and concepts teachers of reading find useful in assisting speakers to become writers and readers.

We find *at* and *it* near each other, to serve as a reference indicating that one may pass from one word to the other by the substitution of one vowel for another. From *at* or *it*, one may pass to *as* or *is* on this Chart by another substitution, this time of a consonant.

From *at* we may pass by *addition* of a sign to either *pat or sat*, which are themselves linked by substitution. A similar exercise could be done with it leading to *pit* and *sit*. The alternative beginnings will help to establish the student's ability to transfer, thus reducing the burden on his memory. If he knows the word *at*, the learner who is capable of the transformations can produce *it, pat, sat, pit*, and *sit* in a variety of different orders. If reversals are included, as one of the transformations, we can add the words *tap* and *tip*.

The following schema shows in another way the links-by-transformation described so far:

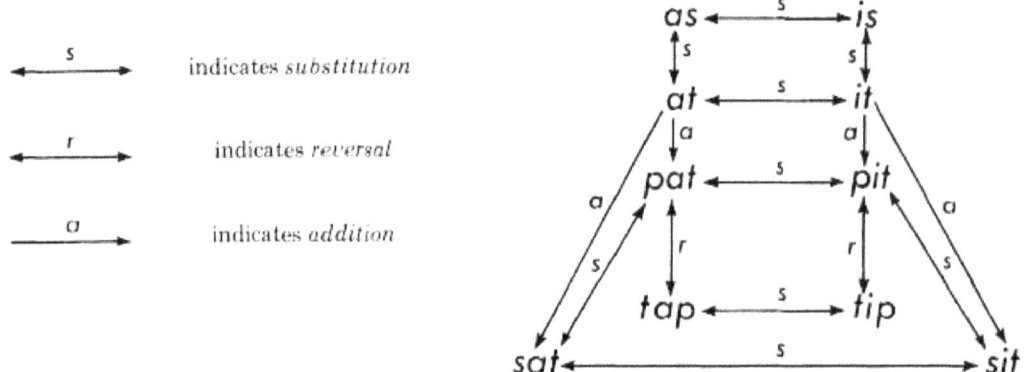

5   An interesting technique for obtaining words beginning with two consonants, as in *stop, spot*, or *spits*, and so forth, is the following:

Let us say we have been able to get *top* and *sat* from the class. We can then ask learners to play variations on *sat* by increasing the length of the sound they make for the first sign *(s . . . at)*, or of the second *(sa . . t)*, or of the third *(sat . . .)*. This, successfully done, demonstrates that the learners are

Chapter I
The First Certificate of Reading

masters of their own vocal chords, and that they can do with them what may help them solve certain problems of learning to read.

We now ask the learners to hold *top* in one hand. At a sign from the teacher, we ask them to open their hands to release it, saying its sound as they do so. While holding *top*, they then return to saying sat with the length of the initial sound increased as before *(s . . .at)*. While they are beginning to say *s . . . at*, there is time for the teacher to give a signal that will release the sound top (and thus interrupt *s . . . at* after *s . . .)* and everyone hears *s . . . top*. This strikes one's ears as *stop*, with the first sound prolonged at will. This technique can at once be applied to *spot, spit,* and *spat*.

6 The power shown by the pupils can be used again, but in another way. We may ask them to evoke *top,* and to see it in their minds with their eyes shut. While their eyes are shut, we ask them to say what word they see if the lime or "curly green" *(s)* is placed on the left of *top (stop),* or on the right *(tops),* or at both ends *(stops)*. We can then ask them to reverse this last word formed in their minds *(spots),* and to remove either the "curly green" *(s)* *(spot* or *pots),* or both *(pot);* reverse the result *(top);* and then start again adding *s* at either *(stop* or *tops)* or both ends (stops). This shows that not only top and pot are known as reverses but also *stop* and *pots, tops* and *spot,* and *stops* and *spots*. Developing awareness of all these links within one's mind enables the memory to be still less burdened. The schema below shows in another way the links vivified by the above game with one's imagery.

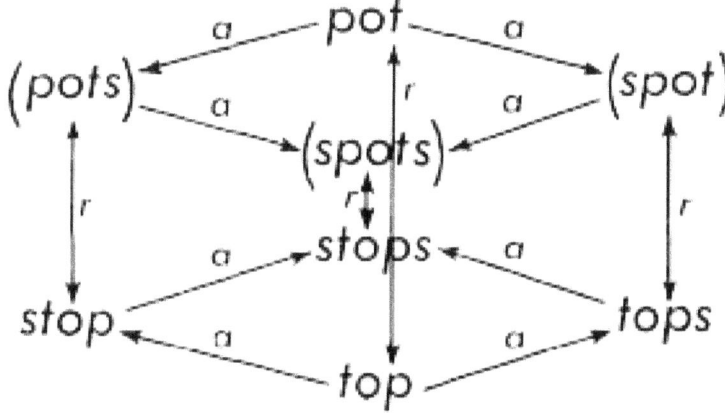

Those words in parentheses in the schema are among those not appearing on Word Chart 2, but which may be created in the mind through this game as well as through Visual Dictation 1 on the chalkboard.

7   We can obtain *steps* from *stops* by substitution of *e* for *o*. We can also get it by starting with *pat*, making it *pet* by substitution of *e* for *a*, then *pets* by addition of *s,* then *step* by reversal, and finally *steps* by addition of *s*.

Word Chart 2 displays the words *past* and *pest*, obtainable from *pat* and *pet* respectively, by insertion of the "curly green" between the last two signs of each.

By a substitution, *test* can be derived from *pest*, or from *pet* by insertion and substitution.

It is important to note that it is allowed in our game to pass from *pat* to *pass,* since one sign with one sound *(ss)* is substituted for another with a different sound *(t)*. It is also correct to go from *pass* to *past* by addition, since in this case *ss* and *s* are both signs standing for the same sound and so may be used interchangeably as the conventional spelling of any given word dictates. This will be the beginning of the discovery that in English almost any letter can be a silent or mute letter in some word.

This schema shows the links just described:

$$\xrightarrow{i}\quad\text{indicates } \textit{insertion}$$

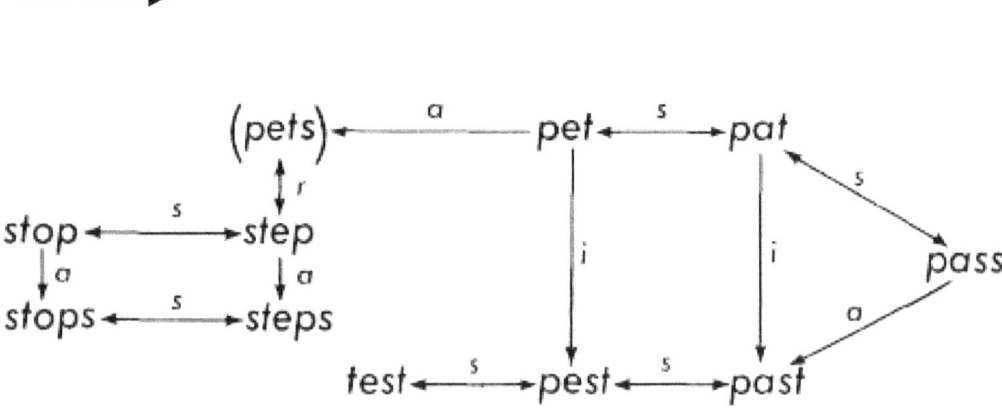

8   Taking any pair of words on Word Chart 2, can we pass from one to another using one or more of the four transformations?

substitution
reversal
addition
insertion

Since subtraction is not allowed[12] in *this* game, we will find that, for example, we cannot pass from *stops* to *at*. In such cases, we reverse the pair and go from *at* to *stops*. At each stage, as we plan our "route," each "station" on the way is required to be an English word. This exercise is called the *Game of Transformations*.[13] That it can be played so early in the program is a remarkable tribute to young children's word sense and linguistic powers. It is the experience of many observers of young children that, early in their lives, they already play with transformation of words when using them orally.

If children learn now that written words, too, can be transformed in this way, this knowledge will give their reading a dynamic dimension that pays high dividends. Later on, this game will serve us in providing a test of mastery of the written language, in particular of spelling.

---

12 Subtraction is not allowed because it would make the game too simple and not challenging enough.
13 See pp. 58-60 and later pp. 109-113.

This schema makes clear all the links-by-transformation described above, most of which are made available using only the words already printed on Word Chart 2:

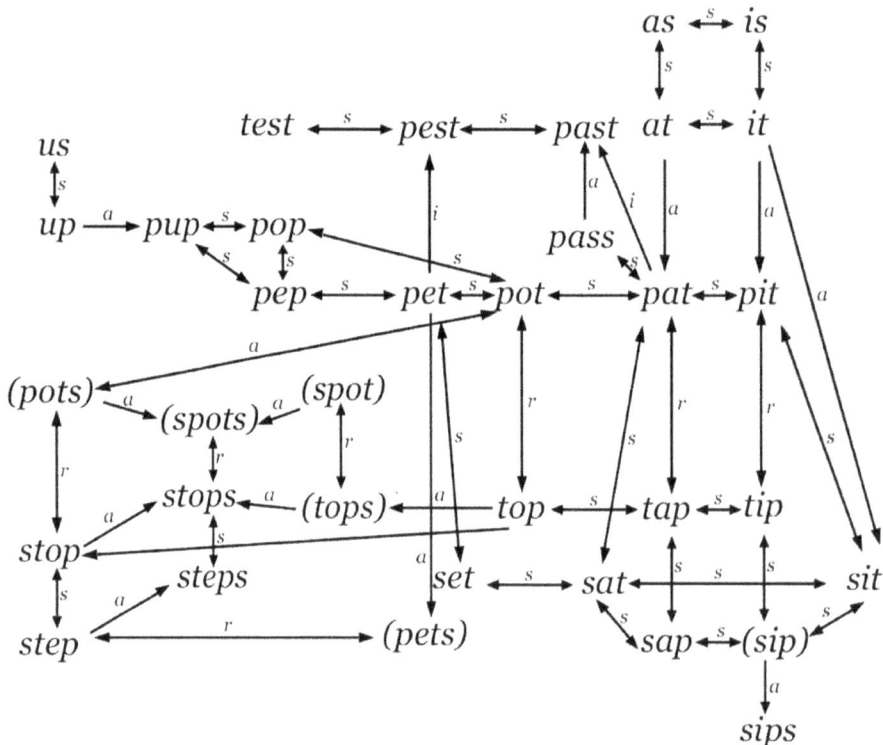

It is this "fabric" (network or web) of interrelationships—dynamic in nature—which, once it becomes part of the mind of the learner through his use of the Word Charts, never allows any written word to be an isolated, static entity held in the mind only by memorization of its appearance. It provides each word with so many supporting links (or connections) to other words that it can always be decoded anew by the use of the understanding present because of these links.

9   The power of the pupils can be developed even further. It is already clear that even with this restricted language—and certainly later on— the Word Charts can hardly begin to include the almost unlimited possibilities for creating words and sentences. Therefore, beside Visual Dictation 1, there is an additional technique which can be used to make more words

available for Visual Dictation 2. It is a development of the game of evoking and transforming words already played with the eyes shut (see above).

1. To begin with, the teacher asks questions similar to these as she makes the appropriate gesture with the pointer of drawing a sign while touching a word on the Word Chart. For example:

    - "What will it be if we look at *pot*, and in our minds put the 'curly green' *(s)* last?"... *"pots"*

      "Or first?" .... *"spot"*

      "Or both places?" .... *"spots"*

    - "What will it be if we look at *pup*, and in our minds substitute the pink *(i)* for the yellow *(u)*?" ....*"pip"*

      "Or substitute the 'curly green' *(s)* for the first brown one *(p)*?" .... *"sup"*

    - "What will it be if we look at *step*, and in our minds reverse it?" .... *"pets"*

      "Or look at *stops* and reverse it?" .... *"spots"*

    - "What will it be if we look at *at*, and in our minds insert the brown *(p)*?" .... *"apt"*

2. The teacher then increases the challenge by asking the pupils to hold in their minds the word (or words) which have just resulted from the mental transformation, and to say this word when the one on the Chart (from which it was just made) is touched. Then she visually dictates a sentence using one of these transformed words, eliciting the intended spoken sentence from the pupils. For example: While the teacher indicates *pat pot us* with the pointer, *pat spots us* is read by the students.

3. Once these two techniques are understood by the pupils, the teacher may find she can change a word while she is visually dictating a sentence.

Thus, by stimulating the imagination in this way, much more of the vocabulary of a given restricted language *(Book 1* and Table 2 of the *Word*

Building Book) can be created from the Word Charts. Indeed, the words on the Chart, or even the Chart itself, seem to take on another dimension. For instance:

- not only is *pot* clearly related to a set of words printed next to it *pat, pit, pet, pop, top, tot*

- but it is related to a set of words which can be "hung" in front of it on an imaginary hook pot (on the Chart) is related to *pots, spot, spots, putt, putts*, etc. (not on the Chart)

- and each one of the words in the imagined set is linked with others printed on the Chart

    as *spots* to *stops* (on the Chart)
    as *pots* to *stop* (on the Chart)

and is linked with other imagined words

   as *spot* (in the imagined set of *pot*)

is linked to

   tops (in the imagined set of *top*)

All of this seems a truly remarkable achievement when we think of all that is involved. Not only have we used positively what is ordinarily a weakness—that is, reading one thing for another—but we have also opened the door to the use of the imagination to control what is in front of us so as to yield by transformation something both possible and new. Teachers who feel uncomfortable when such proposals are made usually become enthusiastic when they see for themselves how easily children accept these things.

This use of the imagination with the Word Charts, and its use with Visual Dictation 1, gives irreplaceable preparation for the games in the Worksheets[14] since it helps to generate in the mind the dynamic and labile imagery necessary for meeting these highly intellectual challenges without difficulty.

---

14 See pp. 54-68 of this chapter.

10 On the whole, *Book 1* has set the trend for the approach which started with the extremely artificial games with signs, involving their repetition and combination, and then moving to sentences read as naturally as when spoken. This covers the ground opened up by the two forms of Visual Dictation.

The vocabulary met so far, included in both Visual Dictations and *Book* 1, is as follows (the italicized words are printed on Word Chart 2) :

two-sign words:	*up, at, it, as, is, us* (ass)
three-sign words:	pap, *pup*, pip, *pep, pop, pat, pit, pet, pot, tap, tip, top,* tat, tit, *tot, sap, sip,* sop, *sat, sit, set,* sot, pus, sis, *its, apt, opt, pitt, putt, tess, pass*
four-sign words:	pips, peps, pops, pups, pats, pits, pets, pots, taps, tips, tops, tats, tits, tots, saps, sups, *sips,* sops, sits, sets, sots, *past, pest, test,* spat, spit, spot, *stop, step,* opts, putts, pitts, tess's
five-sign words:	*stops, steps,* spats, spits, spots, pests, tests, upset, "pepsi," passes
six-sign words:	upsets

There are well over 50 common words and over 80 words in all. With these words at least 150 combinations that are sentences can be made.

It is a characteristic of this approach that much is left to the learner's inventiveness and imagination. It is only the *Word Building Book* (understood through Visual Dictation 1 on the chalkboard) that indicates the possibilities available at this stage. Word Chart 2 and *Book 1* give only some of these possibilities. This flexibility will increase as we move on. Later it will also be indicated fully by the *Phonic Code* (8 charts), which extends the work done on the chalkboard to the scope found on the last table in the *Word Building Book*. We have purposely given much detailed help at this stage because the materials worked on are restricted. Such detail is not necessary as the availability of signs, words, and sentences becomes less restricted, for it would be tedious to continue listing the large number of possibilities. An ever-increasing expansion will be obvious to all.

Book 1 is very brief and is completed very quickly (perhaps in a week with five-year-olds),[15] but its brevity is not to be mistaken for emptiness. On the contrary, in this thin volume it is proved just how much can be done with so little. This is possible because children and other learners bring spoken speech with them, and our job is leading them to master the codification of it as it is today in its written form after slow historic development.

11 We conclude this section with dynamic diagrams summarizing the ground covered thus far. However, even with the restricted language of Table 2 of the *Word Building Book,* the approach is too complex to indicate all of its dimensions in a diagram.

In the diagrams that follow only some of the alternate ways for the introduction of words[16] and sentences are shown—that is Visual Dictation 1. The italics indicate which of the words are printed on Word Chart 2 and which sentences can therefore be given on this Chart by Visual Dictation 2. Of course, as we have intimated, if the teacher and pupils learn to use fully their imagination for transforming words, all the words needed beyond the scope of those printed on the Chart can be generated from it by a gesture with the pointer; to the extent this is done, all the suggested sentences can also be done by Visual Dictation 2. All of these words and others may be used in oral dictation[17] and in writing one's own compositions.

Words Linked to Each Other by Transformations of Sound (and Sign)[18]

These notes and the accompanying diagram are designed to help the teacher prepare for Visual Dictation 1.

---

15 When working with remedial groups (as mentioned in the footnote on p. 11), it may be that nothing but Visual Dictation at the chalkboard is used until we have moved beyond the scope of the restricted language of *Book 1*. In this case because the work is moving ahead so rapidly into less restricted vocabulary, it is often best to omit *Book 1* altogether, or to read only the last page of sentences, and then begin with *Book 2*.
16 A list of these words appears on p. 41.
17 See pp. 48-50.
18 Notes contributed by D. E. H.

Circled portions of the diagram indicate the only clues the teacher will find *she* needs to give. If she gives these, she should try to give them only once, so that the learners will feel responsibility from the beginning for taking in and using what assistance is given.

As before, the arrows marked with a letter (*s, r, a, i*) indicate one of the four transformations—two of them always reversible as the arrow shows. Where ⟶ is found, it indicates some other transformation or combination of transformations which are allowed in Visual Dictation 1 but not later on in the Game of Transformations.

Numbers in squares □ indicate the group of sentences listed on page 47 which relate to this point in the word study. Italicized words appear also on Word Chart 2, to be used in Visual Dictation 2.

Description of alternative directions

Alternative directions for the very beginning lessons of Visual Dictation 1 are given because feedback from a particular group of learners may indicate their lack of readiness for one direction at a given moment, yet their readiness for another. A teacher must have all the alternative sequences well enough in mind so that, when some difficulty occurs in one direction and is not resolvable immediately, she can take her pupils in another direction *so as not to bore them*. That will make them feel equally confident of their powers, and thus strong enough to return to the point of difficulty from another angle and conquer it easily.

For example: Some pupils have difficulty blending syllables to form a word like *pop* or *pat* on the first encounter, yet be equal to a long sentence like *is it as it is*.

The teacher does *not* tell the answer if pupils have some difficulty. Telling does not help.

Alternative 1: This alternative is essentially the progression outlined in this chapter. It is the one to be followed first, since it is the most direct, and it has been proved to work well with most pupils.

Alternative 2: This alternative may offer sufficient help by suggesting how the blending of syllables can also take place by using *pa* and *at* to form *pat;* working in this way with two different consonants and the very familiar white *a,* may be easier for a certain group of learners. It also immediately generates a name useful in varying sentences. The name *pitt* can follow, and others, if needed. Since these pupils may have shown a slower pace in working out reversals of syllables, it may be easier for them *not* to take the reverse of *at* now, but to take the syllable *sa,* which requires only substitution from *pa* and makes *sat* by addition. Since they have *it, sit* is readily obtained. Moving in this way, one can reach a number of more interesting sentences, so that more headway is made in relating all of this to spoken speech, even though the vocabulary is more restricted than in Alternative 1.

After this, it seems easy indeed for the learners to return and find *pip* from *pit,* or *pop* from *pot,* and then *pep, pap,* and *pup.* The latter may also come by addition from *up.* From *sit* we easily deduce *sip;* from this, *tip, tap, top,* (and *tot)* ; or from *sat, sap* and from this, *tap,* then *tip, top,* (and *tot).*

Alternative 3: This alternative is for a very few students finding difficulty even with blending *pa* and *at* into *pat* when first encountered. Since they have *at, it* is easily found. The teacher may give *is* to introduce the "curly purple" *s,* and then *as* is found. Immediately, *is* can be used with *it* and *up* in four sentences made only with words of one syllable with the vowel in the initial position. 1 Once *as* has been found, two more sentences 2 are possible. If blending is still a problem, *us* might be given, and it is easily understood since it is only a slight change from *up.* This yields two more sentences. 3

At this point, enough of the game would be understood to make it easy to blend *pa* and *at* into *pat* or *pi* and *it* into *pit.* From these, *pap, pip, pop, pup,* and *pep* can follow. Now a reservoir of sentences is available. From *pa,* we go to *sa* and *sat* as in **Alternative 2**, and continue in the same fashion suggested there to find *sap, tap, top,* (and *tot).*

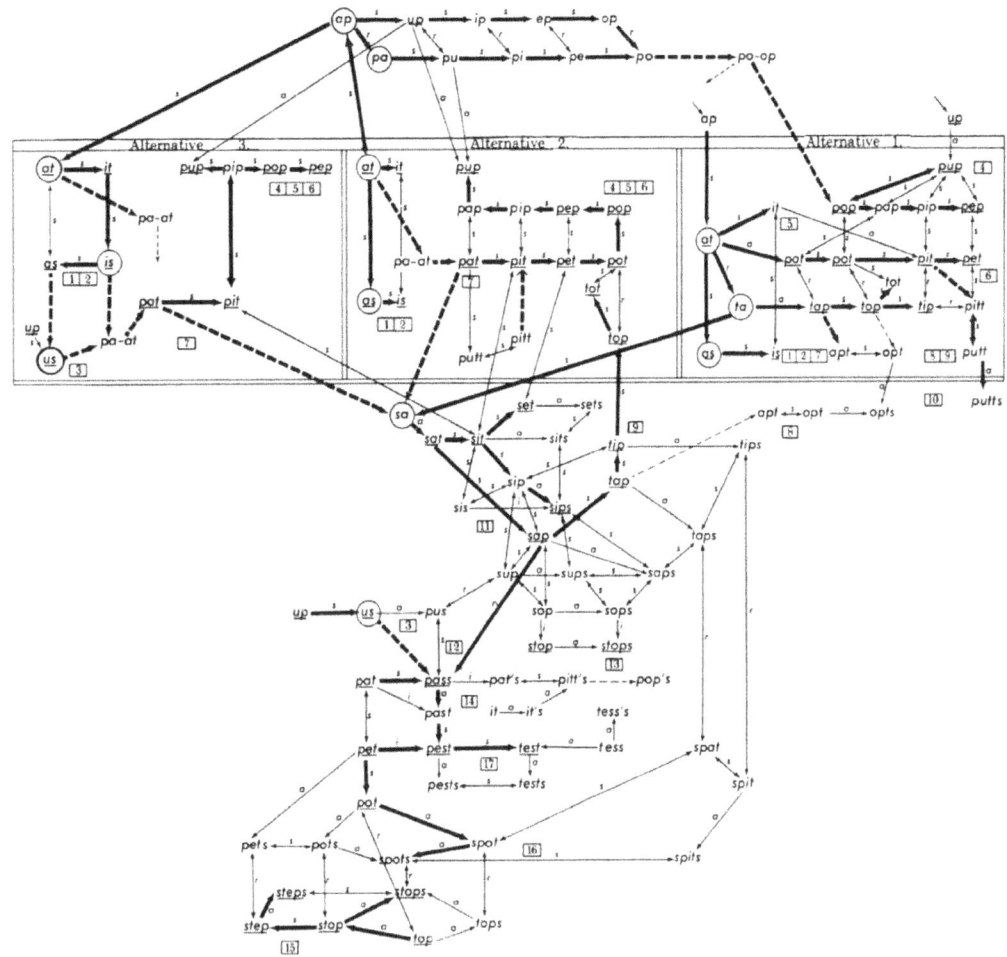

Words Linked by Meanings and by Structures into Sentences

When the symbol (*r*) is used, it indicates that the reversal or change in the order of the words will create another English sentence.

Parentheses ( ) around a name in a sentence indicate that the name added at the beginning or the end creates two slightly different English sentences. Thus from

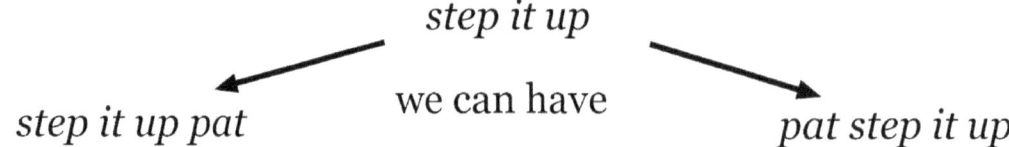

Parentheses ( ) around a word mean it could be substituted for one preceding it to form a new sentence.

Wherever one name is used, one or more names (or nouns) that use some of the signs met already could be substituted, thus producing more sentences. Specifically:

pat, pop, pitt, sis, tess and sometimes *pup, spot, tip, pet*	can all be substituted one for the other, depending on the meaning of the sentence

Numbers in squares ☐ are for cross-reference to the preceding diagram introducing words in Visual Dictation 1. The appropriate time for introducing the sentences may best be estimated by referring back to this diagram. Italicized sentences can also be generated (without mental transformations) through Visual Dictation 2 on Word Chart 2.

Chapter I
The First Certificate of Reading

|1|— it is
— is it
— is it up (it is)

|2|— it is as it is
— is it as it is (it is)

|3|— it is us
— is it us (it is)

|4|— pop up
— pep up

|5|— pep it up
— pop it
— up it

|6|— pat pop it
— pat it (pat)
— pet it (pat)

|7|— pat is up (r)
— it is pat (r)

|8|— pat is apt
— pat is as apt as pitt

|9|— tap it
— top it (pat)
— tip it
— tip up
— tip it up (pat)
— pat is top
— pat is up top
— pat is tip top
— it is tip top

|10|— pat opts
— pet opt pop
— pat opts pitt (it)
— pop putts
— pat tips it up
— pat pets pup (it)
— pat peps up
— pat peps it up
— pat is tops (r)
— it is tops (r)
— its tip is top

|11|— sit up (pat)
— pat sits up
— pat sat up
— set it up (pat)
— pat sets it up
— pat is upset
— pat upsets *tess (us)*
— pat is as upset as pitt
— sip it up (pat)
— pat sups
— pat sips sap
— pat taps sap
— it saps it
— sop it up
— pat sops it up
— pat sits at its top

|12|— pass us (pat)
— pass us up (pat)
— pass it (pat)
— pass it up
— pat passes

|13|— it is pat's (r)
— pat's pup (pet, top, pot)
— pat is at pitt's
— pat's up
— pat's pet's top's
— it's pat
—pop's pet is pat
— pat is pop's pet

|14|— pat is past (r)
— it is past (r)

|15|— stop it (pat)
— stop pat stop
— pat stops at stops (steps)
— step up (pat)
— step it up (pat)
— pat steps up (r)
— pat steps past it

|16|— spot it
— pat spots it
— pat spots us
— pat stops at spots
— spit it up
— sis spits up
— sis spits it up
— pat spat
— apt sis spots tess
— pat pets spot
— pat's pet is spot
— pop spots pat's pet
— pat's pet spits

- test it (pat) — tess tests pitt's pups
- test pat — pests test tess
- pat tests pitt — spot tests top

Section 4
Oral and Visual Dictation Visual Dictation 3
The Worksheets and Testing

1   With the language restricted as it is at present, we can do little more than read isolated sentences such as those which appear at the end of *Book 1*. But we can nevertheless introduce writing and two types of oral dictation.

2   Writing has two meanings. One is concerned with the activity of making the designs of words. This is a power resulting from the coordination of senses, muscles, and imagery, and is primarily an activity of drawing. The other involves putting down a sequence of designs, which one considers to be the equivalent of certain spoken statements, in such a manner that anyone can read it (turn it back into speech) and find the equivalent of the spoken statements originally in mind before writing. This requires a continuous control of a process of transcription of ideas.

We make a distinction between these two meanings because the second, which involves a higher intellectual activity, is the one which makes the writer, while the first makes the scribe.

Exercises of coordination can be separated during the learning process from those concerned with the second meaning of writing, if the teacher abstains from any comment on legibility so long as it can be guessed that the words put down are what has been intended by the writer.[19] If coordination *cannot* improve, reading should not suffer from this. If it can, improvement will come with practice. It *does* pay to ignore bad writing in the first sense when one is engaged in the activity of the second type, because this requires all the energies available for its correct performance. Indeed it is only practice, and not stress on errors, that helps legibility if it can be helped. It is the author's experience that legibility *does* improve in due time through the practice that comes as a by-product of

---

[19] See Appendix 1 for examples of six-year-old pupils' writing.

Chapter I
The First Certificate of Reading

involvement in numerous intellectual challenges that require writing all the time—as in this approach.

3   Since in writing there is physical activity that places demands on the pupil over and above those of reading, it may be wise to start oral dictation in a way that requires only the purely intellectual activity of reading words. The only outcome then is to know which words should be associated with the sounds uttered by the person dictating.

Since Word Chart 2 is already on the wall, the teacher says one of the sentences already met through Visual Dictation 2—for instance, *is pat up*. Then the pointer is offered to whomever thinks he can come up and touch these three words on the Chart in the right sequence.

If a volunteer attempts it, it should be left to the class to agree or disagree and to produce corrections if any are needed. Sometimes questions such as "Is it the one?" or "Do you agree with him?" will assist the pupils in checking the reality of what was shown against what is dictated by their own criteria and those of their peers, suggesting another solution if needed and analyzing his or their own difficulties. The teacher should not show approval or disapproval but proceed to another sentence if all goes well, or assist pupils in analyzing difficulties if any arise. In such cases, for example, the teacher could ask for the sounds when she points to *pat is up:* or for each of the words separately; and then ask for the solution to the original problem of *is pat up*. In this way, she takes the pupils back to a simpler challenge already met so that in their own minds they can bridge the gap to the new insight.

Once it is clear that any sentence dictated by the teacher from words on the Chart can be shown on the Chart by the pupils, the teacher can increase the intellectual challenge by dictating sentences whose words are not all there but can be formed by the transforming gesture of the pointer.[20] For example:

> *pat sits up,* which requires adding *s* to *sit* as the pointer touches the words;

---

20 See technique outlined on pp. 39-41..

or, more difficult,

> *is pat as apt as tess,* which requires, while pointing, the insertion of *p* in *at* and indicating that *tess* is the reversal of *set*

The third challenge can then be for pupils to suggest their own sentences within the restriction of the signs met, and to ask the rest of the class to find these sentences on the Chart with whatever corresponding transformations need to be indicated by the pointer.

4   At any point in this sequence of challenges, the activity of writing may be undertaken at the level of the challenge mastered (i.e., words on the Chart, words transformed from these, sentences dictated by peers). It may be well to start on the chalkboard where one person at first and then perhaps part or all of the class can work, since the results of the written forms are then seen by everyone and are close to the Word Chart which may be needed for comparison. The class again is the judge of correctness. The teacher accepts what is offered and asks pupils to compare what has been written with the words on the Chart only if the writer or any other student cannot put right the slip or error or omission in writing without his suggestion. But, even with this assistance, the pupils correct themselves.

5   After some time is spent on this, the ordinary oral dictation can be undertaken with the whole class now writing on paper. The teacher says each statement only *once* but clearly, at the speed of speech, starting with such simple examples as:

>   *is it us*   or   *as pat is*

and progressing to

>   *pitt spat at spots*   or   *pat stops at steps*

Pupils will need time to write, and it should be given freely. Experience will teach us how long a time is required for writing by different pupils. The need for time may be due to the level of coordination and not at all to the existence or nonexistence of an image in the mind for what needs to be put down. Since teachers cannot really know at first which is the cause of the delay, the wisest course is to give the pupils enough time and learn about their difficulties by observing them during this period.

Correction of work written on individual papers should be done by the pupils themselves. Different procedures may be used as the work progresses. The aim of all of them, however, is to cause each pupil to compare what he has written with something suggested as the correct solution by another student, and also to discover whether he agrees or disagrees. If he finds he disagrees, he must then sort out whether he now agrees with what he himself wrote or, on reconsidering the situation, can agree with the other solution proposed. Fruitful discussions may result in this way which show the learners more and more what it is to rely on their *own* criteria and to sharpen these rather than to depend on the teacher for any judgment or approval. Here are some procedures:

- after each sentence is written under dictation, a volunteer can offer a solution through Visual Dictation 2 on the Word Chart (with whatever transformations may be required)

- or, after each sentence, a volunteer can write his solution on the board

- or, at the end of the oral dictation lesson, one or more volunteers can write on the board one solution for each sentence, and all can check their own papers against this record

- or, pupils may work in pairs and compare papers, raising for class discussion disagreements they are unable to solve between them

6   During this beginning stage, it may also be valuable to do some oral dictation of words and simple sentences, followed by asking pupils to volunteer to dictate a solution visually by moving the pointer over the arrangement of signs on the chalkboard—that is, by Visual Dictation 1. Such words and sentences could also be written and checked by Visual Dictation 1. This type of oral dictation, leading to solution by Visual Dictation 1, once it has provided additional challenge in this early stage,

should then be dropped for a time, to be resumed usually at the level of the restricted language of Table 11 in the *Word Building Book*.[21]

7   Visual Dictation by the teacher (or later on by pupils who create their own sentences for their classmates) can also lead to writing. In fact, the challenge is even greater to the writer than when oral dictation leads to writing, because he must perform a *double* transformation within his mind instead of a single one:

- he must rapidly transform into speech (i.e. read) the sequences of signs he sees dictated visually

- then hold the *exact* words (as well as the meaning) of what has been read long enough to transcribe it back into signs on his own paper through writing, made slower than reading because it requires not only mental activity but physical activity coordinated with it

Therefore, the outcome in terms of the increased power of the pupils is also greater.

Visual Dictation 2 is the more valuable at this time and may involve transforming some words on the Chart with the gesture with the pointer if one wishes to complicate the challenge even more. Visual Dictation 1 using the chalkboard arrangement of signs is useful at this stage, but, as with the oral dictation leading to solution through Visual Dictation 1, it should then be dropped until the restrictions of the language met in Table 11 of the *Word Building Book* are met.

The results of Visual Dictation should be checked by the pupils by reading aloud to others the solutions written on their papers. This (1) insures comprehension of what has been put down, and (2) uses again one medium (speech) to check another (signs), rather than the same medium to check itself—thus assisting in catching errors.

8   As an outcome of oral and Visual Dictation, either led by the teacher or by pupils developing their own sentences, the pupils become confident in

---

[21] See pp. 75-77 and pp. 143-152.

their own power to write. They will then easily progress to writing on paper many of their own sentences either on their own initiative or in eager response to a suggestion. They frequently accompany these with unusual illustrations. Parents often report on the occurrence of this spontaneous activity, sometimes even before the teacher notices it in class! In this, we surely have a real beginning of independent writing and a true test that it has now become an integrated aspect of the linguistic powers of the learners.[22]

9   Now we are ready to begin a new form of Visual Dictation although we cannot go very far with it with so restricted a language. As we progress in the program, however, it will become easier and more interesting.[23]

On Word Chart 2, the teacher may point to a sequence of statements such as:

> *sit up pat*
> *pat is up*
> *pat steps up*   (All of these use the words just
> *pat sips pop*   as they are printed.)
> *tip it up pat*
> *pat stops*

or she may point to

> it is *pat's* pup
> *tess pets* it
> *pitt pats* it
> pop *tests* it
> it *sits* up   (The italicized words are made
> it *steps* up   by transforming gestures while
> it stops   pointing.)
> it sips (pepsi)
> it *sups*
> *pat's* pup is *tops*
> it is as *apt* as *pitt's*

---

22 See footnote on p. 97 of this text referring to *Creative Writing* by Sister Leonore.
23 See pp. 102 and 141

Because they concern one or more persons undergoing a succession of states or performing a sequence of actions, such a set of sentences is the nearest we can come to writing a story in this restricted language of nine sounds.

We give to this technique the name of Visual Dictation 3, because it is using the pointer to make a sequence of sentences whose joined meanings produce a story.[24]

What is of interest here is that we can conceive of doing all of this with such a restricted language. The result is the preparation of the pupil for more complex sentences and stories as the language becomes less restricted without requiring that new principles and insights be acquired. Pupils soon become skilled enough to retain at one time a number of short sentences or a few quite long ones, then reading their story as a whole and naturally as it would be spoken. The relation of all of this to comprehension in reading books is obvious. A variation sometimes can be to ask them to tell the story in other words.

All of this prepares the way for giving oral dictations and visual dictations involving more than one sentence to be written by the pupils. It is obvious, also, that the beginning of spontaneous and creative story writing by the pupils is stimulated naturally by such extensions based on Visual Dictation 3.

10   It may be felt, while working in this way, that a very slight addition to the range of words available would make a great difference. Indeed, if the indefinite article *(a)* were present, the quality of sentences would be greatly improved and more could be written. This feeling is a good preparation for the next stages and, if felt necessary, the teacher might take such a step without loss.[25]

But as author of an approach which *proposes restrictions as a stimulus for creativity* I do not see the need to do today what will become possible

---

[24] Visual Dictation 1 is using the pointer to make a sequence of signs whose sounds produce a word. Similarly, Visual Dictation 2 is using the pointer to make a sequence of words whose joint meanings produce a sentence.
[25] By looking on Word Chart 3, the teacher will note that the word *a* is colored to sound as in speech, like the first sound in *upon*.

tomorrow, and prefer to explore the full possibilities of the present circumstances. The possibilities so far are:

- that we can use the signs of the restricted language for reading and for writing

- that we can read fluently and naturally, understanding most of what is said, written, or read

- that we can take sentences under various forms of dictation, observing spellings and accurately relate graphemes and phonemes with mental images

11   We can now turn to *Worksheet 1*. The preceding activities have created a background of experience that can lead the learner through the Worksheets to (1) enriched and extended intellectual activity and (2) individual ingenuity and creativity. Worksheet 1 also provides a test of what has been learned about the written language.

Since the fundamentals of playing these games have already been used and mastered in the beginning stages of the reading program, the games here should not pose any special problems. But even so, learners need to be introduced to each different type of game in the Worksheet the first time it is played, so that they are clear about the rules—especially since beginning readers are not yet expected to read the printed instructions. The first seven Worksheets deliberately have the same types of games appearing in the same order so that once a game is understood in Worksheet 1 and the pupil knows from the format of that page which type of game is intended, there should be no need for special introduction of each Worksheet.

All sixteen pages of each Worksheet are meant to be worked on within the limits of the restricted language indicated by the table of the *Word Building Book* referred to on the first page of each Work-sheet. At a later time, pupils may come back to any given Worksheet and work without any restriction (except the limits of their own understanding) and see what additional examples or answers can be found for the challenges—recording their improved "score" at the bottom of the page.

Page 1 of Worksheet 1 is concerned with assessing if the pupil understands how to form words by combining signs using Table 2 in the *Word Building Book* as a basis. He is allowed simply to combine signs and to put down his suggested words—non-English as well as English. This gives him practice in writing the signs in sequences, using reversals, permutations, and combinations within the restricted set, and provides the opportunity for writings that cannot be anticipated here. When the pupil feels really free to put down whatever he sees as an answer to the instructions, his awareness may produce the unexpected!

The teacher has nothing to correct; she only needs to note for herself whether the pupil:

- uses the script of the Word Charts and *Books* and the signs of the table in *Word Building Book* that are in front of him

- inserts signs beyond those asked for

- writes horizontally or otherwise

- separates signs and words

- needs time to shape signs and words

- can keep his score

The teacher need *only* note for herself in *her* notebook the pupil's performance on the Worksheets. She should comment directly to the learner only if she is sure that such a comment will not hamper him in his future work by making him aware of what he interprets as the teacher's disapproval. We do not want him to increase his dependence on the judgment of others.

Page 2 of Worksheet 1 is an exercise on the previous work and poses the challenge: Can this pupil recognize which of the written designs can be sounded, which of those look like English, which sound like English, and which he understands? His own score will reveal his insights through his eye and his ear into those words he uses, those he may recognize he has heard but never uses, or those he may not recall hearing and so never uses.

For example, *opt* and *apt* are English words that are simply permutations of *top* or *pot,* and *pat* or *tap* respectively, but may not be recalled or used by many young children, and so they may not list them on page 2.

Page 3 proposes, in contrast to the learner's intuition used to guide him on the previous page, a method of inquiring that can be developed to insure a deeper understanding of words. The pupil must look closely enough at the words to distinguish between them and utter them correctly, in order to yield their meaning (examples are *pots* and *tops, steps* and *pets).* At the same time, he must illustrate the ideas they represent. Of the six words offered, only one *(tot)* may pose a problem which may be interesting to let learners solve in their own way. (They may think it is *taught, tort,* or *tart,* depending on the region where they learned to talk.)

What matters here is *not* that the task suggested is performed and finished, but that the learners gain ways of working that will develop into research and inquiry tools. The results of work on page 3 may well be an exhibition of children's contributions that display treasures of imagination, inventiveness, and observation. All this could be lost if the exercise were treated as a pure stimulus-response situation in which one certain correct answer is expected. Teachers' sensitivity to the value for the individual of a rich experience, as against a good mark for answering the question, will serve their charges well.

Page 4 tests recognition of signs seen already and also recognition that some signs have not yet been seen. It also tests previous experience that may well include, in particular cases, an unsuspected extent of knowledge of signs which can guide the teacher in what to except from that particular learner.

Pages 5 to 10 test:

- that images of words have become sufficiently flexible to provide a number of answers to an incomplete word pattern

- that signs can be removed from any place in words, and yet pupils are still able to evoke them

- that one can take stock of one's knowledge within a restricted language and find that the same word can provide an answer to a number of differently formulated questions

- that not all questions have the same number of answers

Additional classroom games or techniques may be used to introduce these "gap" or "completion" games. For instance: *pat* may be written on the chalkboard, the middle sign erased, and pupils asked if anyone can put in a sign that will make another word *(pit, pet,* or *pot* may be generated). Now the middle sign can be erased again and again to find alternative solutions—and the last sign can also be erased.

s ___ t

is put up, and the students are asked to find all the signs that might be substituted to produce an English word. Then,

sa ___   and next   **___ at**

This game can also be played with two signs missing:

s ___ ___ t,   s ___ ___ s,   ___ a ___ ,   s ___ t ___

These pages of Worksheet 1 are *not* completed when pupils are still on Table 2 of the *Word Building Book*. They can go back to them whenever they feel their new experience is relevant to the questions that they contain. Hence teachers must *not* mark corrections on these pages, but allow students to add to them and correct them on the basis of their further experience. If teachers wish to keep a record of the learners' answers, it may be done in a separate notebook. The progress of the pupils may then be reviewed from time to time.

Pages 11 to 13 give examples of what we have called the *Game of Transformations*. What matters here is:

- that pupils are led gently into a difficult and challenging game through questions of gradually increasing complexity

- that pupils be encouraged not to think of a question as answered once and for all, but attempt to find alternative answers and compare their merits in terms of length, inventiveness, and elegance

The function of this game is to bring together within the dynamics of the mind the products of the activities so far experienced. Through this game, the power of *imaging* is maintained at the center of the activity, while the forming of a network of linkages between words generally unrelated by either sound, shape, or meaning is stimulated.

The psychological significance of the exercises lies in their use of the natural analytic and synthetic powers of the mind, calling on these to work simultaneously.

The mysterious way words are recalled, that is, recognized either by shape or by sound as having something in common with other words, is at the center of the mental operation. But since words may also be altered physically, permitting a willed relationship to other words of which one is yet unconscious, worlds are opened to the imagination. It is also possible that playing such games may have a lasting effect on the flexibility of the mind, the imagination, the intelligence of verbal communication, one's sense of mystery, and may lead everyone to a better acquaintance with the working of one's own mind.

It should be clear that the basis for learners' finding individual solutions to the Game of Transformations has been implicit in all the work done by the teacher with the pupils through Visual Dictation 1 and on the Word Charts in which the links-by-transformation between words have been studied. In addition, the learners have been encouraged continuously to apply their full imaginative powers to evoke in their minds and use an imagery far more extensive than was possible within the limits of the Word Chart or even *Book 1*.

Even so, introducing the game itself is necessary so that its rules now become explicit and thus usable by the pupils. Up to now, the procedures of transformation have served mainly as a guide to the teacher in choosing alternative directions for the Visual Dictations where words are related to each other through the same transformations—something pupils have not been made aware of. A way of beginning work with this game using Word Chart 2 has already been described.[26]

As presented in the Worksheets, this game is still one of considering various pairs of words. The object is to pass from the first member of each pair to the second, by making only *one* of the allowed transformations at a time (substitution, reversal, addition, insertion, but *excluding* subtraction) and with each transformation generating a new and proper English word. Note that *pass* $\xrightarrow{s}$ *pat* is *not* a subtraction, but a substitution of one sign for another, as we have seen above.[27]

Before working with the full game, teachers may find it helpful to do some work with *each* of the four transformations allowed, so that pupils are completely clear about them. Once this is done, teachers may want to move gradually into using all of them in the full game. The following indicates one possible introductory approach:

    1   The work on *substitutions* done by erasing signs to introduce the "gap" or "completion" games may be developed further by the teacher, writing on the chalkboard, for instance

$$pat \xrightarrow{s}$$

and asking, "What is this one?" then, "Who can change it into another word by substituting a different sign in the middle (or at the beginning or the end)?" Then, "Write it here," indicating the space after the arrow.

As many examples can be used as the feedback from the pupils indicates are needed.

The teacher writes *s* in a corner of the chalkboard.

---

26 See p. 36.
27 Discussion of this game in its full complexity is found on pp. 110-111, Chapter II.

Chapter I
The First Certificate of Reading

2 The teacher can now (or in the next lesson) work on *reversals*. She can write one word on the board followed by an arrow

$$pat \xrightarrow{r}$$

and ask, "What is this one? Who can write its reverse?" (repeating examples as often as needed).

Other examples might start with:

$Set \xrightarrow{r}$ (*tess*), $sap \xrightarrow{r}$ (*pass*), $pets \xrightarrow{r}$ (*step*)

r is written under the *s* in a corner of the chalkboard.

3 Similarly, *addition* can be developed by writing on the board:

top

and asking, "What is this one? Who can make it into another word by adding a sign at the beginning or the end?" Someone adds an *s* to the word and makes either

stop   OR   *tops*

"What did he make? Who can add another sign at one of the ends and make another word?" Someone comes and adds in the appropriate way to the work on the board to make it into

stops

Now this could be put on the board:

$$pot \xrightarrow{a}$$

"What is this one? Who can write another word after the arrow that is this word with one sign added to it?" Someone writes

spot   OR   *pots*

"What did he make?" Then the teacher puts a second arrow with *a* over it, as below:

$pot \xrightarrow{a} spot \xrightarrow{a}$ OR $pot \xrightarrow{a} spot \xrightarrow{a}$

and asks, "Who can put another word after the arrow that is his word with one more sign added to it?" Someone comes and completes the task, so the board shows:

$$pot \xrightarrow{a} spot \xrightarrow{a} spots \quad \text{OR}$$

$$pot \xrightarrow{a} pot \xrightarrow{a} spot$$

Other examples of double additions are:

$$up \xrightarrow{a} pup \xrightarrow{a} pups$$
$$pit \xrightarrow{a} spit \xrightarrow{a} spits$$
$$pit \xrightarrow{a} pits \xrightarrow{a} spits$$

Now *a* is written under *r* in a corner of the chalkboard.

4 In the same manner, insertion can be worked on, first writing, for example:

$$a \quad t$$

and asking, "What is this one? What will it be if I insert the 'brown' between two signs?" actually doing this as she says it to make

$$apt$$

Then perhaps writing:

$$pet \xrightarrow{i}$$

and asking, "What is this one? Who can write another word after the arrow that is this one with the 'curly green' inserted between two of its signs?" If there is understanding on the part of the pupils, this should result in

$$pet \xrightarrow{i} pest$$

Other examples if needed:

$$sop \xrightarrow{i} stop \qquad sis \xrightarrow{i} sits \text{ (or } sips\text{)}$$
$$sat \xrightarrow{i} spat \qquad pat \xrightarrow{i} past$$

Now *i* is written under *a* in the separate list on the board.

5   Looking at this separate vertical listing, the teacher may now ask questions to summarize the understanding of which sign stands for which transformation, asking, for instance:

> "Who can point to the sign we use over the arrow to show we have used substitution (or addition or insertion or reversal)?"

That subtraction is not allowed may then be clarified, since it is not on the list.

6   We may then try sequences of two different transformations, two of the same and one different, or three different, and so forth. The teacher starts by writing a word followed by an arrow which is marked to indicate the type of transformation. After a solution is found, the teacher puts another marked arrow after this word, and after the next solution, another arrow, etc. At any point, a new sequence of operations may be started. (But we are not, in this preparatory game, concerned about what word we end with—as we are in the stage just beyond this.)

7   Now the full game can be played.

The teacher asks pupils to look at the pair of words she has written on the board:

tap
stop

and to think how they can transform the first one into the second by making only one transformation of a sign at a time, and at each step producing an English word.[28]

She may rewrite the problem thus:

$$tap \longrightarrow \longrightarrow stop$$

---

28 In a special case where children are very young or work slowly, the restriction of having to form an *English* word at each step may be lifted for a few lessons and added later on.

so that the learners will see that they have one or more intervening steps. Here they might quickly see that they can make *tap* into *top,* and then make *top* into *stop.* Someone can write *top* in its place, and he or someone else can mark the arrows properly. If there is any difficulty in marking the arrow, the teacher can ask, "What did we do to change *tap* into *top?"* and point to the vertical list of signs on the board, which is there to act as a ready reference:

s

r

a

i

Students usually can quickly analyze which letter is needed. They then can be asked, "What did we do to change *top* into *stop?"* and mark it.

8 A few more simple examples should serve to help most learners to work on their own in these games and to analyze from the start the type of transformation used. For instance:

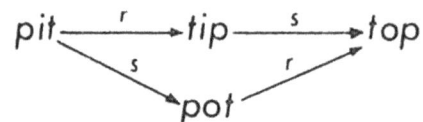

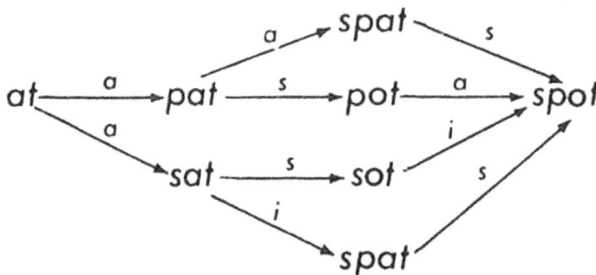

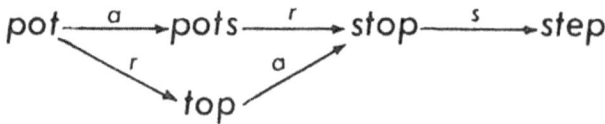

The teacher can ask, once one "route" is completed, if there is another way, and another, and another, etc.

Chapter I
The First Certificate of Reading

The Game of Transformations on Worksheet 1 should not now pose a challenge that is too difficult. For this first Worksheet, we show several possible solutions to assist the teacher in seeing that there may be *many* alternatives. There is rarely *one* answer only, even though we are restricted to the signs of Table 2 of the *Word Building Book*.

1 from *pat* to *pits*

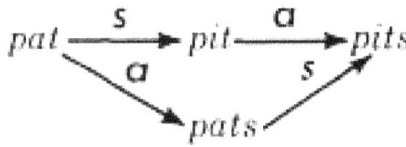

2 from *top* to *stops*

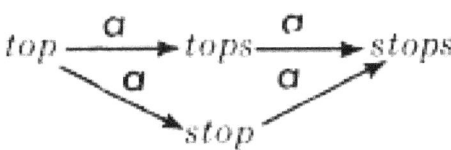

3 from *pet* to *sat*

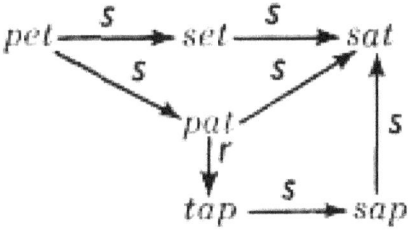

4 from *pit* to *step*

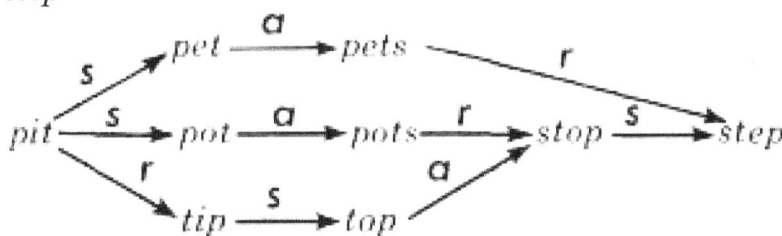

5 from *pot* to *tip*

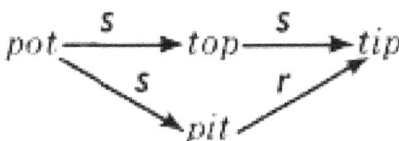

6 from *top* to *pit*

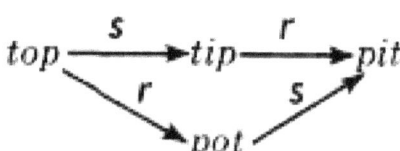

It is suggested that when pupils first work by themselves on their Worksheets, they all work at the same time, and that the teacher circulate among them and give individual help where needed. After each example is done, it can be very interesting to collect the answers on the board and discover that there are *several* possible correct solutions among them. The challenge from now on can be to see how many solutions one can find for each game, rather than to focus on finding one solution quickly or on finding the shortest one only. Teachers may, in fact, find themselves amazed at solutions found by their pupils beyond what we have shown here, and even beyond what they themselves have thought out.

Additional solutions may be added a day, a week, a month, or much later when the insight into these games is deeper. The improved score may then be shown at the bottom of the page.

Page 14 of Worksheet 1 opens the door to the pupils' own proposals for this game. Here their autonomy is tested as well as their aptitude at choosing pairs of words that are close to those studied, or those that are more challenging or even impossible according to the rules of the game. Teachers may again find themselves surprised at the inventiveness shown in meeting this challenge, including the many additional pairs of words the pupils may suggest to challenge their classmates beyond what can be put on this page.

Pages 15 and 16 encourage the learner to compose sentences and, implicitly, stories. Thus making use of all the ground covered in taking pupils in their education from spoken speech to its written form within the restricted language of *Book 1* and Table 2 in the *Word Building Book*. The Visual Dictations and oral dictations have prepared the way for this beginning in creative writing within the restrictions of what has been mastered. Indeed, most children soon fill more pages with their spontaneous efforts than those provided in the Worksheets.

12 The content of this first Worksheet is obviously usable as test material, but it has more uses than that of providing a score. Teachers are reminded that what matters is to see children or other learners grow in awareness of their powers, and hence of themselves, rather than to score here and now at a particularly high level. We are looking at learners involved in the process of acquiring a code for their speech through a number of activities designed to mobilize their senses, their intuition, the intelligence, and hence to stimulate observation of words and their behavior within the whole dynamics of the self.

The materials, including the Worksheets, have a built-in power to keep us as teachers in contact, to a certain extent, with what goes on in the learning process. Through this, we can gain a degree of control of the teaching situation rarely possible in other approaches.

It is for this reason that we may talk of *subordinating teaching to learning,* even though prepared materials are offered to educators.

We wish to test at every moment, by the achievement of our pupils, whether *we* are doing a good job. This will be the case if, as a result of joyful and powerful activities, we find the pupils reading fluently, naturally, and with proper intonation the materials produced from the restricted language we have been considering in this section.

If they do so, we award them their first reading certificate.

13 One last remark about this section must be added. To retell what is seen in one second from a window, or what has been experienced in a momentous minute, may take hours or months. Likewise, in this *Guide* we have needed many pages to attempt to describe what takes in fact only a relatively short time in the classroom. *The implementation of this program, leading to the first reading certificate, need not require more than the first few hours at school for ordinary first graders, being completed as part of the first week's work.*

Chapter II
Meeting the Sounds of English

1   In this program, the stage of progress takes us next to meeting the full range of sounds used in English, together with some of their spellings, leaving the remaining spellings until the next chapter.

2   English, in the analysis proposed here, presents some 51 well distinguished sounds though, speaking strictly in terms of the most refined linguistics, many more sound components could be isolated. But for the purpose of teaching reading, this list will prove adequate. With each sound, a different color is associated. While this rule was also applied throughout the last chapter, it was not apparent except in the case where the two s signs were introduced. To distinguish the different sounds that these signs with the same shape have, a lime green color was adopted for the s in *us* and lilac for the s in *is*. Then, to indicate that the same sound—the one given the lime green color—may be spelled in three or more different ways (as in *sit, pass,* and *pat's)*, we placed s, ss, 's in a single column on the chalkboard all in the same shade of green.

These principles for applying colors will be observed up to a point. By blending three primary colors in varying strengths and combinations, we can produce a range of colors that are secondary, tertiary, and so on. The difficulty is in obtaining shades that are readily distinguishable since 51 is a large number to select and control for consistent matching and contrasting within single charts and between different charts. This question of color control was a major commercial and technical problem in producing a set of twenty-nine separate colored Charts, relatively low in cost and yet sufficiently consistent in color for easy use.

3   A number of considerations relating to the use of color as an additional dimension indicating sounds in words can be of use to readers:

- The principle of sound-color correspondence can be restated: like sounds are identified by like colors whatever their spellings, and unlike sounds are distinguished by the use of unlike colors even if the same sign is used. The following two sentences illustrate each of these aspects respectively:

    *a*ll w*a*s d*a*rk *a*s m*a*ny h*a*res r*a*ced *a*round the vill*a*ge sw*a*mp

  The sentence above gives, in some regions, up to ten distinct sounds (more commonly nine) to the letter a, while in the sentence below, one sound is represented by ten different italicized signs!

    he s*ays* men s*ai*d m*a*ny fri*e*ndly l*eo*pards b*u*ry d*ea*d h*ei*fers for *ae*sthetic reasons,

- Related sounds can be represented by related colors. It is not possible to follow this principle with complete consistency in view of the number of colors involved. But, for example, the sign *th* as in *that* is given a color close to that of *s* in *is* since this latter sound becomes identical to the one in the first word if sounded with the tongue between the teeth. Similarly, and for the same reason, *th* in *thin* has a color close to that of *s* in *sat*.

- Color should not create new problems, but it may solve some:

    1   Color-blind people are not hindered by their color-blindness. Whatever existing sensitivity to color they have, they spontaneously develop their own clues, using shapes and shades. Color-blindness has never been reported as an obstacle to learning with *Words in Color*.

    2   Many teachers report that children confuse the signs *d* and *b*. It would have been valueless to have given these two signs, so similar geometrically, colors that were very

distinct, since the power of retention might then have been focused on the color clue, leaving the shapes still to be confused. So the colors for these two signs are intentionally very close, attention being drawn to shape by other means. One such means is by the mastering of one of these signs before introducing the other. This is the path followed in this program: *d* occurs for the first time on Word Chart 4, while *b* appears first on Word Chart 7. Words such as *burden,* which use both signs, challenge the learners soon after.[1]

- Where, as in the case of diphthongs, the sounds associated with some signs involve a merging of two otherwise distinct sounds, this phenomenon is reflected by including the tint selected for each of the sounds concerned in the representation of the sign in color, applying the color of the first sound uttered to the top half of the sign and that of the second to the lower. Examples:

  in *hour* — the sign formed by the first three letters of the word contains both purple and pale aqua, using in the uppermost portion the same color as used to denote the sound of *a* in *father,* and below, the color used to indicate the sound of the sign *w* in *with;*

  in *quick* — *qu* is in two colors, the top being that of the *ck* in *truck* and the bottom again that of the *w* in *with.* Later on, in *quay,* the *qu* has only one color, since the sign has only one sound, that of *k,* as we also find in the word *conquer;*

  in *next, exist,* and *anxious* — the signs *x* employ in each case different pairs of colors found in signs already met, making each *x* different in appearance from the others, while at the same time reflecting faithfully the particular sounds each indicates. Later on, in *anxiety,* *x* has only one color and one sound, that of *z* in *zoo.*

- Of all the materials associated with this project, only the twenty-nine Wall Charts are in color. Words appear in color on twenty-one of these Charts. The remaining eight

---

1 See also, in this connection, p. 99.

form a tableau called the Phonic Code, on which only a few whole words appear coincidentally. Here, only those parts of words, or signs which indicate the separate sound-components of words are seen, the various spellings for each particular sound being arranged in a single column. Since there are fifty-one sounds in this classification of English, fifty-one columns are used on the tableau, and these include, in all, over three hundred and fifty signs. On the twenty-one Word Charts, more than six hundred words provide the phonetic clues for reading English. All materials other than the charts are printed in black, just as ordinary reading materials are.

In this chapter, we shall be mainly concerned with meeting sounds of English not introduced in the very restricted language discussed so far. In Chapter I, the central techniques of the approach have been described quite fully with the hope that teachers will see that (1) as the language becomes progressively less restricted, and (2) as Word Charts 3-21 and *Books 2* and *3* are met, the approach has the *same* dimensions but is now extended and developed to meet the needs of a continuously expanding reading vocabulary. It is these extensions of the techniques that are discussed from now on, based upon the understanding of what has been offered in the previous chapter.

Section 1
Word Charts 2 to 12 Visual Dictations 2 and 3
Oral Dictation

1 The following Charts are introduced progressively and, once introduced, remain on display as a gradually expanding group. They are hung up on a vertical surface in the classroom following one arrangement or another. The following frames in black on white correspond to the Charts and are numbered accordingly, and arranged in order from 2 to 12 when viewed from left to right and top to bottom. This is one of several arrangements teachers find very useful. The content of each chart is clearly visible.

Chapter II
Meeting the Sounds of English

pat pit pet pot at it up tap tip top pep pup pop tot as us is sat sit set stop step pass stops steps past sap sips test pest ₂	mat tim met tom mom must mumps miss mast mess map am stamps a mops pump sum sam pam not nut net ten men man an sun in on tent upon sent ₃	fan fun fist fit if of fat puff fuss spend spent dad I sad mad fed and send mend sand mud fund stand end dust did that this them then than the thin yes yet fifty ₄	let lad sell tell lots smell spell slap list slit doll dull mill ill until till lend lent land less unless filthy funny wet wit with swim was will sunset slept ₅	pant wins thus rat ran red fur strip my sister wild mind rest kid kit kill neck milk skill silk kiss pile mile skip sick line fine truck track struck run rust strike ₆	her his has hat him hot bat but brick promise flat simple impossible suddenly horror worry word work world there burden back black sorry brother son from little ₇
hate same late male more fatal home bone woke he me we date egg use unite fuse girl first go got get leg globe make made nose any like fire nine ninety ₈	sold thirty no gone dirty off hundred seven april usable five give tiger thanks hose thirsty hungry dog gold bankrupt front firm duty loss so horse robe big gum bigger ₉	shop she ship china church chin shall shred michigan chicken wish cherry for or nor chorus child children hotel far shut channel charm shell shot done does chips goes chill have ₁₀	cat crime blood cry quickly question call all by watch small false clutch next orchestra capable criminal character garden phrase catch fantastic box match are were such air ₁₁	father mother able animal family ate to do too potato two tooth look fool took tomorrow school education soldier generation gem john judge joan jack adjective ₁₂	

2   A look at the actual colored Charts will quickly evoke the feeling that each of these Charts has an atmosphere of its own. This is due to the impact of the new colors that make their appearance in succession as, on each new Chart, several words using new sounds occur. This atmosphere which each Chart has introduces a new feeling which is readily associated with the words encountered on each, enhancing their retention. Pupils rapidly learn which words are to be found on which Chart and can locate any particular word in a very short time—much shorter than would ever be possible through memorization. Visual Dictations 2 and 3 and their complementary oral dictations maintain this knowledge at a level of immediate availability.

3   The set of Word Charts is so designed that most of the consonants are first met in conjunction with the five vowels introduced on Word Chart 1. Two exceptions are, first, the *schwa* or unstressed vowel found so commonly in English, and, second, the sign and word / that permits so many sentences referring to the readers themselves. The schwa sound is introduced very early (Word Chart 3), as it is involved in the ordinary usage of the indefinite article *a*. In this scheme it is always identified by its bright yellow color.[2] This color was chosen since the pale yellow u of *up* must register a change when left unstressed as in the word *upon* (Word

---

[2] May we suggest again that teachers *not* burden the memories of their pupils with the specialized *names* of the colors. These names are used in this guide merely as a cross reference for the teacher to the colored Charts. Work on the Charts requires only that the students *see* which colors are alike and which are different—a discrimination that a few-months-old baby makes without attaching a label to his perception.

Chart3). The bright yellow is maintained for all spellings of the schwa which, in English, can include practically any sign or combination of signs using vowels as the following list shows:

a —	fat*a*l	*u* —	*u*pon
o —	pot*a*to	*e* —	th*e*
i —	penc*i*l	*ea* —	pag*ea*nt
y —	eth*y*l	*ou* —	numer*ou*s
ei —	for*ei*gn	*ie* —	consc*ie*nce
oi —	tort*oi*se	*io* —	quest*io*n
ai —	mount*ai*n	*ia* —	mart*ia*l
eo —	pig*eo*n	*eou* —	right*eou*s
he —	ve*he*ment	*oa* —	cupb*oa*rd
iu —	nasturt*iu*m	*iou* —	consc*iou*s
au —	rest*au*rant	*eau* —	bur*eau*crat
ah —	halleluja*h*	*ough* —	thor*ough*ly

4 In this program, reference is not made to "long" and "short" vowels as such. In all, twenty-one vowel sounds are isolated and the principle is followed of introducing new sounds when the material already presented has been thoroughly assimilated and sufficient practice given. If it is true, however, that a great deal can be achieved with only seven vowel sounds, then this should be attempted before the others are introduced. And if the obstacles raised by the demands of learning to read are more readily overcome by keeping the number of ambiguous situations to a minimum through the restriction of vowel sounds available, it will pay us to proceed as far as we can with these only. Later, we can introduce the remaining vowels several at one time because of the increased insights into the reading process acquired by the pupils, further illustrating the concept of the cumulative effect of learning.

Once the sound for *I* has been met, a number of its useful spellings, such as occur in the words *my* and *line,* can be brought in without mention being made of the "long *i.*" The color used will indicate that in the words *mind, wild,* and so on, this new sound for the sign *i* is required rather than that found in *till* and *with*. Indeed, in the program, the question "Why this sound?" is answered by "Because this color is there." If the sign is lemon colored, you make the sound for 7; if it is pink, you make the sound used in *it*. But whatever consistency there is in the behavior of sounds and spellings in English, the learner will *discover* this consistency through observation of the color changes between a number of words such as *my, mile,* and *mill*.

Up to Word Chart 8, then, only seven vowels are met. But on Word Chart 8, five more are introduced together:

e as in *he*	*u* as in *use*
a as in *hate*	*o* as in *more*
o as in *home*	

Their colors are new ones and thus indicate that they differ in sound from the same signs met previously. The sound is ascertained by the learners when they hear the teacher utter one of the new words in which it appears. (For example, learners quickly deduce the sound for the different colored *a* by listening to the teacher pronounce *hate* and comparing it with their own pronunciation of *hat,* met on Word Chart 7.)

5   When Word Chart3 is introduced and displayed alongside Word Charts 1 and 2, it can be used with or without reference to Visual Dictation 1. To do so, the teacher draws on the chalkboard the new signs *m* and *n* in their respective colors, and then utters such words as *am* or *an* at the same time as she touches the appropriate signs in the appropriate order with the pointer. Then, by linking signs with the movement of the pointer, she can elicit from the class all the words found on Word Chart 3 and many additional ones, such as *tarn, tan, pan, pin, pen,* and so forth, just as was suggested in the last *chapter* for the introduction of Word Chart 2.

But since this procedure was thoroughly explained in Chapter I, let us concentrate here on alternative means, where the second stage of the teaching is begun by displaying Word Chart 3 and using Visual Dictations 2 and 3 as the techniques for mastering its content and its possibilities. The awareness of a growing systematic organization of new sounds and signs begun on the chalkboard is maintained through work in the *Word Building Book* as it is used in conjunction with the Worksheets.3

This alternative of Visual Dictation 2 and 3 is the procedure suggested for most groups when they are ready for Word Chart 3—that is, at this point, dropping Visual Dictation 1. However, in *two cases*, the use of Visual Dictation 1 for the introduction of sounds is advised:

- With remedial students who know several small words by sight, it is suggested that Visual Dictation 1 be continued through the introduction of the sounds found on Word Chart 3 *(m, n, and schwa)*, with no Word Charts in view until this is completed. This forces these pupils to think of sounds instead of trying to rely on superficial visual clues. When Word Charts 2 and 3 are then displayed together, following the extension of Visual Dictation 1, too much is presented for the learners to rely only on superficial clues. Much more than a cursory reaction is needed to read correctly *pat* and *pet; sat* and *set; stop, step,* and *stamps; set* and *sent; is, it,* and *in; in* and *on*.

- With those few five- or six-year-old children who may be much slower than the majority during the beginning stage of the program, it is suggested that Visual Dictation 1, used to introduce Word Chart 2, be continued for the introduction of the new sounds on Word Chart 3, and perhaps even those on Chart 4. Otherwise, the introduction of Word Chart 4 or, at the latest, Chart 5, is through the alternative procedure of Visual Dictation 2. This is the one focused on in this section.4

6 When a new Word Chart is hung up, joining the set already displayed, it can be seen that there are many alternative routes to be followed by beginning with words on one of the familiar Charts and proceeding to new ones on the new Chart.

Each successive new Chart can be viewed at first as new territory, but with landmarks on it similar to some of those on preceding Charts. These links can provide a starting point for exploration on the new Chart. Some people

---

3 See p. 55.
4 Contributed by D. B. H.

Chapter II
Meeting the Sounds of English

feel it is the coloring of the sounds which creates the most consistent clue to these landmarks, since it makes more vivid the identities and similarities.

Teachers can look at the new Chart and try to see what landmarks will be recognized by *their pupils,* who as yet do not read many words but who do understand from their work on the previous Chart how the color is used for sound, as well as how to turn a written word into speech. This will indicate to teachers how to move their pointer in the introduction of one new word after another so that hardly anything need be told the pupils. If a teacher takes all this into account, she might perhaps, on introducing Chart 3, only say some things like this:

"What was this one?" (touching an already familiar word on Chart 2 such as *at)*

"If I tell you this one is . . ." (touching a new word on Chart 3 which has only one new sound, such as *am)*

". . . then what will this one be?" (touching a new word on Chart 3, using the new sound and others known already, such as *sam)*

"And this one?" (touching again a new word on Chart 3, such as *pam,* in which all sounds are now known, although pupils must also use what they already know about transforming one word into another by changing these known sounds by substitution, reversal, addition, or insertion)

"And this one?" (touching a new word on Chart 3 which requires only one transformation — perhaps a reversal, as in *map)*

This can continue until all the words on the new Chart have been explored in this way.

Alternating with the above study of how words are linked by the sounds they have in common is the study of how words are linked by meanings or by their use in sentence structures. If the pupils easily read on Word Chart 2,

sit up pat   then, if the new words   *sit up sam*
is pat up   have been decoded,   *is pam up*
it is pat   they can obviously   *is it tom*
pat sat up top   read sentences like   *tim sat on a map*
these, made by Visual Dictation 2

The second set of sentences is generated by transforming the first set in one or more ways—by substituting one word for another, or by reversing the order of the words in some way, adding a new word, or inserting a new word (and, in some cases, subtracting a word). Here, it is the related meanings of words and their relations to the structure of one sentence and another one that guides the teacher in choosing how to make new sentences. These relationships form the basis for the teacher's expansion of Visual Dictation 2.

Each new Chart stimulates consideration of its words in terms of their equivalent sounds[5] and their equivalent meanings and structures.

In this *Guide,* more assistance is given the teacher with the first type of study—that is, the word study, and more initiative left to her for developing fully the second—that is, the sentence study.

pat pit pet	mat tim met tom
pot at it up	mom must mumps
tap tip top	miss mast mess
pep pup pop tot	map am stamps
as us is	a mops pump sum
sat sit set	sam pam not nut
stop step pass	net ten men man
stops steps past	an sun in on
sap sips test pest	tent upon sent

---

[5] See Appendix 3.

Chapter II
Meeting the Sounds of English

Here are some examples of how the study of Word Chart 3 can be developed:

1. Since the pupils know the word *at,* the teacher can give *am.* From *am* the operation of addition can be used to form *sam* and *pam.* Reversing *pam* gives *map.* From *map,* substitution gives *mat,* and the same kind of transformation again gives *met, mess,* and then *miss.* From *map,* substitution also gives *mop* (the teacher should cover with her hand the *s* of *mops* on the Word Chart until the following step) which then gives *mops* by addition.

    From *sam* we can find *sum,* and then *sun,* all by substitutions.

    Using these words in conjunction with those on Word Chart 2, we find several sentences are possible by Visual Dictation 2. Among them are:

    pam is up   *pat mops a mat*

    sam met pat   *sum it up*

    is it a map

2. Starting with words on Word Chart 2, *tip* could lead to *tim, top* to *torn, at* to *mat, pup* to *pump,* and so on, deriving the second word by substitution, addition, or insertion, respectively. From *top, mop* (by the use of hand to cover s on *mops)* can be derived, leading to *mops;* and from *mop, map* can then become *pam* by reversal, and then *sam* by substitution—this linking up with the sequence developed in (1) above.

    A number of suggestions for comparisons between Word Charts 2 and 3 could be tried out in turn:

    pet and *set*   leading to   *met* and *net*

    at and *as*   leading to   *am* and *an*

    it and *is*   leading to   *in*

These open up alternative routes for the conquest of words on Word Chart 3. Teachers should refrain from giving more than one word as an example to introduce *m* and *n*. Discovering how the other words are read should be left to the inquiring minds of the learners.

3. Through *mat,* we can find *mast,* from which we can derive *must*. We cover the last two signs of *mumps,* the word *mum* appears. One sign is uncovered to make *mump,* then the other to show the full word *mumps*. From *mump, pump* can be derived, but it can also be found from *pup*.

   From *stops, stomps* can be formed by insertion (using the transforming gesture of the pointer) and then *stamps* by substitution.

   The following sentences are only a few of those that could be given for practice:

   tom must pump it up   *mom mops up a mess*

   pam stops as it is mumps   *tom met sam up a mast*

4. The word *pot* could lead to *not* as the first word used on Chart 3; this leading naturally to *nut, net,* and by reversal, *ten.* The words *met* to *net* could be continued to yield *not* and *nut*. More sentences are possible including:

   tim stamps on a nut

5. The word *man* could be arrived at by addition from *an* or by substitution from either *mat* or *map*. From *man, men* follows, then *ten, tent, sent,* or *ten* and *net*—thus linking with the sequence in (4) above. But *men* could also be obtained from *met,* and so on.

In choosing alternative routes between words, teachers need to keep in mind those which require only *one* transformation (substitution, reversal, addition, insertion) between words. For instance, it is preferable to approach *must* from *mast,* requiring one substitution, than from *us,* which requires two additions. But sometimes, as seen above, unless one or more mental transformations are made by a gesture with the pointer (or by covering part of the word with the hand), it is impossible to shift from one to another of the words printed on the chart without more than one transformation. For example:

stops ----▶ *stamps* requires an insertion and a substitution

mom ----▶ *mumps* requires a substitution and two additions

The following sentences are only a few of those that can be found by knowing all the words on Word Chart 3 (not in Book 2):

- *it is not sam*
- *tim sat upon a pump*
- *ten men sip pop in a tent*
- *as mom mops a mess on a mat tom stamps on a nut*
- *is it mumps*
- *pat sets up a sum*
- *a pest is in a tent*
- *sam sent tom in*
- *is a mast a must*
- *it is a must*

All of this shows how flexible the materials can be and how much richer the Word Charts are when worked on in this way rather than read from left to right and top to bottom as a page of unrelated words. Teachers using these Charts will gain a great deal if they recognize the flexibility and make use of it wherever an opportunity presents itself. This flexibility even allows us to pass on to a new Chart before all words are known on the old one. Those remaining can be learned with some of the new words.

In Appendix 3, teachers will find a diagram which summarizes the links by sound among the words on Word Chart 3 and between the words on that Chart and the preceding one. To some teachers, this will be helpful in sorting out alternative routes for introducing a new Chart which have not been indicated above, or in sorting out possible routes for playing the Game of Transformations as done in the Worksheets. Others may find it too complicated even to consider at this time (which is why we put it in an appendix), but may find it very helpful a month or two after beginning their use of the approach—or even a year later.

7   Though attention has so far been concentrated mainly on words, the few examples of sentences given hint at the extensions of Visual Dictations 2 and 3 possible as new Charts are added. As soon as a new word has been

uttered by the class, and thus becomes usable in conjunction with previously mastered words, sentences and stories can be dictated visually with the pointer. Teachers must make an effort to dictate sentences that avoid a sense of boredom due to the ease of the challenge in the new words, but must not hinder progress by using in rapid Visual Dictation words not yet fully decoded.

In the pupil books, the pages follow this same alternation of word study with sentence study, but the challenge is increased by the removal of color clues and by the inclusion of additional words.

- *Book 2,* pages 2 and 4 offer for study not only words on Word Chart 3 but also additional words which can be made from the new signs introduced there (such as *stump, mass, nap, nest, ant,* etc.)

- *Book 2,* pages 3 and 5 give many more sentences than those suggested in this text or even by the content of the new Chart, since they include words not on the new Chart even though within its restrictions.

Our overall sensitivity to how a lesson is moving, based upon continuous feedback we get from the learners—since we move the pointer silently and *they* respond orally—is essential at every moment, so that the appropriate alternation of activities is chosen to avoid boredom or too difficult challenges for these learners. This alternation not only involves the word and the sentence study on the Charts, which has been outlined, but the reading in *Book 2,* the games in the Worksheets, and oral dictation. The oral dictation suggested earlier can now be expanded as Visual Dictations 2 and 3 are developed. These are the natural stimuli for the generation by the pupils of their *own* sentences, which are either made on the Charts with the pointer, produced on paper, or done in the Worksheets.

8   These remarks on the techniques associated with the introduction of the study of Word Chart 3 apply equally to subsequent Charts, and the approach outlined should be maintained throughout the series. The materials contained in particular Charts may occasionally necessitate detailed description for treatment of specific new challenges encountered, but the process sketched above will not in each instance be repeated in this text for teachers. Though each new Chart is different in character from the

Chapter II
Meeting the Sounds of English

previous one each can be tackled through a variety of entries leading to a variety of routes and a multitude of sentences far beyond what is possible to record. The type of detailed diagram mentioned above for the study of the words on Word Chart 3 is also provided in the Appendix for Word Charts 4 through 6, but is left to the teacher for subsequent Charts. Sentences for Visual Dictations are now left entirely to the ingenuity of teachers and pupils, since such sentences are almost unlimited.

9 In the top two lines of Word Chart 4, the signs *f* and *ff* both mauve-colored are introduced and sound as in *fan* and *puff*, respectively. At the same time, *f* in *of* appears, distinguished by the new color khaki to indicate the difference in its sound. This color is found later in *seven*, where it is used to denote the sound for *v*.

> *fan fun fist fit*
> *if of fat puff fuss*
> *spend spent dad I*
> *sad mad fed and*
> *send mend sand*
> *mud fund stand end*
> *dust did that this*
> *them then than the*
> *thin yes yet fifty* 4

Word Chart 4 introduces four consonants. These are the green-colored *d* as in *and*, the light-purple-colored *th* as in *that*, the very pale green *th* as in *thin*, and finally, the pale pink consonant y as in *yes* and *yet*. In *fifty* we find the y in the same pink we have met before in *pit*. On looking at this last word, one might think at first that the value attributed to the sign y is incorrect. But if one says "fifty-four" or "fifty-seven" the short vowel sound is the one that is heard. It has been necessary on more than one occasion in selecting colors to make a choice between the sound of the word when pronounced in isolation and its sound when uttered naturally in a sentence. In some cases the first principle was adapted, in others the second, with the object of providing points for discussion to increase the pupil's awareness of sounds and of their spoken language. Teachers are invited to exploit these opportunities in their own classrooms.[6]

10 Should any pupils be lagging behind in word recognition, exercises such as the following can be given them, asking them:

- to indicate with the pointer all words on these three charts containing the sound *a*, represented by the sign colored white, and so on for each of the other vowels studied;

- to point out all words containing, say, the combination *at*, or *it*, or *et*, or *an*, or *en* and so on;

- to point out all words containing, say, *and*, or *end*, or *if*, where these are words in themselves (as are *it* and *an* and *at*), but which we have not yet practiced finding on the Word Charts.

Since, in this approach, word transformation is a technique for the generation of bonds between words as well as for the introduction of new words, on these Charts it can be seen that such examples as *fan* and *fun* are intentionally placed near each other, and *fund* appears soon after the *d* has been introduced *sad* and *mad* and *mud* provide other examples of links, while *and, sand,* and *stand* illustrate one unfolding sequence of words, and *end, mend, send,* and *spend* another, and so on. The "confluency" of routes to produce some words is obvious and can serve as another exercise. For example: *spent* can be obtained from *sent,* or from *end* via *send* and *spend*.

Further study of this colored Word Chart 4 will make clear to the teacher alternate ways of introducing its new sounds or spellings. For instance, one can see that *an* is known from a previous Chart, and, therefore, *fan* could be given to introduce *f; and* to introduce *d; than* to introduce the light-purple-colored *th*. Since *in* is known, then *thin* can be given to introduce the other sound for *th*.[7]

---

[6] See, in particular, *from* (Word Chart 7) and *to* (Word Chart 12) discussed on p. 88.
[7] Some teachers may find Appendix 3 helpful. It contains a diagram that summarizes the links by sound among the words on Word Chart 4, and between those words and some on the preceding Charts.

Chapter II
Meeting the Sounds of English

The game of transforming one word into another on the same Chart, sometimes calling in a word from an earlier Chart, can be followed easily up to Word Chart 12. The links discovered will help learners call to mind whole groups of words every time just one is seen or thought about, producing out of verbal material a network of connections in the mind. The game will at the same time prepare pupils for later games of substitution where synonyms are demanded.

11 By maintaining some aspects of the work and changing others, it is possible to keep flexibility at the center of the program. To play the Game of Transformations to excess or to concentrate on it for too long will generate fatigue and boredom. But to spend some time examining each new Word Chart when it appears, in order to see what sorts of problems it presents and what discoveries can be made from it, does have value and serves to enliven the class and keep the game attractive.

Teachers may find it worthwhile to play the Game of Transformations for a while when pupils have taken note of some specific words on the Charts, which can then serve as landmarks or starting points from which to try to deduce the sound of others through the operations of transformation. For example, on Word Chart 5, the sound for the royal blue may be understood if the teacher gives *lad* (since *sad, mad,* and *dad* have already been met). Then *let* can be decoded by analogy with *pet, met, set,* or *net*. From *let, less* can be obtained by substitution (as it can from *mess* and *yes).* By reversal, *tell* can be found from *let*. The last transformation is another example of what happens to some *spellings* in English when sounds are reversed (as Word Chart 2 showed earlier with *sap* and *pass).* On Word Chart 6, a still more interesting observation can be made when reversing either *kiss* or *sick,* which mutually require changes in spelling. Written English demands in these cases that a *mute* letter *s* be added at the end, on the one hand, and the *mute* letter *c* be inserted after the vowel and before the *k,* on the other. These are examples of two general rules for spelling which, however, need not be pointed out to the pupils, as they will be discovered after a few weeks with this program and will remain much clearer in the mind as a result.

let lad sell tell lots smell spell slap list slit doll dull mill ill until till lend lent land less unless filthy funny wet wit with swim was will sunset slept 5	pant wins thus rat ran red fur strip my sister wild mind rest kid kit kill neck milk skill silk kiss pile mile skip sick line fine truck track struck run rust strike 6

Word Chart 5 shows that if *un* (met already in *sun* and *fun*) precedes *less*, no alteration of *less* is required; but that if it precedes *till*, the single sign *l* is substituted for the double sign *ll*. Examples of this can be studied to enliven the Game of Transformations, should this have been played for too long.

Likewise, Visual Dictation 2 could be used to relieve the teacher and stimulate the interest of the class, either through sentences that may be amusing, like:

I am a dull nut   and   *did the madman land in the sand*

or those that stir the imagination, like:

I will swim at sunset

or sentences that make people thoughtful, like:

I am sad as dad is fed up with this man

Readings from *Book 2* and answers to questions from the Worksheets will provide, on their own, all the variety one could wish for.

Chapter II
Meeting the Sounds of English

12   The game of transforming the printed words in the imagination by a gesture with the pointer, and then using these transformed words in sentences[8] can greatly increase the scope of Visual Dictations 2 and 3.

For example:

- in the case of *will*, what would we have said if the blue *e* had been used instead of the pink *i*
- with *wet*, what would have resulted had the lilac *n* been inserted between the blue e and the magenta *t*
- or, alternatively, with *sent*, had the aqua-colored *w* replaced the lime-colored *s*
- *slap* can easily become *slip; ill* can become *pill; spell* can become *spill;* and *filthy* can become *filth*

Such transformations which have not actually taken place on the Charts are carried out in the mind and retained in readiness for use. If these are used in Visual Dictations 2 and 3, the capacity of the learners to use their imagery rather than their vision is brought to bear on the extension of the sentences that can be produced from Charts. Now, sentences like the following may be elicited from the pupils:

sam fell in a dam, not a well

while showing

sam tell in a mad, not a will

and perhaps

did ted slip on the sill and spill the pills

while showing

did fed slap on the sell and spell the ill

---

8 See p. 39.

13 One can review as a whole the first twelve Word Charts now displayed on the wall. Each has individually offered opportunities and challenges different from those found on the others.[9]

The following additional points may be mentioned here:

- In the word *from* (Word Chart 7), the coloring adopted for the sign o is not that customarily found with the word pronounced in isolation; the use of yellow rather than orange for this sign indicates its sound when it occurs in sentences, as in the examples below:

    tim must go from his home

    he ran far from the hungry tiger

- On the other hand, *to* (Word Chart 12) is colored so as to sound the same as *too* or *two,* though it is pronounced like this only when used in isolation or stressed. Ordinarily, as in the infinitive form of verbs (e.g., *to sit, to run, to go,* etc.), it has simply the indeterminate sound of the *schwa*. This point has already been discussed, but it is nevertheless useful to consider examples that are met when the sounds of English are studied.

her his has hat	*hate same late*
him hot bat but	*male more fatal*
brick promise flat	*home bone woke he*
simple impossible	*me we date egg*
suddenly horror worry	*use unite fuse*
word work world	*girl first go got*
there burden back	*get leg globe make*
black sorry brother	*made nose any like*
son from little 7	*fire nine ninety* 8

- Whenever it seemed appropriate, words such as *till* and *until, egg* and *leg, big* and *bigger* have been printed as close to each other as possible on the same Chart, to attract the attention to irregularities of spelling for the

---

[9] Some teachers may find Appendix 3 helpful. It contains diagrams that summarize, for the words on Word Charts 5 and 6, the links by sound with one another and with words met previously.

Chapter II
Meeting the Sounds of English

same sound. In Word Chart 10, for example, the three sounds of *ch* can be viewed not only as introducing a new sound, but also differing spellings for sky-blue *sh* (of *shop*) as found in *michigan,* and for the gold-colored *k* (of *kid*) and *ck* (of *chicken*) as found in *chorus*. Word Chart 11 gives two new spellings for the dark-magenta *ch* (of *chip*)—*tch* found in *match,* and *t* found in *question*.

- *qu* and *x* each appear as double-colored signs.[10]

- *n,* in *thanks, hungry,* and *bankrupt* (Word Chart 9), is found to have the olive color which will later be used for the *ng* in *young* and *sing* (Word Chart 13), indicating its equivalence in sound to this sign and at the same time distinguishing it from the sound it has when colored lavender, as first given in *man* and *sun* on Word Chart 3.

- *child* and *children* show a unique relationship by their difference in color of the *i;* later on, *crime* and *criminal* are related in a similar fashion.

- Long words appear sufficiently early to permit an attack to be made on them in a variety of. ways.

14 Let us consider, in particular, the point about long words. From the start, we have involved the learners in the solution of the problem of sounding new written words through using the techniques of substitution, reversal, addition, and insertion. In the first week of reading, they attacked *pat* or *sat* from their knowledge of *at,* and *pest* from their knowledge of *pet*. In the second week, they met and solved by themselves the reading of:

stamps and *mumps* and *upon* (Word Chart 3)

stand and *fifty* (Word Chart 4)

filthy and *until* and *unless* (Word Chart 5)

struck and *strike* (Word Chart 6)

brick, promise, impossible, suddenly, burden (Word Chart 7)

fatal, unite, fuse (Word Chart 8)

usable and *bankrupt* (Word Chart 9)

---

10 See p. 71.

sold thirty no gone dirty off hundred seven april usable five give tiger thanks hose thirsty hungry dog gold bankrupt front firm duty loss so horse robe big gum bigger	shop she ship china church chin shall shred michigan chicken wish cherry for or nor chorus child children hotel far shut channel charm shell shot done does chips goes chill have

Next, we reach:

> *michigan, hotel, chorus* (Word Chart 10)
>
> *tomorrow, family, soldier, education, generation, judge* (Word Chart 11)
>
> *clutch, orchestra, character, phrase, question, fantastic,* and *criminal* (Word Chart 12)

The challenge presented by short words should not be underestimated, but neither should that offered by long ones be exaggerated.

What may be involved here is the stubborn pursuit by some pupils of false trails suggested by elements that may or may not be related to what they are looking at. If anyone really looks at a word in color on the Charts, all the clues for its pronunciation are there, and only the right sound can be uttered. But some learners, after a time, can no longer keep themselves at the task, so follow any clue they seem to find in a word. For such pupils, what is needed is a re-education in looking and listening. For beginners, it is, rather, an education that requires them to offer a solution only after they have processed all the clues and are sure that they are right. To help them, it is advisable for teachers to relate the problem on hand to problems already solved, but never to tell them the answer. In this connection, let us consider some of the examples above:

> *Chorus* can be found through linking *or* and *us,* and seeing that the beginning is the same color as the *ck* in *chicken;*

orchestra	its colors can be easily solved by recognizing that *or* has been sorted out, that *ches* has the same color pattern as *kiss*, and that "or-kiss" carries the *tra* to give the right sound;

cat crime blood cry quickly question call all by watch small false clutch next orchestra capable criminal character garden phrase catch fantastic box match are were such air ₁₁	father mother able animal family ate to do too potato two tooth look fool took tomorrow school education soldier generation gem john judge joan jack adjective ₁₂

hotel	transformations from *no* to *nose* and then to *hose* yield the first syllable, while *tell* yields the second;
michigan	which a number of older boys read as "machinegun," can be divided into mich-igan, and *miss* yields *mich*, once we see that the *ch* here is the same color as the end of *wish*;
soldier	move from *sold* to sold, in which this *d* has the color of the *g* in *gem*; add the ending of *sister* for the sound of *ier*;
education and *generation*	are usually decoded with the same ease—*gem* serves as an entry to *gen*, *ed* is taken from *red* or *fed*, though the *d* has the sound of the one in *soldier*. The ending *ation* is recognized because of the colors, the *t* having the color *sh* in *shut*.

Naturally, not all pupils follow the same path. Often it is very difficult to know how they have succeeded, since success is the least revealing of events. Errors, on the other hand, help us by revealing the problems of our pupils, since we cannot force them to be right or wrong to please us.

15. In the remaining sections of this chapter, reference will be made to the same Charts considered here, but the emphasis will be on the other materials.

Section 2
Book 2—Words, Sentences, Stories

1   The sections of *Book 2* are arranged, as far as possible, to show in the conventionally printed form (that is, the left to right spatial ordering of the signs and the words) the two Visual Dictations: the first page of a section shows signs linked into words (as in Visual Dictation 1), and the second one shows words similarly linked to form sentences (as in Visual Dictation 2). At this stage, it is more convenient to make sentences with Visual Dictation 2 for, while possible with Visual Dictation 1, it is less time-consuming here.

This does not mean that on a number of occasions teachers will not resort to the well-practiced exercise described in detail in Chapter I. It simply means that since the formation of words has, through practice, been established, we may, for the most part, omit this game and at the same time increase the yield, reserving Visual Dictation 1 mainly for work with the signs in the *Word Building Book* when it may be necessary. This can happen, for example, during group work, when there is need to generate words wanted for producing sentences by Visual Dictation 2 on the Word Charts.

In the various sections of *Books* 2 and *3* words are introduced after the new signs have been met, although the particular words in the books are only examples. Some of these can be seen in color on the Charts, or may be generated from them; others are new and can be studied as soon as the group disperses for individual work on the relevant page. More words still can be generated by the pupils from the signs in the corresponding table in the *Word Building Book*.[11] This study of words leads not only to their careful decoding, but to awareness of their spelling, since it focuses attention on their structure, and leads as well to greater understanding of the set of meanings which goes with each.

---

[11] A list of the new signs being considered appears at the top of each page of separate words in *Book 2,* making it easy to locate the particular table in the *Word Building Book* which includes the new signs.

For the most part, the sentences which follow in each section of the pupil books contain words just introduced on the preceding page as well as those met in the classroom sessions. Occasionally words are used that can be decoded by analogy.

2   It is clear from a perusal of the word-pages of *Book 2* that the rule of restriction is observed throughout. No sign is used whose sound has not already been introduced in the preceding pages or at the head of the section concerned. In this way, ambiguities are avoided and practice in only the sounds already met is given.

3   The first four pages of *Book 2* refer to Word Chart 3. This has been described in detail in the preceding section. If the Word Chart and the *Word Building Book* are introduced first, and then *Book 2,* it is easy for the teacher to ask the group she has just introduced the Chart to to work at their seats with the words on page 2 of *Book 2*. While they are doing this, she may go around and visit those whom she knows take longer to recognize words already met, and to look at new words. If the first group of learners still have difficulties, reference to the words in color on the Charts should suffice to eliminate them. Teachers should *never* tell pupils what to sound for any of the printed words.

The pupils who can read page 2 of *Book 2* are asked to read page 3 in conjunction with Table 3 of their *Word Building Book,* and to proceed with individual work in Worksheet 2.

4   It seems reasonable to ask teachers to devote more time to the pupils who are struggling with some point not yet fully clear, and to let those able to engage in their own education by individual creative work to proceed with it. The result of this subdivision of a group, however small, into smaller groups, will be to reduce the gap between pupils, since the difficulties being encountered at this stage are only of an understanding of how signs reflect sounds. Insight into this relation, once achieved by a few minutes of intensive individual or small group work, often permits those who have met difficulty to proceed successfully from then on. That some pupils will devise as many as thirty new words while others produce as few as five may have no bearing on future work, since it is possible for principles to be understood equally well regardless of the number of

examples. Quality in work is rightly valued by teachers, but differences of this kind may merely indicate the easiness of the work and the filling of available time. Quantity of words produced does not necessarily point to a deeper insight by one student which would set him ahead of the others on every occasion. While teachers should note who does what, they should refrain from drawing immediate conclusions, waiting instead for other events to suggest whether this productivity really reflects power and insight, or simply the use of time in generating words exemplifying one relation of sign to sound.

5   Page 4, being interchangeable with page 2, can be considered first, or they can both be taken in the same assignment. These two pages, with their accompanying sentences, are to be looked at as a first step toward a second reading certificate.

This should be understood to mean that the pupils beginning *Book 2* are those who have graduated from *Book 1*. They are no longer the beginners they were a week earlier. They know that signs are used to suggest sounds, and they know that some games generate noises sounding like speech, and have transferred from the one activity to the other a number of times.

All this knowledge of rules and procedures makes the learners incomparably more effective than they were when they first began. To meet this new competence, teachers should show their awareness of it in the way they work with their class at this stage.

The author was not able, in pages 2 to 5 of *Book 2,* to reflect the increase in competence of the pupils, but if teachers look at *Book 2* as a whole, they will see that though spacing and type size are not different from that used in *Book 1,* the ground covered in the 24 pages is greater, proportionally, than in the 16 pages of *Book 1*. The awarding of a second reading certificate, in perhaps two weeks from the start of *Book 2,* should be justified by the ground covered. This can be achieved if teachers do not inhibit their pupils' progress by setting aside the same amount of time for each sign or new page, but allot time for the different sections of *Book 2,* with progress based realistically on the increased power of the learners.

The cumulative effect of learning will be evident when

- less time and effort are taken to resolve the problem of reading each new page;

- pupils increasingly visualize more new words and sentences than are actually shown;

- the number and variety of words used by pupils when writing or using the Worksheets increase.

Naturally, pupils needing more time should not only be given more time, but also greater variety.

6   It is already clear that, while there are on page 2 of *Book 2* many of the words from Word Chart 3, page 4 presents a number of new words. Stress could be put on this difference, and pupils made to look for more and more new words. Thus, more and more new sentences will follow as asked for in one section of the Worksheets.[12]

Pages 6, 7, and 8 are, respectively, devoted to signs appearing on Word Chart 4. Treating these signs separately is an artificial device, as will be seen by what follows in the book, but it can be useful at this point if only to prove to the learners that it is possible and interesting to work on each new extension of the restricted language to expand their vocabulary.

It must again be noted that many more words exist than are given and, therefore, that many more sentences could be proposed by including such additional words. The pages of the book, and the Word Charts, only indicate examples of what is possible, leaving pupils free to do more. If teachers understand this from the start, when the task is still manageable, they will let pupils forge ahead on their own, since the restricted language is wider and the possibilities vastly more plentiful than the scope presented in the books and Charts alone.

7   Pages 9 and 10 go together, although they do not face each other. Page 10 offers a new test of the ability of pupils to work mentally, rather than in

---

[12] See p. 120.

the presence of selected words, and also of their aptitude in forming sentences with these words. When practicing Visual Dictation 1, we developed the skill of composing sentences mentally from lean material. Now, we meet a similar application of the mind, since we have to use a set of words we *have* seen, but can no longer see, to form sentences. How often pupils will need to turn back to page 9 will indicate both their level of dependence on the visual sign and how well their imaginations are working.

Since many more words and sentences exist potentially than are offered, the gathering of additional examples could be one of the aims of these pages. A logbook, in which new words are entered as they are thought of, could be started by each pupil.

8   We must stress the fact that, through comparing words on the Charts with those in the pupils' books, teachers will become aware that these materials are complementary and mutually reinforcing and, at the same time, will become better users of both the Charts and the books. We have taken advantage of each medium to broaden the learner's insight.

Space on the colored Charts is at a premium, but sufficient examples of words have been given to help establish phonetic clues and relationships. While space is not so restricted in a book, nevertheless only a small number of additional signs and words are provided, since the Worksheets and classroom opportunities are the means intended for extending the field of experience.

Let us note that *dd* appears on page 7 of *Book 2* but no example of this sign in a sentence is given before page 8; *pp* is indicated on page 12, but no such sign appears on the Word Charts before Word Chart 15. To become strict and uniform in such matters might create boredom, and it is in any case unnecessary, since pupils learn very quickly to work well with the flexibility of the materials and have the feeling that no restriction is imposed on them.

9   With page 12, we resume the practice of reserving two pages for each set of new signs. On the left are the words chosen as examples, on the right a selection of sentences. At the top, in heavier type, the new signs are

displayed. There is no fixed rule for the presentation of these signs, nor for the placing of the words in a particular line, other than that signs in one column are related to each other by one common sound. Note that much more ambitious sentences are now attempted on page 13. The way is open for teachers and pupils alike to take flights of imagination in the creation of their own sentences with the signs available. Naturally, it is not easy to regulate the imagination, and some classes will be more at ease than others with this opportunity.[13]

10 Page 14 reflects the cumulative effect of learning in presenting a considerable number of new signs to be studied. The author's confidence that pupils can learn this rapidly and retain it all should be tested thoroughly by every user of the method. If the increased pace of learning is found to be realistic, teachers will gain new insights with respect to the amount of material learners can assimilate that will enable them to speed up progress.

11 Though the so-called "long *I*" sound was first introduced on page 7 (and Word Chart 4) in the shape it takes when it forms a word, and, more thoroughly, as *i* and *y* on subsequent pages, all the other "long vowels" are introduced together on a single Word Chart and on one page, 16, in *Book 2*. It has been shown in practice that learners are able to take a development of this order in their stride, that it is unnecessary to consider the contrast between letters, which is in effect a complication, and that it is helpful to present a block of signs and words all at once. The book is now a mine, revealing its wealth in the quality, length, and number of sentences possible. On page 19, in particular, the example

my older brother uses logarithms in his math, I don't

is given both to indicate that in our experience this level of reading *is* the child's, and to offer one example of what could be done by teachers using this approach.

---

[13] In *Creative Writing* by Sister Mary Leonore, R.S.C., of Sydney, Australia, and in other volumes in the series *Words in Color in the Classroom,* ample examples of pupils' work within a restricted language show what can be achieved when the teacher is sensitive and free (see Bibliography).

12 It is not necessary to describe in detail what each pair of pages offers. A quick glance provides this information. It may be useful to stress once more that when the sign *b* is introduced, no confusion must be left between *d* and *b*. The care taken here consists in first presenting a list of words with only *d's* in them, then a second with *b's* only, and then one including both *b's* and *d's* at random, and, in particular together, in such words as *bad, bud, dub, band, blind, burden, abdomen,* and so on. Very soon the learners may create others such as *bed, dabble, board,* and *subdue.*

13 An interesting feature seen to be developing is the triplet of spellings for each consonant sound: the single sign, the double letter, and the sign with the "silent *e.*" The corresponding types of signs for each consonant, whenever possible, are arranged to appear in one horizontal line of the Phonic Code or in the *Word Building Book,* making three horizontal lines of each type.[14]

In a later section of the Game of Transformations,[15] we shall see how consonants that are given a double-letter sign can be treated to generate greater insight into spellings. Here we see their systematic appearance. Teachers are thus given opportunities to observe how images are formed, and how these help spelling.

On pages 20 and 21 of *Book 2, oe* as in *goes,* and *oe* as in *does,* are introduced. On page 20, several sounds for the sign *ch* are introduced. Two of these offer no difficulty, but *ch* as in *chrome* presents a problem. Reference to *ch* in *chorus,* on Word Chart 10, may be necessary.[16] All of this is met on the Charts and in *Book 2* before *orchestra* and *character* are met on Word Chart 11, both of which occur later in the book.

The book concludes with another set of new signs.

---

[14] See also p. 124.
[15] See p. 109.
[16] See p. 91.

Chapter II
Meeting the Sounds of English

14 With the exception of the few sounds listed below, we have, in this small volume, *Book 2,* met under one or more guises all the sounds of English.

	Vowels		*Consonants*
ow	as in *cow*	*j*	as in *jug*
oo	as in *book*	*s*	as in *leisure*
oy	as in *boy*	*x*	as in *exist*
oi	as in *reservoir*	*x*	as in *obnoxious*
o	as in *one*		

The signs for the sounds met so far are reproduced here from Table 9 of the *Word Building Book*.

a	u	i	e	o	a	u	I
o	y	a	a	e	e	y
a				u	o	i
oe				o	i
				i

p	t	s	s	m	n	f	f	d	th	th	y
pp	tt	ss	ss	mm	nn	ff		v	dd
pe	te	se	se	me	ne	fe		ve	de
		's	's

Chapter II
Meeting the Sounds of English

a   o   a   u   e   o   e   o
                             oe   a   oo
                                       ai

l   w   k   r   b   h   g   n   sh   ch   qu   x
ll   ck   rr   bb   gg   ch   tch   xe
le   ke   re   be
              ch
              c
              che

$\overline{l}$ $\overline{re}$
le

15   The earliest stories in the *Book of Stories* are interesting in a special respect. The *first story* is as follows:

- at sunset pat and pam went in with sam

- tim and tom were still on the sand

- sam sat on a step and pam on a mat

- pat was upset because she lost ten stamps

- the sand was full of wet lumps, but tim and tom sat on them

- mom and dad told them to run in as it was dinner time

While the *second story* opens with a single descriptive statement, the sentences that follow reveal a principal characteristic of these stories: each adds its meaning to the previous ones:

- in the family there are mom and dad and five of us, sam, pam, tom, pat, and tim

- sam is up first, tim last

- sam has a bed and tim and tom a bunk

- pam and pat have a room on the first floor

- pat is tall and tim is small

- tom is as tall as pam, but pam is older

- sam is nine and tim is five, tom is seven

- sam is the oldest and his sisters and brothers love him very much

The reader now anticipates that the *third story* will be a continuous narrative, since the rereading of the first after the second gives the feeling that the first story *is* meant to be the beginning of a longer narrative. The third passage, still more than the second, is what one would call a story:

- pat has a pet, it is fat and sits on mom's lap

- sam has a thin and dull cat found on the rocks, pat's cat is not his friend

- sam's cat wants to go out, pat's cat wants to stay in

- when sam's cat is out, pat's cat starts to jump around the house and to drink and eat

- when sam's cat is back, pat's cat hides in mom's lap

- pam, tom, and tim have no pets

From now on, the *Book of Stories* unfolds as a continuous narrative, as its title suggests. But, for the present, this set of stories is not the principal concern, as it will be later on when it can be used for exploring their meanings and in the beginning study of composition and style. The pupils, having manipulated the restricted language of *Books 1* and *2*, will, like the author, have ideas of their own that are story-like and can be written down.

16 Every teacher will receive the spontaneous gifts of her class if she makes it natural for them to write as freely as they can within the limits imposed by each successive restricted language. Since the learning moves at a swift pace, pupils find themselves less restricted in the language every day. Since writing freely is not simply a question of vocabulary, teachers will need to find means of letting their classes use Visual Dictation 3 (and its complementary oral dictation) as early as possible, allowing the pupils to judge the results as a story, rather than as a set of sentences.[17]

To begin with, two sentences can be put together by one pupil or several pupils working in a team. Then the class could be invited to join in and suggest additional lines, developing a theme which unfolds further as each new sentence is added. After such group work, the pupils could return to their desks to write down on their own whatever comes to them. Reading aloud to the class what they have written could take place as an immediate sharing of experience in the following session.

---

17 See p. 53 for examples of Visual Dictation 3 and footnote on p. 78.

There are many variations on this procedure, any of which might be preferred by teachers. Each teacher may wish to develop her own way of stimulating pupils so that each pupil develops *his* approach to writing within the restricted but developing languages that form the sequence of the approach. Eventually a class—or even an individual—"Book of Stories" might be added to the classroom bookshelf. Such books could prove to be among the most creative ever written.

Section 3
Worksheets—Control of Progress

1   Of all the materials included in this program, the booklets of Worksheets are potentially the most valuable to the learners, since so much latitude is allowed in the research they can do to answer questions and so much opportunity is given to be inventive.

2   The Worksheets were conceived as a tool which changes as the learners advance. Worksheet 1 has been described in the previous chapter.[18] For the study of sounds and of the words used in *Book 2*, Worksheets 2-7 inclusive make a number of proposals which steadily increase in difficulty and complexity and, therefore, in the demands they make upon the powers of the learner.

Since Worksheets 1-7 follow the same pattern, pupils become efficient in handling their tasks and can use the Worksheets as a steady record of their own progress. But they can also be used as a battery of tests of linguistic power, not only for the pupils themselves, but for the teachers and for researchers, once a sufficient number of completed Worksheets are made available. From such a study by researchers, there may emerge a possibility of studying, in a complex way, the complex act of learning to read as well as that of learning to speak one's mother tongue.

3   If we look at *page 1* of Worksheets 1-7, it will be seen that learners are asked on each occasion to make up "words," using signs from the tables in the *Word Building Book* that are different from those on the Word Charts and those found in the relevant sections of *Book 2*. They are therefore

---

18 See pp. 53-54.

Chapter II
Meeting the Sounds of English

required to make combinations of the various signs whose sounds have been studied in class. With the knowledge that the words to be produced here must be different from those met in class and in the pupil books, pupils are thrown back on their use of the wider tool of combination and permutation of signs in order to obtain the words asked for. There should be no end to the production of answers for the exercise on page 1. The freer, more imaginative, minds will produce the most creative responses without special encouragement. We need only to leave pupils alone and observe what they do with the challenge, noting what they offer. A question at the foot of the page asks for the number of "words" found. This is the only question that can legitimately be asked of all learners engaged in such a task. It will measure the interest in the game, the degree of understanding of it, and how well time has been used.

Page 2 of the Worksheets goes deeper into the material produced on page 1, and asks for the recognition that some of the above "words" produced by permutations and combinations of signs are actual words in the English language. The results of work on this page will test:

- whether the words produced can be sounded by the learner;

- whether, once he has sounded the words, the learner has inner criteria for deciding if a word is either a word known to him or one that could be part of the language as he views it;

- whether the learner accepts random words as English or is guided by random criteria.

4   The insight into the difference between groups of signs, on the one hand and words one knows on the other, will grow as the first pages of the successive booklets are considered. This insight is much more important than the objective product formed using the signs on the paper. It is this insight that we should cultivate in each learner. Teachers will see that they should refrain from correcting what is proposed by the pupil and instead study it in order to increase their own understanding of their pupils. To correct is to reduce the value of the efforts and to interfere with the data.

In order to enable pupils to recognize their progress, they should be allowed to go back and take a deeper look at what they have done on previous occasions. Could anyone exaggerate the importance of the recognition by a learner that he himself now possesses criteria which permit him to make up his mind about the accuracy or inaccuracy of what he believed to be right not long ago? He will be master of the criteria teachers apply in order to *know* what is right or wrong in a certain situation. To test this *is* important and should not be interfered with.

5   The question of recognition of words has two meanings: one is concerned with insight into their shape as it relates to the sound of speech; the other relates to the ability to evoke experiences, images, and other materials in response to the sounds found hidden in the signs of the written word.

The exercise on *page 3* of these Worksheets shifts from the first meaning, partly covered on page 2, to the second, by asking for drawings or for newspaper clippings or for actual objects (to be found and brought to school) that illustrate what meanings are evoked in the learner's mind by the sound of a word. When a word is abstract, as, for example, *empty* (page 3 of Worksheet 3), it may really challenge the imagination of learners, producing whatever is in their minds as an answer.[19] This precious aptitude of the imagination should not be interfered with. The results should all be accepted by the teacher, errors being handled by the class in full session.

It may be possible in some classrooms to display on a board the various solutions found by the class members. Such a display would be like an objectification of a section in a dictionary where several different meanings are given for one word. These displays may occasionally be of such quality that teachers will want their colleagues to share in their delight; photographs of the displays could be taken and sent to language journals, through the medium of which the work of a single child could serve to enrich all.

---

19 See footnote on p. 97. In Sister Leonore's book, *Creative Writing* (and other volumes in the series *Words in Color in the Classroom*), we find records of the interesting ideas children brought to this game (pp. 27, 36-37).

6   *Page 4* serves as a test of recognition of signs within words. Because words here are printed in black, compound signs (digraphs, trigraphs, etc.) such as *oa* in *boat* could appear to some learners not as one sign, but as two letters whose two different sounds have been met. Through such exercises we can find out whether pupils learning by our approach consider letters as separate parts of words or consider signs made of a group of letters as the units of sound in words.

If it is true that pupils have learned to associate graphemes with phonemes, we should expect some to recognize graphemes in words, rather than letters of the alphabet that have been ignored altogether as such in this approach. The fourth page of these Worksheets, therefore, provides a double test. On the one hand, it measures the degree of success learners have achieved in mastering an important aspect of the program, and, on the other, whether pupils at this stage can keep the sign concept in mind, rather than just see isolated letters in words. The *Word Building Book,* if well used, can help establish this idea, assisting in the perception of signs as related to sounds, rather than letters to sounds (or to their names). The second section of this exercise, on the lower half of page 4, asks the pupil simply to write down any words he can and then to draw a circle around those signs not to be found in the *Word Building Book* table being studied. This provides a further opportunity to learn about the pupils' experience outside school. But it also gives the learner a chance of knowing that this experience is acceptable to his teacher.

For the teacher, the answers to such questions can provide clues both about what every pupil brings to his work, and also where this might prove a help or a hindrance. The exercise also makes it easier to insist on the importance of looking again at each word, considered as a combination of the units we call signs. This will have the greatest impact on the retention of shape, which is equivalent to saying that it will turn spelling into a game.

7   This insight into word formation will be enhanced by the game extending over *pages 5-10* of each Worksheet. This game is to be considered as a whole; that is, pages 5-10 of each Worksheet represent the progression of the game from one Worksheet to another, as do the twenty-four columns (four to a page) available to be filled in, in each Worksheet.

The game, known as the "completion" game, presents various combinations of signs with spaces to be filled in by other signs to be chosen by the pupil. The object of this game is to propose in each column as many standard English words as possible which come to mind at this stage from what has been studied.[20]

Since each attempt at the Worksheets is dated, pupil and teacher will know (1) what has come to mind on each of the various occasions concerned, and (2) how the passage of time affects the results by allowing for extension and self-correction.

Examination of the pages in the successive Worksheets shows that it is possible to make pupils aware of what words look like when truncated in a variety of ways by asking them to evoke one or more words whose shape can integrate the form presented. This exercise has a tremendous potential, particularly since every pupil can return to any of the questions as his experience develops.

What is requested of teachers is that they understand that any dynamic vision of a word can only add strength to its retention, and that the exercises presented here show each word in a number of aspects. There is at least one example on the Word Charts or in the pupil books for each proposal, so that mere reference to such an example will lead pupils to understand that images of shapes change if we cover up parts of the shapes. Here again, the unit is the *sign,* not the letter, though it often will be found that the sign required is also a single letter. With practice at imagining completed answers and seeing them as fully printed words in place of the partial combinations, pupils will come to appreciate how it is possible for one word to be a solution in more than one column.

Among the exercises, some suggest immediate solutions, while others are more demanding for learners who are new to the game. But for those whose imagination is of the kind required here, the task of relating a partial signal to particular words from a set stored in the mind as sounds and shapes will be demanding however the challenge is presented. What is meant, here, is that there are some pupils who, while completing

---

[20] See p. 58 for a detailed description of how this game may be introduced.

Chapter II
Meeting the Sounds of English

— *et*

at once find words such as *pet, met, set, net,* or *let,* and so on; but, when working on

$$f\text{———}y$$

may find much more of a challenge, requiring the scanning of Word Charts or pages in *Book 2* before *filthy* or *fifty* are found as possible solutions. If *funny* was offered as an answer, it would be pointed out that in this word *nn,* being a single sign and having one color only, would only be a solution for

$$f\text{——}y \quad \text{and not for} \quad f\text{———}y$$

Sometimes, for a long period, only one example may be found to satisfy a request for a word, as in the case of

$$\text{——}l\text{——}s\,s$$

which can be answered by reference to *unless* on a Word Chart. Eventually, *useless* or *aimless* might be found as alternative solutions.

When teachers undertake seriously to present such games to their classes, refraining from making suggestions themselves, they have at their disposal a means for testing linguistic growth and, at the same time, a teaching tool leading to continuous development.

Scoring here is so simple that it can be done by the pupil; the teacher needs only to check the scoring.

8   In the previous chapter we have already discussed thoroughly the function of the *Game of Transformations* found on *pages 11-14* of each booklet and have given a detailed description of how the game may be introduced. Here, we give some additional assistance, needed for playing with ease the game in its more complicated forms.

A deeper understanding of the four operations of transformation used — *substitution, reversal, addition, insertion*—and of the one not allowed (subtraction) may be helpful. In performing these transformations the rule is that they must be transformations involving single *signs* as defined by their appearance as a single unit in the *Word Building Book* or later on in the Phonic Code. This is important because although most signs have only one sound, a certain number have two sounds (as shown by the double coloring on the Phonic Code) and the majority of them have two or more letters even though they have only one sound. We have already understood that *subtraction* of signs is not allowed in *this* game.[21] However, many routes in actuality *are* allowed which are not seen as that because they appear superficially as subtractions or double transformations to teachers used to thinking of the spelling of words in terms of the letters rather than in terms of signs. These possibilities are increased by the following *two types of equivalence:*

- *horizontal equivalence:* If the same sign is maintained when effecting a transformation, even if the sound is not kept, this is not counted as a change. Since color represents sounds, the above equivalence expresses that there would be an additional change in the word if the transformation were written in color. (It can be considered "horizontal" because the sign that is maintained would appear in different columns which are side by side in either the *Word Building Book* or on the Phonic Code.)

to —s→ so   *o, f,* and *le* are all maintained

if —s→ of   with a change in the associated sound.

mile —s→ male

- *vertical equivalence:* When signs are different but represent the same sound (that is, belong to the same column in the *Word Building Book* or on the Phonic Code), they can replace each other without it's being counted as a transformation.

kit —s→ cat   *k* and *c* represent the same sound

all —s→ off   *a* and *o* represent the same sound

---

21 See "allowable exception" below.

Chapter II
Meeting the Sounds of English

There is one *allowable exception* to the rule of performing transformations with single signs (and in some cases also to the rule of no subtraction of signs). But only if there is *no* alternative route can one make the following types of transformations via sound which do not conform to the rule. Some teachers may rightly object to them because they do not find them fun nor do their pupils find them easy, while others may delight in the additional challenge they contribute to finding solutions to difficult games of transformation.

won —a→ once   fire —i→ flyer
packs —s→ tax   scoff —r→ fox
fatal —s→ fable

Because of these equivalences, far more is done in one step than in other examples in which the operations are taken more strictly according to the definition. These make the game possible when otherwise not, and more challenging and fun.

Let us now give a full analysis of the operations in the Game of Transformations:

1 SUBSTITUTION of one sign for another:
When both sign and sound change in the substitution, it is counted as a transformation. Examples:

pat —s→ pet
OR
high —s→ hay

In the following, besides substitution we have used:

struck —s→ strike   *vertical equivalence,* since we do not count the substitution of *ke* for *ck*

whose —s→ shoes   *vertical equivalence,* since we do not count either *o* to *oe* or *se* to *s*

gone —s→ lone
thin —s→ then   *horizontal equivalence,* since we
ire —s→ are   do not count the changed sound
pile —s→ pale   of the sign *o, th, re,* and *le*

But the following are *not* allowed, since they are not substitutions of sign for sign, but of two signs for one:

$$\text{ship} \xrightarrow{\;/\!/\;} \text{slip}$$

$$\text{tames} \xrightarrow{\;/\!/\;} \text{taxes}$$

2   ADDITION of a sign at either end of a word:

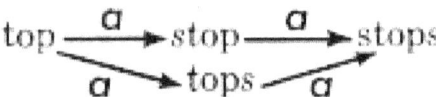

In the following, besides addition we have used:

go $\xrightarrow{\;a\;}$ goes	*vertical equivalance*
go $\xrightarrow{\;a\;}$ g*o*t	*horizontal equivalence*
lose $\xrightarrow{\;a\;}$ clothes quay $\xrightarrow{\;a\;}$ quee*n*	both *horizontal* and *vertical equivalence*

sigh $\xrightarrow{\;a\;}$ si*re*, but not bit $\xrightarrow{\;/\!/\;}$ bit*er* or bite $\xrightarrow{\;/\!/\;}$ bit*er*

3   INSERTION of a sign between other signs:

at $\xrightarrow{\;i\;}$ a*p*t   sap $\xrightarrow{\;i\;}$ s*l*ap   sooner $\xrightarrow{\;i\;}$ s*c*hooner

pet $\xrightarrow{\;i\;}$ p*e*st   stuck $\xrightarrow{\;i\;}$ st*r*uck

In the following, besides insertion we have used:

fist $\xrightarrow{\;i\;}$ fi*r*st sale $\xrightarrow{\;i\;}$ sa*b*le	*horizontal equivalence*
pack $\xrightarrow{\;i\;}$ pla*q*ue	*vertical equivalence*

4   REVERSAL of signs:

$$\text{pat} \xleftrightarrow{\;r\;} \text{tap}$$

$$\text{spots} \xleftrightarrow{\;r\;} \text{stops}$$

In the following, besides reversal we have used:

Chapter II
Meeting the Sounds of English

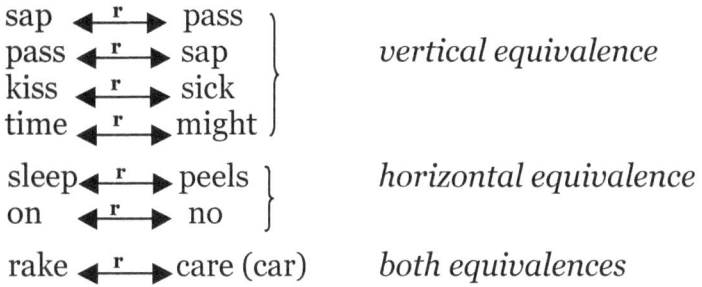

The following is not allowed since it is not reversal of the signs, and the two words have only one sign in common. One is made of two signs and the other of three.

$$\text{saw} \longleftrightarrow\!\!/\!\!/\!\!\longrightarrow \text{was}$$

5 *NO* SUBTRACTION is allowed; that is, a word proposed in a sequence of transformations must *never* have fewer signs than the word preceding it. Therefore, additions and insertions are never reversible operations, while substitutions and reversals are.

$$\text{mist} \longrightarrow\!\!/\!\!/\!\!\longrightarrow \text{miss}$$
$$\text{sworn} \longrightarrow\!\!/\!\!/\!\!\longrightarrow \text{sword}$$
$$\text{slip} \longrightarrow\!\!/\!\!/\!\!\longrightarrow \text{ship}$$

The following are *not* subtractions, as we have shown above, since the number of signs in the first and second words is equivalent.

$$\text{high} \xrightarrow{\ s\ } \text{hay}$$
$$\text{knit} \xrightarrow{\ s\ } \text{kit}$$
$$\text{sew} \xrightarrow{\ s\ } \text{go}$$
$$\text{sing} \xrightarrow{\ s\ } \text{sin}$$

9 Here we give a number of possible solutions for the Game of Transformations in *Worksheets 2 and 3*[22] and propose only one possible solution among many for each of the transformation games proposed in *Worksheets 4-7*.

---

22 See p. 65-66 for solutions for Worksheet 1.

Worksheet 2

1 from *pat* to *not*

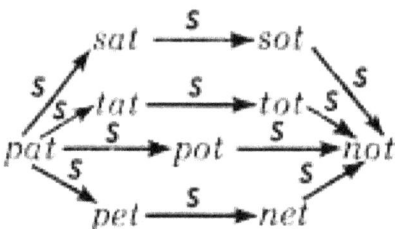

2 from *net* to *nuts*

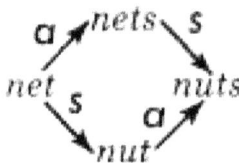

3 from *tin* to *mints*

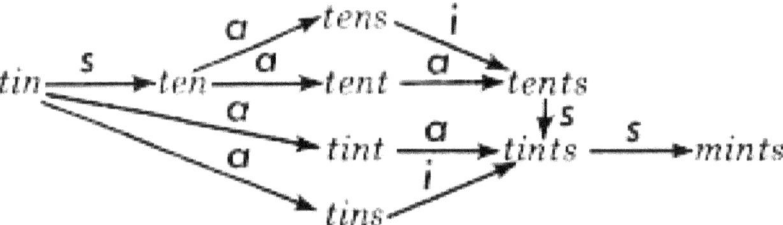

4 from *sent* to *tents*

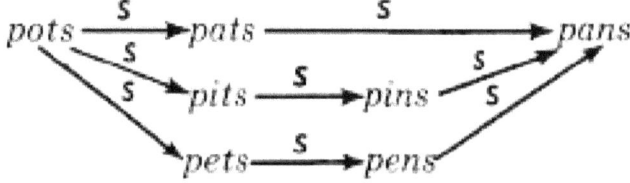

5 from *pots* to *pans*

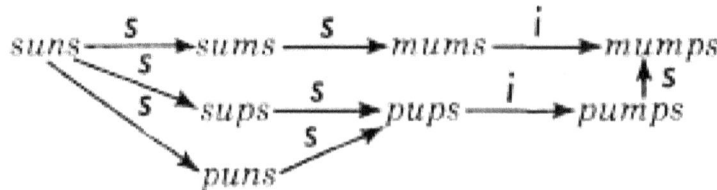

6 from *suns* to *mumps*

Worksheet 3

1. from *fed* to *funny*

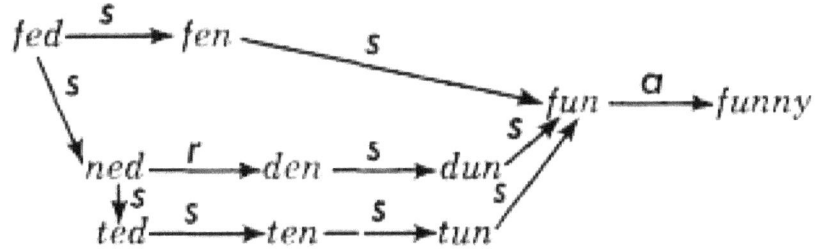

2. from *did* to *fund*

$$did \xrightarrow{s} dud \xrightarrow{s} dun \xrightarrow{s} fun \xrightarrow{a} fund$$
$$did \xrightarrow{s} dad \xrightarrow{s} fad \xrightarrow{s} fan \xrightarrow{s} fun$$

3. from *end* to *stand*

$$end \xrightarrow{s} and \xrightarrow{a} sand \xrightarrow{i} stand$$
$$end \xrightarrow{a} send \xrightarrow{s} sand$$

4. from *fat* to *thin*

$$fat \xrightarrow{s} that \xrightarrow{s} than \xrightarrow{s} thin$$
$$fat \xrightarrow{s} fan \xrightarrow{s} fin \xrightarrow{s} thin$$
$$fan \xrightarrow{s} fen \xrightarrow{s} then \xrightarrow{s} thin$$

5. from *of* to *left*

$$of \xrightarrow{s} if \xrightarrow{s} it \xrightarrow{a} lit \xrightarrow{s} let \xrightarrow{i} left$$

6   from *lot* to *well*

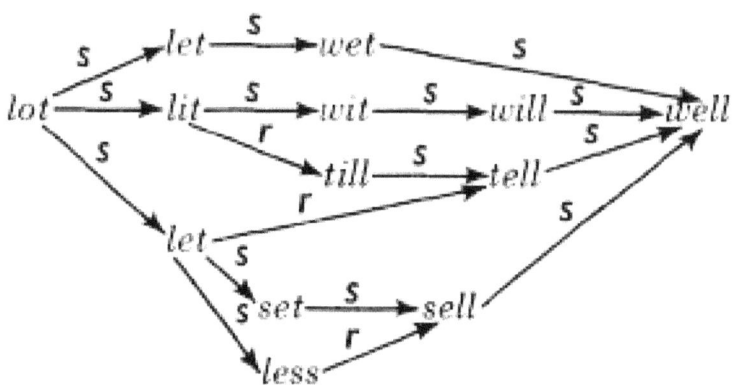

Worksheet 4

1   from *red* to *don*

$$red \xrightarrow{s} rod \xrightarrow{s} nod \xrightarrow{r} don$$

2   from *kit* to *silk*

$$kit \xrightarrow{l} kilt \xrightarrow{s} silt \xrightarrow{s} silk$$

3   from *fur* to *work*

$$fur \xrightarrow{a} firm \xrightarrow{s} form \xrightarrow{s} fork \xrightarrow{s} work$$

4   from *wild* to *skill*

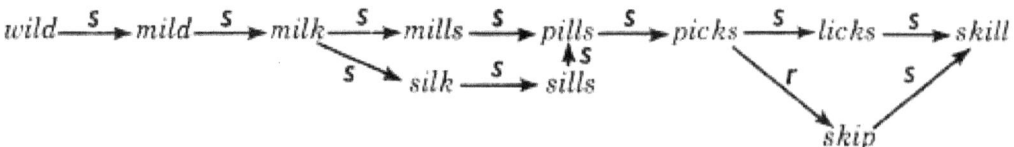

5 from *hot* to *brick*

hot —s→ hat —s→ pat —r→ tap —s→ tip —s→ tick —l→ trick —s→ brick

6 from word to sorry

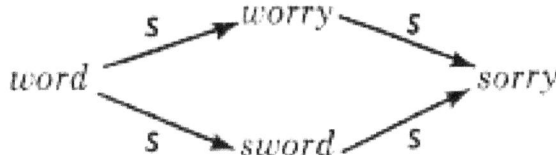

Worksheet 5

1 from *bone* to *stone*

bone —s→ tone —a→ stone

2 from *go* to *globe*

go —a→ gone —s→ lone —s→ lobe —a→ globe

3 from *home* to *nine*

home —s→ hose —s→ nose —s→ none —s→ nine

4 from *ship* to *child*

ship —s→ chip —s→ chill —s→ mill —s→ mile —a→ mild —s→ child
ship —s→ shape —s→ shale —s→ male —s→ mile

5 from *make* to *bank*

make —s→ bake —i→ bank

6 from *dog* to *misty*

dog —s→ log —s→ loss —a→ lost —s→ most —s→ mist —a→ misty

Worksheet 6

1 from *chin* to *tell*

$$chin \xrightarrow{s} tin \xrightarrow{s} till \xrightarrow{s} tell$$
$$\searrow_{s} chill \nearrow_{s}$$

2 from *ate* to *cable*

$$ate \xrightarrow{s} ale \xrightarrow{i} able \xrightarrow{a} cable$$

3 from *or* to *worthy*

$$or \xrightarrow{a} for \xrightarrow{a} forth \xrightarrow{s} worth \xrightarrow{a} worthy$$

4 from *does* to *robes*

$$does \xrightarrow{i} dopes \xrightarrow{s} ropes \xrightarrow{s} robes$$

5 from *home* to *camel*

$$home \xrightarrow{s} come \xrightarrow{s} came \xrightarrow{s} car \xrightarrow{a} carl \xrightarrow{i} carol \xrightarrow{s} camel$$
$$\searrow_{s} core \xrightarrow{a} cora \xrightarrow{a} coral \nearrow_{s}$$

6 from *are* to *host*

$$are \xrightarrow{s} ate \xrightarrow{a} hate \xrightarrow{i} haste \xrightarrow{s} host$$

Worksheet 7

1 from *might* to *salt*[23]

$$might \xrightarrow{s} mate \xrightarrow{i} malt \xrightarrow{s} salt$$

2 from *hall* to *front*

$$hall \xrightarrow{s} ball \xrightarrow{s} bell \xrightarrow{a} belt \xrightarrow{s} bent \xrightarrow{s} bend \xrightarrow{s} bond \xrightarrow{s} fond \xrightarrow{i} frond \xrightarrow{s} front$$
$$\downarrow_{s}$$
$$bolt \xrightarrow{s} bold \xrightarrow{s} fold \xrightarrow{s}\nearrow$$

---

[23] In the earlier printing of Worksheet 7, the words must be reversed, since as they are printed, the game requires subtraction.

Chapter II
Meeting the Sounds of English

3 from *axis* to *flames*

$$axis \xrightarrow{s} alleys \xrightarrow{s} allays \xrightarrow{s} flays \xrightarrow{i} flames$$

4 from *jar* to *saddle*

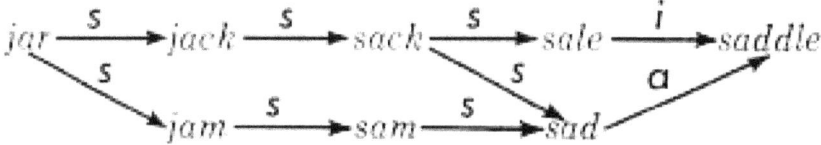

5 from *quit* to *think*

$$quit \xrightarrow{s} sit \xrightarrow{s} sick \xrightarrow{i} sink \xrightarrow{s} think$$

6 from book to spoke

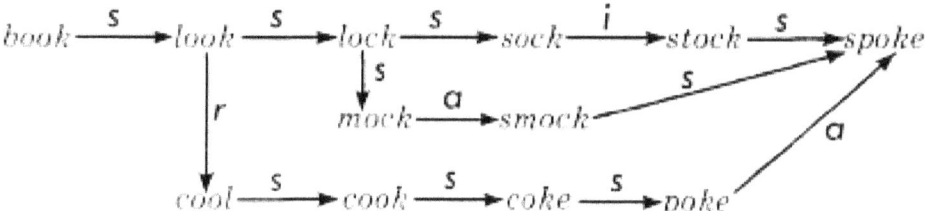

10 The test of progress in the Game of Transformations is to be found in:

- the speed developed in the game;

- the variety of alternative routes proposed;

- the aptitude in relating one word to a large number of others through a succession of standard English words, by utilizing the four operations of transformation discussed fully above.

Ample space is allowed in the Worksheets for the recording of a variety of different routes from one word to the other. No criteria are imposed for judging any particular route as preferable to any other, and scoring for the game is based simply on the number of different ways found for making each of the transformations asked for. Pupils (and even teachers) will find themselves able to go back to the game weeks, months, and even a year or so later, and discover additional routes—especially once the language is no longer restricted and the *whole* of the Phonic Code is available.

As a further elaboration of point (3) above, the exercise on *page 14* of the Worksheets is provided. The learners are requested to choose pairs of words themselves, and to try to link them through a succession of words derived from them, using the four operations of the game.

11   As an overall test of progress and experience in general, *pages 15* and *16* are left virtually blank, the space being intended for use in the most comprehensive exercise of all: free writing. Pupils are asked, in the first place, to make up sentences with words formed from only those sounds and spellings included in the particular table they have reached in the *Word Building Book,* selecting the correct spellings from the restricted range available. Then, on *page 16,* they are asked to compose other sentences, availing themselves now of whatever words they happen to know, regardless of the signs or sounds involved.

The author believes that, in addition to testing what has been learned through the program, it is useful to establish what else the pupils may have acquired through either their wits, their enhanced awareness of words, or their own linguistic behaviors. Thus, these two blank pages are an essential part of the tests presented in the Worksheets.

12 While the various exercises in the first seven Worksheets follow a similar pattern from one booklet to the next, each has been carefully composed for use in conjunction with a particular stage reached with the accompanying materials. It is the author's view that these sheets present the outlet for individual work and growth, permitting the pupil to contemplate, on his own, what he has done and is doing, and what is at work in himself. By being asked questions, the learner is led to a succession of deeper awarenesses; these ultimately represent the full extent of the education he will gain through this program. Reading and writing result as a by-product of the activities as a whole.

In each Worksheet, there is an inner development taking one from a contact with the unknown through the broadest and widest net of algebraic operations on sounds to flights of free imagination through a succession of analyses and syntheses that mobilize the whole self. The structuring of each Worksheet by the stages of learning—*contact, analysis,* and *mastery*—makes this material far more useful than other ways of recording or other forms of individual work.

There is, further, an inner development of the seven booklets as a whole. Together, they aim at using increasing powers that become instruments of the mind for meeting the ever-growing challenges as wider and wider areas of the language are taken in. To become aware of oneself involved in a certain task requires that the whole of the self be not fully taken up by the task. This is made possible by maintaining the format of exercises in successive booklets as closely invariant as possible and allowing the learner to go back as often as he wishes to his earlier attempts, to modify and revise them. But it is also achieved by moving, stage by stage, from challenges of one order that evoke responses as an immediate intuition to those of another that would tax anyone. Learners of a particular task differ from masters of it only insofar as the first have not yet gone through it while the others have. While going through the task they come to know it, to know about it, and about their own minds' struggling about it.

By the time they have completed their work on the first seven booklets, the pupils as individuals will have been involved in sufficient experiences for them to be expected to function much better linguistically in the use of their mother tongue—written as well as spoken.

The remainder of the program will take care of other attributes of their minds, such as noting etymological origins, criteria for the structure of speech, etc.

Section 4
Word Building Book—Phonemes and Some of Their Graphemes

1   In this section, we shall consider the first nine tables of the *Word Building Book,* together with some of their uses. We shall be less concerned here with learners than with teaching, but hope we will serve learners in the end through an improvement in the teacher's understanding of this tool.

2   The *Word Building Book* reflects, more than any of the other materials, the novelty of this approach to the English language and toward learning to read. The reader will find no words in this book. These have to be supplied by *him,* after the manner of chemists who, with a table of atoms and isotopes in hand, must seek particular combinations to produce the substances that make up the world. Here, there are algebraic rules permitting words or groups of words to be obtained through the combination, permutation, and repetition of signs.

There are conventional rules in English that associate one sound with the set of signs in each column—and different sounds with the sets of signs in different columns, and that make it understood that consonants sound only in conjunction with one of the vowels already introduced. These two sets of rules produce groupings of signs and sounds which we shall call "words." Since some of these combinations, when sounded, trigger *meaning,* we shall retain these as "words" of the English language.

The linking of signs to form words is *not* done by physically cutting up signs and pasting them side by side (or writing them together), but by generating subsets of the set represented by any table in the *Word Building Book.* Such subsets may be generated by touching signs with a pointer to form temporal sequences which correspond with the temporal order of sounds reflected in the spoken words.[24] The forming of an image of a word structured in time in this way will permit its transcription into the conventional spatial sequence of signs as well as its utterance—both temporal activities. We can easily associate graphemes with phonemes through these images-structured-in-time. They should, therefore, be our prime concern if reading and writing are our aim.

3   In the next chapter, we devote particular attention to spelling. Here, we wish to note only that the *Word Building Book* is a tool with a number of useful characteristics.

- It indicates a sequence of restricted languages, growing through successive steps toward the whole of English.

---

[24] This is the extension of Visual Dictation 1, which was first described on p. 21, and can be done by the pupil using the unsharpened end of his pencil as a pointer and his *Word Building Book.*

- It enables us, as we move toward including all the sounds of English, to introduce a number of different signs that correspond to the same sound, and a number of signs each corresponding to a number of different sounds.

- It shows that with the seven sounds of the so-called vowels—the "short vowels" plus the schwa and the sound of the first person singular *(I)*—*we* can introduce almost all the consonants, and form words and sentences that are English.

- As the pupils advance, the increase in the number of new signs introduced from one table to the next is much greater—a fact justified by, and justifying further, our concept of the cumulative effect of learning.

- By Table 9, the complete content of *Book 2* is covered, as well as that of eleven of the Word Charts.

- The *Word Building Book* shows that, from signs m each restricted language, many *more* words can be obtained and recorded in the Worksheets than have been suggested by this program or by the teacher in class through the Visual Dictations. Words of recent origin or recently in common usage can, therefore, be generated and used (for example, "pepsi," "jet set").

- The signs met, up to and including Table 9, do not display the wide range of spellings that are left for the last five tables associated with *Book 3* and the last ten Word Charts, but they do prepare for these spellings by developing an organization of the sounds and spellings met so far—which need only be added to.

- Certain types of spellings for consonants—for instance, the double-letter signs and those with the "silent e"—are placed on the same horizontal line on the tables to indicate that similar alterations apply to a number of consonants.

- The *Word Building Book* reveals that, in English, almost any letter can be a *silent* one.

4   Although, in the study that follows in the next chapter, we shall have to extend the content of the tables considerably to include all the graphemes

of English, we have already established the fact that, in English, a large number of signs are used to represent a large number of words. A certain respect for words is shown when we have met them for what they are and as they have developed through time under the varied historical influences that cannot be fully known or understood. The feeling is imparted to learners that their language has a unique set of representations, and that by selecting the accepted signs for making particular words they are analyzing and synthesizing in a way that leads to a better and deeper acquaintance with a living language.

5   Let us now look at the state of mind of learners who have met a number of graphemes for the phonemes introduced up to Table 9, which include practically all those used in English. Since words have always been organized into sentences in this program, the learners know how their speech can be codified, and they have grown familiar with the overall appearance of individual words through the particular character (shape and sound) of each. They have experienced that to read is:

- to look at signs aligned;

- to receive from each of these a signal which the learner's experience has now made implicit in them;

- and because of this, to make sounds with a certain melody that, when heard, resembles speech enough so that it delivers a meaning —*its* meaning.

They have found that to write spontaneously what one thinks is:

- to know and understand a meaning;

- to let this meaning select the words (of speech) for its expression;

- to see the images of those words in the mind as signs arranged in particular orders;

- to let those arrangements of signs order the muscles of the hand to transcribe them onto paper or chalkboard.

In the learners' experience, *images* closely knit together, *actions* (of the organs of phonation, or the muscles of the hand and arm), and *meanings* have been combined to form as strong an association as possible. Together they relieve memory and assist in the coordination of automatic responses to the appearances of words in the media of speech and writing.

When we place our teaching emphasis on understanding rather than memorization, the problems of spelling encountered by so many learners are eliminated. Words have "character," which is derived from their form. When beginning to *write,* the learner must recognize the singularity of each word design, as when entering the realm of *speech,* a baby has to recognize that sounds have characters of *their* own, and through these retains them.

The energies of the learners have been used to the best advantage. The pupils have shown at every stage that they can accomplish proportionately more because they have been left free to do all the jobs which are merely analogous or immediately extensions. No repetition has been necessary. No mistakes due to lack of attention have been made, only slips which are recognizable immediately by the mind which is kept alert by the variety and intrinsic interest of the exercises. Each stage of progress has increased the already heightened awareness of oneself at work to the extent that now each learner is ready to forge ahead and complete the task in hand.

The learners are now entitled to receive their Second Certificate of Reading, which indicates that practically all the sounds of English have been encountered, and all the aspects of the language have been met time and again in the successive restricted languages, each broader than the last.

Chapter III
Meeting of Spellings

This chapter covers the study of the remainder of the Word Charts and completes the survey of graphemes used in English as presented in the *Word Building Book* and *Book 3*.

What has been attempted so far, described in the previous chapters, involves what seem to be the deeper aspects of reading and the analysis of the spoken language insofar as sounds are concerned. What remains to be treated is simpler and will be covered more easily although the area is much greater than that examined so far. A path of controlled teaching and extensive learning has been closely followed, yet contact with the linguistic aspect of the language has been maintained throughout. In this chapter, the field will be extended to involve the learner in the language as a means of broadening experience as a whole. This is achieved through the *Book of Stories*.

Following from what has been learned up to this point, linguistic dimensions will develop naturally while oral dictation is considered. Progress will be tested as the new study advances. The freedom given by greater power and greater means at the disposal of the learners will permit much more of the written language to be covered in less time than hitherto.

The next and final chapter will consider widening still further the awareness of what language means and does, both in particular and as it behaves as a whole.

Section 1
Word Charts 13-21—Visual Dictations 2 And 3

1 A glance at the words on the remaining Charts gives an idea of the extent of the ground covered as far as spellings are concerned. Only a few of the spellings of English are not included. Leaving out geographical and personal names has made the task manageable. The few words omitted are, for the most part, to be found in *Book 3*, and these and the remainder can be constituted in color from the signs in the Phonic Code.

Teachers, whenever the need arises, may put such words on the board (even using colored chalk in the appropriate colors for the sounds, if necessary). In so doing they will avoid any delay while the value and flexibility of the materials will in no way be lessened.

2 In Word Charts 13-21, as the occasion arises, each new Chart presents different sounds for a single spelling, as well as several different spellings for a number of sounds previously met. Through this type of contrast, learners may become aware of sets of sounds for one spelling, or sets of spellings for one sound. This expands the network of relationships between words which already exist in the learners' minds—and which we have been concerned with developing throughout the program. On Word Chart 13 we have several interesting studies.

Chapter III
Meeting of Spellings

> elephant physics
> photograph foot be
> see sleep feet been
> why where when
> who whom whose
> these between you
> youth our your soup
> hour young sing
> house courageous₁₃

In this chart, we find that:

- four words contain a red *ee* sounding as *e* in *be*, while one word *(been)* has a pink *ee*, sounding as *i* in *pin*

- three words contain a pale aqua *wh* as in *when* or *while*, and three contain *wh* colored pale blue, as in *who* or *whole*

- six words contain five colorings for *ou*, indicating five of its different sounds

- two words contain *ng* in olive color, sounding as *n* in *thanks* and in *hungry* (Chart 9)

Other words are included so that the students can make sentences with these words and with those already available. Teachers will at once be able to make a number of sentences incorporating these new words in association with those of previous Charts, through Visual Dictation 2.

Pupils can likewise be given the opportunity to use this Chart for their own sentence formation and also to alter some of the words on it or on previous Charts in order to assist in forming whatever sentences should come to mind. They might derive *sang* or *sings* from *sing, yours* from *your, seed* from *see,* and so on.

Here is one of several sentences that could be produced from the words on the Charts available up to this point, if mental transformations are included:

this youth thinks that he sings well but he sends me to sleep with his songs

In the sentence above, *thinks* came from *thanks* (Chart 9), *sings* and *songs* from *sing* (Chart 13), and *sends* from *send* (Chart 4).

3   Word Chart 14 proves very useful for every group of pupils. Even very slow learners in remedial classes attack promptly and with enthusiasm the words offered.

> *eyes day may*
> *high thigh night*
> *they saturday*
> *gray greyhound*
> *money honey prey*
> *prayers wood would*
> *should cool field*
> *aged finished*
>
> 14

It is recommended that pupils refer to the lemon-colored *i* (on Chart 4) to reestablish this sound before opening the new Chart with *eyes* or *night*, which involve the same color (and therefore the same sound), but with very different spellings. The pupils may find *thigh* difficult to sound, but reference to *thanks* on Word Chart 9 may assist them with the first sound. The teacher should try to help the learners understand the meaning of *thigh,* perhaps by asking them which part of the body it names.

Chapter III
Meeting of Spellings

Teachers often question our writing of *Saturday* with the pink ending (as in *fifty*) rather than the sea-green coloring for the ending *ay* (as in *day*). Our writing of *Saturday* reflects the sound of its final syllable in normal speech (as, for example, in the utterance *Saturday night*). A number of interesting links can be found in words with *ey* and *ay* endings on this Chart.

The words *conceived* and *conceit* test the learner's capacity to attack unusual words. The teacher may decide to help the students analyze these words by going back and pointing at *see*. To contrast *wood* and *would*, the teacher can dictate orally to the class a sentence containing these two words. A pupil can then point to the sentence on the Charts and show which shape of the word goes with which meaning. The class can be the judge, and the teacher the witness. Since *l* is mute in *would* and *should*, they may be contrasted with *field*.

Of further interest is the ending *ed* which, when Chart 14 is contrasted with Chart 15, can be seen to be treated in a number of different ways. In English, the sign *ed* has sounds that link it with the magenta-colored *t* (as in *finished*) and the green *d* (as in *rolled*), so we color *ed* accordingly on the Word Charts. But the *e* can also be associated in sound and color with the preceding consonant. This occurs in cases where the infinitive form of the verb already ends with a mute *e,* as in the case of *conceived* on this Chart, where only *d* is in green, or as it would be handled in a word such as *priced* where only *d* would be given the magenta color. The word *aged* on the Chart with the blue *e* is a challenge which can benefit the learners by forcing them to look more carefully. It is obviously not the one-syllable word (which would have only three colors with the division between colors coming either as *a-ge-d* or *a-g-ed),* but a different word where *e* and *d* form a separate syllable together and therefore e has a separate color to denote a sound of its own. Either the yellow *schwa* or the pink *i* found in unstressed syllables (as in *chicken* on Chart 10) might have been used, since the particular color chosen for the *e* here simply reflects the amount of stress applied to the sign in pronouncing the word.

Interesting examples of all of these ways of sounding *ed* could be collected, since in each category many examples can be found. For instance:

stabbed, hugged, banned, hummed for the green *ed*;

sniffed, hopped, picked, hissed for the magenta *ed*;

robed, dodged, timed, stored for the green *d* since *e* is associated with the preceding consonant;

diced, sliced, faced, roped for the magenta *d* since *e* is associated with the preceding consonant;

learned (as in "learned man"), *posted, started, mended* for a separate coloring for the sign *e*.

4 Word Chart 15, rich in signs and links between words, deserves careful study.

> **stopped rolled told**
> **talk walk sigh lie**
> **listen lesson push**
> **fast fasten door**
> **sugar sure busy**
> **business heir one**
> **once england lamb**
> **ocean dumb put**
> **good better well**
> 15

The word offering the greatest challenge is, in our experience, *heir;* learners are mesmerized by the letter *h* even though this is not isolated by the use of a separate color. Several ways of working are possible here, all valid and all useful.

- If the pupils say *hair* for *heir,* the teacher may point to *heir* several times, looking at it but saying nothing and waiting patiently until the sheer passage of time suggests a revision of their proposed sound.

- The teacher may preface the pointing by asking how many colors are used for the word. Receiving the answer, "two," for the turquoise-colored *hei* and the dark orange *r*, she may then ask for the number of sounds that can be expected to be heard when the word is read correctly.

When "two" is again offered, she asks the pupils to read the word and listen carefully to their own voices to see how many sounds they actually do hear. When all pupils read *heir* as it should be sounded, a new task can be begun. But if some do not, the teacher has only to bring their attention back to the need for a two-sound word, which can then be achieved by contrast with the three-sound word they are producing.

- The teacher can touch *air* (Chart 11) and ask the students to say it, or she can touch *there* (Chart 7) and ask students to say it without its first sound *(th)*. Then, if *heir* is studied, its two colors indicate almost immediately that its two sounds are the same as those just produced.

- This word may be put into circulation in the class verbally; for instance, the teacher might ask someone, "Are you your father's heir?" thus stimulating recognition of meaning or provoking discussion of the word before she asks someone to find it on the chart.

Other features on this chart are:

- the three spellings for the sound of the sky-blue in *push*, in *sugar* and *sure*, and in *ocean*

- the two examples of lime-colored *st* sounding as *s* in *listen* and *fasten*

- the mute *l* in *talk* and *walk*

- the similar color sequence of *rolled* and *told*

- the mute *i* in *business,* forming part of the lilac sign, and the pink *u* in *busy*

- the mute *b* in *lamb* and *dumb*

- the sound of *o* in *one* and *once,* where it has a combination sound forming a syllable (pale aqua over pale yellow)

This Chart also provides many new possibilities for sentence formation. The inclusion of *good, better,* and *well,* in particular, suggest many possibilities for developing the students' awareness of sentence structures.

The new coloring of *the* (in contrast to *the* on Chart 4), for use before words beginning with a vowel, also suggests special sentences.

5 Word Chart 16 presents a number of insights in a very compact way.

> *write right written*
> *wrong sword sworn*
> *know new knew*
> *knowledge knee tea*
> *news great pear*
> *tear pearl tear*
> *lead bread lead*
> *people hear here their*
> *ear weird heart buy*
> 16

In this Chart:

- each of the six sounds of *ea* is used in one or more words

- a new dark orange-colored sign, *wr* in *write,* is contrasted with *r* in *right*

- a new lavender sign, *kn,* in *knew,* is contrasted with *n* in *new*

- a lime *sw,* in *sword,* is contrasted with the lime *s* and pale aqua *w* used in *sworn,* where s and u; have two different sounds

- a wide variety of signs, for comparison and contrast of color, spelling, and sound, is provided in the confined area of this Chart by:

  lead and *lead*   *lead* and *people*
  hear and *here*   *their* and *weird*

Chapter III
Meeting of Spellings

> *tear* and *tear*   *know* and *knowledge*
> *tea* and *tear*

There is, as usual, more than one way of effecting an entry into this Chart. In fact, there are at least four "entry routes," any of which may be taken first. The teacher may want to begin by having the children either compare spellings with sounds, or sounds with spellings. Or she may want to start with *tea,* which is short. A fourth alternative is to start with *know,* which has the same colors as *no* (previously met on Word Chart 9). Wherever the start is made, this Chart reveals a great deal about written English and paves the way for similar encounters in the following three Charts, where many new and related forms for sounds are introduced. Making sentences using these words will develop a better acquaintance with each individual word. One such sentence is:

> *I will buy new pearls for my earrings, said pam*

To the sentences given on page 25 of *Book 3,* many other examples can be added.

6   Word Chart 17 introduces one of the few sounds of English still to be met—the cobalt-blue s in *measure.* Three words on the Chart include this sign.

> *measure leisure*
> *either treaure*
> *plateau beauty paul*
> *lawn because said*
> *mail maintain paid*
> *doubt laugh taught*
> *bury daughter water*
> *paw poor pour pore*
> *raw therefore quiet*
> 17

New spellings for sounds already met include:

- ochre-colored *eau* in *plateau*, contrasted with pale-green *eau* in *beauty*

- blue *ai* in *said*, contrasted with sea-green *ai* in *paid*

- many spellings for the brown, as shown in *w<u>a</u>ter, p<u>au</u>l, t<u>au</u>ght, p<u>ou</u>r, p<u>o</u>re,* and *p<u>aw</u>,* among others (complementing the experience in the previous Chart of many sounds for one spelling, *ea*)

It is interesting to note that there is a distinctive atmosphere of "brown" about this whole Chart, because of the concentration of spellings of the sound that goes with this color.

7   Word Chart 18, while mainly concerned with spellings, introduces a new double-colored sign found in two spellings, in *boy, buoy, moist,* and *oil*. Colored brown over pink, it represents a merging of the vowel sounds of *off* and *pit* respectively.

> flown flowers boy
> sew sow sow buoy
> fruit suit suite
> sweet moist isle
> zip zoo zero oil
> eight eighty height
> freight board bored
> boar soar sore saw
> cloak broke
>
> 18

Chapter III
Meeting of Spellings

Of special interest on this Chart is the play made on signs and sounds in words within lines and between them:

second line: *sew* and *sow* are both colored lime with ochre, but *sow* and *sow* are differently colored, the second being lime with purple over light aqua

third line: *suit* and *suite* are seen to have different sounds, despite their very close spellings, and *suite* and *sweet* on the next line involve identical color sequences, giving an example of the sign u with the sound of the pale aqua *w*

sixth line: *eigh,* sea-green in *eight* and lemon-colored in *height,* illustrate the different values of this spelling in these example words

seventh line: *board* and *bored* sound alike and are colored alike, despite different spellings

eighth line: *soar* and *sore* are another example of the same phenomenon

Vertically, the proximity of *soar* and *cloak, sore* and *broke* add to the feeling of many that there is little point in formulating rules for pronunciation, and that it is better to fix word images indelibly in the mind when sounding them.

The lower section of this Chart contains, like the last, many examples of the brown sign. When Charts 17 and 18 are placed side by side, their eighth lines form almost a continuous row of similar words for comparison:

paw, pour, pore, boar, soar, sore, saw

8   From the top three lines of Word Chart 19, reproduced below, it would seem that the problems presented by the sign *ough* are the principal concern of this Chart. But, in reality, the most significant contribution it has to make is the further illustration of the concept of the cumulative effect of learning.

> **tough cough though
> thought through bough
> examination thorough
> anxiety half mix exist
> thursday woman true
> women wednesday
> halves calves loaf
> hiccup taxi cramp
> loaves borrow swamp**
> 19

Here, the whole set of sounds associated with one spelling are introduced at the same time. Color plays a decisive role in that its use clearly distinguishes the spellings from each other, showing how different sounds are associated with each. Note that it would be incorrect to classify the first two words as equivalent in structure to the next five using the letter-group *ough*. In the first two words, the letter group is composed of two signs, *ou* and *gh*, each with a separate sound, while in the other five, *ough* is a single sign. When such words are printed together in black, they seem, of course, to suggest the same characteristics;

- *tough* and *cough* also have different vowel sounds and colors (pale yellow and brown, respectively) in the sign *ou*, but the same final consonant sound in the sign *gh*

- *tough* has three differently colored signs: *t-ou-gh*. But so has *thought*, as indicated by three differently colored signs: *th-ough-t*

These next four pairs of words are related by transformation since horizontal equivalence applies in each case:

- *though* leads to *thought* by addition of the final consonant *t*, along with a change in the vowel (ochre to brown) and the change in the sound of *th*

Chapter III
Meeting of Spellings

- *hough* becomes *bough* by simple substitution of the first sign, along with a change in the vowel (ochre to purple over pale aqua)

- *though* leads to *through* by insertion of *r*, along with the change of the vowel (ochre to leaf green) and the change in the sound of the *th*

- *through* becomes *thorough* by insertion of o, along with a change in the vowel sound in *ough* (from leaf green to yellow or to ochre)

This can be shown schematically as follows:

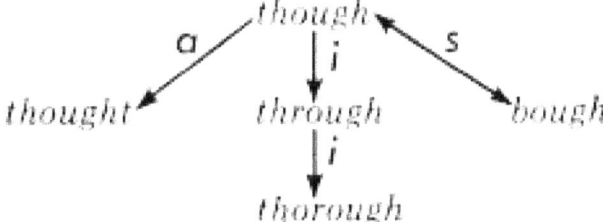

Other aspects of this Chart are also of interest and can be noted:

- *hiccup,* which some people misspell "hiccough" by analogy with "cough," is included and presents the first example of the spelling *cc* for the sound of gold

- three colorings for the different sounds of *x* are given in close proximity to each other in *anxiety* (lilac), *mix* (gold over lime), and *exist* (gray over lilac). A fourth sound for the sign *x*, as found in *obnoxious* and *anxious* (gold over sky blue), is *not* shown here, but could be mentioned at this stage by the teacher or developed when these words are met in *Book 3*. (This sign is also found on the Phonic Code and in the *Word Building Book*.)

- the allocation of colors to signs in *half, halves,* and *calves* presented a problem, and the ultimate choice could have been different without affecting the result. The colors actually appearing are white *a,* mauve *lf,* and khaki *lve*. Here, the letter *l* has been associated with the consonants *f* and *ve,* but it could equally well have been combined with the vowel *a* to produce the sign *al* sounding as in *pat*

- the words *cramp* and *swamp* are place one above the other to draw attention to both their similarity and difference in coloring and pronunciation

- the pairs *half* and *halves*, *loaf* and *loaves* are included for comparison, *f* in each case being replaced by *ve* on forming the plural

- a striking change of color is used when *woman*, with a beige-colored *o*, becomes *women* with the pink *o* (the same color as the second vowel in this latter word)

9   Word Charts 20 and 21 can be taken together, since these present a large number of words selected simply for the opportunities they provide for illustrating, studying, and forming a photographic image in the mind of sounds with varied spelling.

| guard calm shoes
guarantee scissors
scythe ghost adieu
service diaphragm
hymn yatch aisle
science indict prosaic
sieve friend yield
debt straight seize
siege reservoire receipt
20 | pneumatic cage scheme
schist rhythm jewel
righteous hallelujah
tissue amoeba psalm
azure bathe vulture
trekked pension quay
blithe clothes awkward
cube queue clique
vision region mayor
21 |

For example, on Word Chart 20:

- the sound of the magenta is found in four different spellings: *ya*ch*t, in*dic*t, de*bt*,* and *recei*pt

- the sound of the tangerine-color is found in three different spellings: *ca*lm*, hy*mn*,* and *diaphra*gm

- the sound of the lime-color is given three times as *sc*

- the seventh line gives three sounds for *ie*, to be contrasted with *receipt, science,* and *adieu* (elsewhere on the Chart), and *lie* (Chart 15)

- the new diphthong of pale aqua over purple makes its appearance in *reserv<u>oi</u>r*

On Word Chart 21:

- the sign *sch* is contrasted in *scheme* and *schist,* since it has two sounds in the first word and one quite different sound in the second. In *schism,* the *sch* (found in the lime column on the Phonic Code) has one sound but it is different from that in *schist*

- in *righteous* and *vulture,* the sign *t* (dark magenta) has the same sound as in *question* (Chart 12) and as the *ch* in *chin*

As each work poses its own problems, these two Charts are a good test both of the growth in the pupils' awareness and of their speed of attack on unusual words. These Charts also oblige the learners to look closely at the words and to attempt to retain them.

10 The intention of the preceding analysis of content is not simply to suggest that the sole function of these Charts is to help learners gain a mastery over spellings. If the value of Visual Dictations 2 and 3 is understood, it will be clear that, as each new Chart joins the rest on display, new sentences become possible using either the vocabulary on the Charts or that obtained by the simple mental alterations discussed earlier. Incorporating the new vocabulary in sentence-making increases the range of reading and writing. The use of Visual Dictations with the Charts should become routine, even if far less time is taken up in such exercises than in looking at each of the newly introduced words for its own sake.

Let us state again that reading is a process by which meaning is derived from a temporal sequence of words and, once the meaning is reached, the words used may be forgotten. Spelling, on the other hand, is the opposite process, by which words are retained in the mind both as unified designs and as structures composed of signs related to sounds —since as structures they can be compared with other words similar or somewhat similar in signs or sounds. Hence, it is important to have spatial arrangements like those adopted for the Word Charts, precisely because the groupings of words on those Charts do not make sentences nor produce much meaning. They simply offer a static presentation of words, demanding for the purpose of later recall no more than that the eye should attempt to make a photographic image of each. Spelling cannot fail to be good when the problem is tackled realistically, and when we are aware that it is *not* reading that helps with spelling— except, perhaps, in those cases where the reader examines each word separately when scanning a sentence to arrive at the meaning.

With Visual Dictations 2 and 3, there are increasing opportunities for making more and more extended and interesting sentences with the addition of each Chart on which more varied words become available.

A remarkable observation here is that so-called "slow learners" are able to operate with the large expanse of words displayed by the twenty-one Charts.[1] As the pointer darts here and there, touching one word after the other, even "slow learners" are able to form sentences that are involved and unexpected. These are usually read back to the teacher, with the fluency and understanding of ordinary speech, immediately after the movement of the pointer ceases. This reading is a true extension of the self and shows its value all the time.

Section 2
Word Building Book, Phonic Code, Visual Dictation 1

1   Though the various instruments provided in *Words in Color* are treated separately here, it is to be understood that each complements the rest, and any one instrument may prove more useful than the others in overcoming the particular difficulties faced by different individuals.

Tables 10 to 16 of the *Word Building Book* primarily involve additions to the signs in existing columns, rather than new columns. Nine new columns are, however, added to the forty-two on Table 9, but since six of

---

[1] Actually only twenty Charts are used in Visual Dictation, since Chart 1 has no English words on it—only vowels.

these are double-colored diphthongs, this constitutes in reality only four completely new sounds.

2   Note that, on Table 10, a new consonant column with six spellings has been added.

3   The expansion of the tables of the *Word Building Book* now becomes more rapid, as greater numbers of new signs are introduced at each stage. The cumulative effect of learning is such that large areas of the English language can now be taken in one lesson, where earlier in the program movement forward was made only step by step. In fact, the function of *Book 3* and the last tables of the *Word Building Book* is to bring learners to the contemplation of the full panorama of English as a language. With each new table of the *Word Building Book,* the vista expands until, on Table 16, an almost complete view of the components of written English words is obtained.

4   The way in which each new table is tackled is not different from that already described in the previous chapter, but now attention is concentrated on the increase in the number of spellings in each column.

Whenever a word with a new spelling for a sound appeared on one of the Word Charts or in *Book 3,* the new sign concerned was added to the appropriate table in the *Word Building Book*. Now, starting from the *Word Building Book,* one can single out a sign and ask for words that include the sound it represents, using this particular spelling. For pupils to provide a full answer here involves their knowing or deducing the spelling of many words not yet frequently met in print.

5   Hence, there are a number of new games that can be played in the classroom. The teacher, or any of the pupils, may select one of the new signs added to the table. The corresponding sound is then made for it, *if it is a vowel*. But if it is a consonant, a word incorporating it is chosen, and only in this way is it sounded. The pupils then suggest other words they know which they suspect will involve this spelling of the sign. If correct, these may be added to their logbook of words.

Should the suggested words contain, on the other hand, some other member of the same column in the *Word Building Book* table, it is a simple matter to point this out, saying, "This is the spelling you want." But if a word suggested uses one of the signs still to come, the teacher may inform the students that, while it will soon be possible to write this word, it cannot be done until the new signs it involves have been met. She may also ask the students to bear the suggested word and its spelling in mind until this sign is introduced. Or she may give them the spelling of the word showing the sign in question that will eventually make its formal appearance on a subsequent table. It is now clear that the *Word Building Book* is concerned with spellings of English words.

6   When Table 16 has been reached, the eight Charts of the Phonic Code can be displayed. This presents, in full color, practically the same content as the final table of the *Word Building Book,* but excludes a few signs whose uses are either rare or very specialized. The color code for the columns of signs is the same as that used on the Word Charts. The columns are separated by vertical white lines, except in the case of the four combination consonant sounds (two sounds of *x*, and the *l* and *r* that are half *schwa* sounds), which are separated by horizontal white lines. The upper section of the Phonic Code (Phonic Code Charts 1, 2, 3, 4, in this order) lists of the various spellings of the *vowels,* the lower section (Phonic Code Charts 5, 6, 7, 8, in this order), the *consonants.* The whole Phonic Code includes over 380 different signs. The Phonic Code, as it appears on Table 16 of the *Word Building Book* follows on pages 118-119.[2]

7   When the Phonic Code is hung up, the array of signs is at once much more challenging to the learner than the development provided by successive tables of the *Word Building Book*. For now, in this first and only analysis of the signs in color, a summary of the entire content of the Word Charts is presented at once, while in the progressive stages of the *Word Building Book,* the impact of the full array of spellings was lessened each time, since attention was inevitably drawn to the *new* signs only.

Often, teachers will wait until reaching Table 16 in the *Word Building Book* and Word Chart 21 before putting up the Phonic Code, since a full

---

[2] See Appendix 4 for (1) one word exemplifying each spelling (2) a diacritical mark appropriate for the sound assigned to each column, (3) the names for the color used in this text for the teacher's reference.

understanding has then developed gradually for this summary of the phonetics of English. But frequently, they find it is helpful with a number of groups to put this table up for reference once most of the sounds of English have been met (that is, when they are ready to introduce Word Chart 13[3] and Table 10 in the *Word Building Book),* even though the remainder of the spellings are yet to be introduced.

---

[3] When working with remedial pupils who can read a little when they begin the program, the teacher may want to introduce Word Chart 13 by the second or third lesson, since once the natural flow of spoken speech which carries the meaning has been reestablished in their reading, through Visual Dictation from Word Charts 2-12, the main difficulties of these pupils are with compound words and difficult spellings. If they continue to move rapidly, it is best to take Word Charts 13-21 as quickly as possible, and then return to study these in more detail along with the Phonic Code and with *Book 3*. If the pupils now show they need to move at a slower pace in assimilating the new signs introduced on Word Charts 13-21, it is very helpful to introduce the Phonic Code at this point, and work with it and *Book 3* along with each new Word Chart introduced.

a	u	i	y	e	o	a	u	u	I	a	o	a
au	o	o	ey	ie	oh	o	e	e	y	aa	a	ay
ai	oe	a	ay	ea	ho	i	ea	o	i	ea	au	ey
	ou	u	ui	ai	aw	y	ou	i	igh	e	aw	eigh
	oo	e	ee	u	a	ei	ie	ou	ie	ah	augh	aigh
	a	ai	ia	a		oi	io	ea	eye	au	ough	ei
	up	ei	ie	ay		ai	ia	y	ye		ou	ea
		ae	ea	eo		eo	eou		eigh		oo	ai
		is	hea	ei		he	oa		is		hau	et
		ois	hi	ae		iu	iou		ais		oa	au
						au	eau		ei		awe	
						ah	ough				ao	
											ho	
											oi	

p	t	s	s	s	m	n	f	f	d	th	th	y	l
pp	tt	ss	ss	z	mm	nn	ff	v	dd	the	the	i	ll
pe	te	se	se	ge	me	ne	fe	ve	de		h	j	le
ph	ed	's	's		mb	kn	ph	lve	ed		t		lle
bp	cht	z	c		gm	dne	lf	ph	ld		phth		'll
	ct	zz	ce		mn	pn		gh		'd			
	bt	ze	sw		lm	gn		tte					
	pt	si	st		'm	en		pph					
	tte	thes	sc			in		ft					
	th	x	sch			on							
	d	sth	ps			nd							
	't		sse			mn							
	phth		sce			ln							
			sth										
			tz										

l
le
'll

Chapter III
Meeting of Spellings

u	e	o	ou	a	o	oo	oi	oi	o
you	ee	oe	hou	ai	oo	ou	oy		
eau	ea	ow	ow	hei	oe	u			
ue	ei	owe	ough	ea	ough	o			
ew	ie	oa		e	ou				
eu	i	oh		ei	u				
eue	eo	ew		ae	ue				
ieu	oe	ou		aye	ui				
ewe	ay	eou			ew				
yew	ey	ough			wo				
iew	y	oo			eu				
hu	ae	au			ieu				
	is	eo							
		ot							

w	k	r	b	h	g	sh	ch	ng	j	qu	x
wh	kk	rr	bb	wh	gg	ch	tch	n	g	cqu	xe
o	ke	re	be	w	gu	t	t	nd	d		xc
u	ck	rre	bu	j	gh	s	c	ngue	dge		cc
h	ch	wr			gue	ce	che		ge		
	c	rh			ckgu	che			gg		
	cc	rrh				ss			dg		
	lk	rt				sch			dj		
	qu	lo				sc					
	que	rp				ci					
	cch	rps				c				x	
	che	're									
	cqu										
	kh										
	ca									x	
		r									
		re									

The Phonic Code often helps to clarify the work in the *Word Building Book,* since the major difference is only in the length of columns, not in the number of columns. And it can make easy the reference to an unusual spelling which is occasionally needed for a word suggested by pupils but not yet met in the *Word Building Book*. But, beyond this, it serves to give pupils a general sense of what remains until they have met the entirety of English, and does so at a point when they cannot possibly be overwhelmed, since they are already confident with most of the sounds and only lack full understanding of certain spellings. Very occasionally, for a special reason, a teacher will find with a certain group that she wishes from the beginning to have visible those Charts of the Phonic Code that contain the color for the new sounds being introduced. But on the whole, making this complete table available this early in the program proves either confusing or distracting from the main work, and so slows progress, since the same progressive organization of sounds met is found in Tables 1-9 in the *Word Building Book* in a simpler form.[4]

8   The first form of Visual Dictation is the means of generating words and sentences on the Phonic Code. How the pointer is used in this connection has already been described at length. Visual Dictation 1 can be taken up again at this point,[5] but now so much more is involved in the exercise. The pointer is best moved first very slowly and only to produce short sentences of this kind:

>   *it is*   *he is old*   *is this girl ten*

As the pupils grow accustomed to this new test, it is preferable to concentrate more on the acceleration of the pointer than on the generation of longer sentences. For if one is slow and the pupils manage to read each word in turn, only memory is taxed, but acceleration demands increases in alertness and concentration. However, attainment of dexterity and speed in the use of the pointer over such an area is not a simple matter. Teachers will find it helpful to practice, first, with sentences without complications, and with those which do not lead to hesitations in the rhythm of the pointer's moving to the right signs. When teachers are clumsy in this exercise, they reduce the chances of learners' successfully using the pointer on the Phonic Code to produce their own words and sentences, which, after all, is the ultimate test revealing mastery over spellings. It is, therefore, a requirement of good teaching that teachers do not attempt to use the pointer on the Phonic Code in front of their classes until they are confident of their own reasonable efficiency, and that they are not asking too much from their pupils.

9   When teachers, with the Phonic Code before them, have thought of a sequence of sentences, they can produce each word by linking the component signs with the pointer, pausing slightly to symbolize the break after each word, lowering the pointer briefly at the end of each sentence,

---

[4] To have some reference that can be worked with by the whole class at one time, teachers may want to reproduce the current table in the *Word Building Book* in black or in white on the chalkboard. Generally, color is not needed here any more than in the *Word Building Book*.
[5] See pp. 17-31.

Chapter III
Meeting of Spellings

and finally, stopping (facing the class) to indicate the conclusion of the dictation and to invite the pupils to say out loud what they have read.

Then, a pupil may be asked to change places with the teacher and make the same sentence while the class watches. If this is done without a mistake, another example may be considered in a similar manner. Where a mistake is noted by the class, other pupils can be given the chance to produce the sentence correctly, until the right signing has been proposed and has been accepted by the class as a whole. But if no one notes a mistake made, the teacher can ask the class to read each word aloud after it has been completed by the pupil taking his turn at the Phonic Code, making it clear than an error has been introduced somewhere. The teacher can then ask one of the pupils to point out the sentence correctly.

10 The procedure suggested above can be followed by a session in which pupils make up sentences of their own and either ask one of their fellow students to point out the signs on the Phonic Code corresponding to those used in the words of their sentences, or go to the Phonic Code themselves and indicate the spellings they think are used in the words they have thought of.

It is idle to attempt to forecast what any class of pupils may propose; in the writer's experience, the beginnings are timid, but bold proposals are soon forthcoming.

Pointing at signs on the Phonic Code is a powerful tool in producing mastery of spellings.

11 As pupils advance, teachers may become increasingly demanding, moving toward sentences involving what are usually considered difficult words. Pupils familiar with Visual Dictation 1 tend to judge the difficulty of words by the numbers of different signs they contain, rather than by the complexity of their spellings. In this respect, *taught* may be simpler than *stops,* since the first requires only three pointings (twice at *t* and once at *augh)* while the second requires five. Likewise, *daughter* may prove easier than *sister,* and *thorough* easier than *strike* or *children,* and so on.

12 Naturally, such well established games as the Game of Transformations can be included here as a further application of the Phonic Code. The teacher may also wish to introduce a new game, in which the teacher or any pupil may say just one word, and members of the class volunteer to point out its component signs from among the colored columns. In this game, it is advisable to allow time for pupils, with their eyes closed, to call to mind the word's shape and sound components, before asking for it to be compounded from the Phonic Code. This practice reinforces the photographic use of the mind for spelling, as well as the scanning of words required for reading.

Another useful procedure for focusing the pupils' attention on transformations and the Code is to initiate, through oral dictation, sequences of words that require either a transformation in sound or in spelling from the one preceding. Each of the words in such sequences should be composed from the Code with the pointer by a volunteer pupil, and accepted or rejected by the class. If the spelling (not the sound) changes from one word in the sequence to the next (e.g., *so, sew, sow*), the teacher may need to clarify the meaning of the word she is asking for, so that the pupil may choose the appropriate spelling. Below are several beginning sequences which might lead to longer sequences:

so, sew, sow, sow, bow, bough, beau, bow . . .

tot, taught, taut, tote . . .

ate, rate, trait, strait, straight, eight, weight, wait,

white, height, sight, site, mite, might, fight, light, like, bike,

bake, take, tale, tail, sail, sale, male, mail, fail, pail, pale . . .

judge, fudge, budge, badge . . . *edge, ledge, pledge* . . .

gem, gym, jim, jam, jamb, lamb, lamp, damp, dump . . .

in, sin, sing, sink, slink . . . *song, sung, sang, sand, stand*. . .[6]

Games such as those suggested challenge the pupils' ability to evoke spellings and focus their attention on the structures of, and structure-

---

6 With remedial classes having intensive courses and perhaps fragmented understandings of spellings from their previous experience, such games are more welcomed and needed than in the first grade class where the pace is a little slower and the pupils discover a great many words, sentences, and stories on their own every day.

meaning relationships in, single words far beyond the scope of the Word Charts. Such games can be played seriously and with steadily increasing difficulty throughout the program, but they should be abandoned at the point when the new challenges are not sufficient to avoid boring the pupils.

13 The word games already described can be alternated with a sentence game in which the pupils are asked to use one, two, or three of the homonyms they have studied in a sentence given by oral dictation. When the pupils can complete, with the Phonic Code and pointer, sentences such as the following, teachers will feel that these exercises are proving their worth:

> *the steamboat entered the straits straight after leaving the harbor*
>
> *the fisherman taught the stranger how to keep his line taut*
>
> *the cartrights will write a letter right now about the Indian rites*

14 The Phonic Code may usefully be left on the classroom wall after the Word Charts have been studied and taken down. Its multivalence is obvious. Among other things, it allows easy cross reference and, therefore, is a more useful tool for phonetic analysis than the international phonetic alphabet. Its large print enables students to refer to it quickly, even from a considerable distance.

15 Below are some examples of other exercises or games the class can play with the Phonic Code.

- Looking at any column, pupils can attempt to put down, in a limited time (say, 5 minutes), at least one word exemplifying each of the spellings in that column.

- In a limited time (say, 10 minutes), the pupils can put down as many words as they can think of having a certain spelling for one sound.

- In a limited time, pupils can give as many examples as possible for all the spellings found in each column.

- In a limited time, pupils can take one spelling and see how many words they can find in which that spelling has a different sound.

- The class can be challenged, without a time limit, to form sentences that contain as many spellings from one column as they can find useful examples for. A resulting sentence is considered more skillful the fewer words it uses that do not involve one of the signs in question, and the less it is stilted in meaning.

   he had s*ou*p, gl*u*cose and fr*ui*t for the rh*eu*matism he got through l*o*sing the sh*oe*s he thr*ew* in the t*wo* bl*ue* p*oo*ls

which contains all the leaf green signs on the Phonic Code Chart 4, may nevertheless be considered less skillful than

   dr*ea*ming p*eo*ple bel*ie*ve s*ee*ing k*ey* policemen like C*ae*sars rec*ei*ving qu*ay*side am*oe*bas secretly

which uses all the red signs on Phonic Code Chart 3, uses only one extraneous word, and is somewhat less contrived than the former.

- Conversely, the class can be challenged to form sentences using words in which one grapheme has as many different sounds as possible. Two examples are:

   great overbearing earls fear heaven heartily

and

   this woman is one of the women who worked for only a month.

- The class may also try to find pairs or triplets of words that

    - sound alike but are spelled different and have different meanings (homonyms), or

    - are spelled alike but sound differently (homographs).

16 Thus, effective techniques for increasing the students' ability to associate correct spellings with sounds have been carefully developed in this program, and, if care is taken to employ these techniques from the

start, most children will acquire fairly quickly the desired expertise. Indeed, older learners can be expected to master the association of spellings with sounds in a few hours.

Section 3
Oral Dictation

1   This short section will be concerned with *oral dictation,* which depends on sound, in contrast to Visual Dictation, which is carried out silently through use of the pointer and depends on sight.

2   Anyone who has codified his own speech will recognize that the signs met so far correspond to sounds. Anyone who has succeeded in reading by Visual Dictation knows that every word has one aspect that is part of their spoken language (sounds), and another that is part of their written language (signs).

If *Words in Color* has been used effectively up to this point, the pupils would now be able to hear sounds as they always have done while reading and, at the same time, evoke the correct images belonging to written speech. Testing this new skill is the purpose of oral dictation. At the same time, oral dictation should prove useful in training learners to code speech exactly as they may later do as a stenographer or secretary.

3   During the first exercises with oral dictation, the Word Charts may be left in front of the pupils for reference. Later, this support may be withdrawn and, later still, the Phonic Code, too, can be removed, since the real test of retention is that all this remains part of one's imagery and can be easily re-evoked when needed.

In oral dictation, the teacher utters a sentence in a clear and natural voice, so that its meaning as a whole is conveyed by the speed, pitch, and intonation clues which are part of the integrated experience of hearing speech. The learner can then use the meaning of the utterance as a whole as the key to separating into words, and putting down in writing, the flow of sound. Unless an image of a word is generated in the learner's mind, however, he will not be able to reproduce it in writing. Oral dictation is, therefore, a test of the learner's mastery over spelling via understanding what is dictated and of his ability to evoke immediately the signs, in their appropriate spatial arrangement, for the sounds uttered by the teacher.

The teacher should say a sentence once only, but must act responsibly in choosing and uttering it. This will stimulate responsibility on the part of the learners, who must listen carefully, extract the meaning from the intonation and the words used, and put down, in the most appropriate transcription from sound to sign available to them, what they think they heard.

It is neither necessary nor desirable to count errors and award marks in this activity. If the program is being correctly followed, oral dictation is the last stage of the apprenticeship in each restricted language; therefore, since so many exercises have created imagery in the mind, few mistakes will be made. Those that are made will serve to inform the teacher of what remains to be more fully mastered.

Looking at each pupil's responses to oral dictation will reveal to the teacher a great deal more than a mere total of errors made and the distance remaining to be covered. Mistakes are now symptoms of deliberate reflection on the part of the writer, not results of haphazard responses. Bearing this in mind, teachers will treat errors as indications of what exercises the pupils still need in order to develop inner criteria which function properly to provide correct images for the sounds.

Far fewer errors than may be expected will be produced by learners who have been taught consciously in accordance with the techniques suggested so far. Whenever they do not know how to spell something, the pupils are conscious of it; they know, too, that certain probabilities favor various signs as the correct version, and that a choice has to be made between them. The certainty that produces automatic and correct responses will appear after the learners have had more practice. Such automatic and correct responses, when they do appear, can be taken as signs that the pupils have fully functioning inner criteria for choosing between one spelling and another.

4   Oral dictation is used as an exercise for blending a number of mental activities which produce better spelling. Among the abilities it calls upon, and, therefore, develops are:

- the power to listen with understanding

- the power to visualize written forms corresponding to sounds heard

- the power to put down a sequence of marks on paper that can be deciphered by someone other than the writer, and that satisfy criteria which correspond to the rules of the language

5   Oral dictation is a mental transmutation of Visual Dictation. If Visual Dictation has been carried out carefully, oral dictation will not present any difficulty. Hence, if oral dictation presents obstacles, they should be tackled through additional work with Visual Dictations which strengthen the learners' ability to visualize spellings. If an individual is able to visualize words or do an equivalent mental operation, then writing under someone's dictation is not essentially different from spontaneous writing. The difference may lie only in his ability to write as rapidly as someone else talks.

6   Because some of the usual obstacles to oral dictation have been overcome through *Words in Color,* certain exercises to develop speed in writing can be undertaken much earlier than in other programs. Oral dictation may be able then, without straining the learner's abilities, to becomes as rapid as that given in regular stenography courses.

The ability to write rapidly is not closely related to the ability to read rapidly, since the first requires the use of muscles that customarily do not move as rapidly as the eyes do when scanning the page. Oral dictation is one of the ways by which speed of writing can be acquired, so long as it is done deliberately and thus without tensions.

Section 4
Book 3 and the Worksheets

1   We have assumed that the study of Word Charts 13-21 has been going hand-in-hand with *Book 3,* but we have not yet discussed this third text nor the Worksheets associated with it. Another text, the *Book of Stories,* will be considered at the end of this section, and more fully in the next one when we study the Worksheets that go with these stories.

2   The format of *Book 3* follows that of the two previous pupil books. The only differences are:

- *Book 3* is printed in smaller type, since now it is almost second nature to the pupil to read a text; size of print does not matter when one knows what one is doing and one's eyesight is normal.

- Sentences are no longer made deliberately short for the ease of the learners; they are whatever length their purpose requires.

- On every new left-hand page, the number of spellings for one sound, or the number of sounds for one spelling, are given together.

- When all the spellings of English have been reviewed and the complete Phonic Code has been displayed, the two common elements of printed matter— *capitals* and *punctuation marks*— are introduced.

Except for commas, which are used throughout *Book 3* and the *Book of Stories,* punctuation is introduced only in the continuous text at the end of *Book 3, page 40* in a letter from a girl to her father. The roman type of the conventional printed text is introduced beginning with "Story 36" of the *Book of Stories,* which will be reached when *Book 3* is finished.

By introducing these conventions of writing at the end of *Book 3,* we cover all the ground which the traditional definitions of "reading" and "writing" require of us.

In *Book 3,* on the left-hand side from page 2 to page 35, the new signs (which represent new sounds or for the most part additional spellings of sounds already met) are listed at the top. Underneath these is a set of words using these signs. On the right-hand side of each page are sentences utilizing the new signs. Each set of signs that produce the same sounds are placed in the same column; i.e., if the same sign appears in a number of columns on the left-hand page, it must be assumed that there are this many different sounds associated with this sign.

3   It becomes clear, as one turns the pages of this book, that its study is only meaningful when each new page is introduced *after* the Word Chart introducing the same signs. Visual Dictation 2 will provide sentences similar to those that appear on the right-hand pages. This part of the work has been well covered in relation to *Book 2* in Chapter II, and does not need repetition. But since, in Section 1 of this chapter, we only mentioned briefly Visual Dictation 2, teachers can find in the pages of *Book 3* examples to guide their choice of sentences for Visual Dictation related to each new Chart.

After such examples are worked out in class with the pointer on the Charts, pupils can be asked to work on their own on a particular pair of pages in *Book 3.*

4   Worksheets 8-12 are complementary to Word Charts 13-21, the *Word Building Book,* and *Book 3.* Except for each page 3, which still inquires about the meaning of some words, these new Worksheets take pupils deeper into their awareness of the sounds and the spellings of English. They provide new games calling for different mental qualities than those already used.

Page 1 of each of these five Worksheets asks the same question about three different sets of words which, in black and white, either show the same spellings or give different spellings for the same sound. These exercises are obviously tests for the third phase of the program, when varied spellings are met and must be used. They leave considerable latitude to the learners. Some of the sets of words are diversely related, indicating that we are departing from the strict stimulus-response type of test and trusting the initiative of the learners. Indeed, this is the value of such tests in this program. Since we have from the beginning cultivated multivalence and autonomy of learning, we must allow these aptitudes to be enhanced by the exercises we offer either for practice or for testing pupil progress.

5   *Page 2* of each of the Worksheets gives pairs of words; the problem posed requires reflection before the learner can decide whether different or identical spellings correspond to identical or different sounds. One has to know the particular sounds one has to make as a response to seeing a word, then listen to one's voice and decide whether two designated words present the same sound for the signs which are to be compared. It is most likely that pupils will develop criteria to help themselves by going back to the Word Charts or to pages of *Book 3* to decide if the *s* (same) or *d* (different) sound is present. The possibilities are as follows:

- spellings can be the same but sounds different *(soup* and *house)*
- the same sound can be rendered by different spellings (would and wood)

Scoring 100 percent is not hard. Evidence from a number of classes playing this game will establish whether it is helping to develop their awareness of the sound-sign relationship.

6   *Pages 4, 5, and 6* of Worksheet 8 are examples of exercises with signs that have two or more sounds.

A set of words is given in which the same sign appears sixteen times. The pupil must decide, by listening to his voice, in which words he has to make sounds in one way and in which in another. Anyone who knows the words and can listen to his voice will score 100 percent. With the learners, we shall discover the range of obstacles which this very simple game presents.

Corrections can be made in a number of ways, two of which are suggested below:

- First, the teacher forms pairs of pupils among those who state that they have gone through pages 4, 5, and 6, and lets one pupil give his answer and the other accept or reject it. After pupils find that they agree that the work is done properly, or that they disagree because of their doubts, then

- The teacher forms a group, of which he may be a part, to listen to the sounds made by individual pupils reading one word of the list in turn and waiting for the group to respond. This procedure relieves the teacher from having to be the sole and final assessor, and gives the pupils a number of chances to discover the criteria that make one sure of one's answers.

7   An alternative way of playing such games is found in *page 4* of Worksheets 9-12. Pupils are asked there to rewrite lists of words so that they group together those words which contain the same sound in one or various spellings. This game is presented again in a slightly different way on page 4 of each successive Worksheet, in order to indicate that there are a number of ways of playing the game.

But all ways of playing this game serve the same purpose: to make pupils aware that, in English, each word one learns must be known for itself—known "personally," as it were. This intimacy with a considerable number of words creates a fondness for the personality of words, and no longer generates resentment and impatience when one is confronted with the multiplicity of English spellings. The playing of such games will, naturally, also yield evidence that words are accurately known.

On *pages 5 and 6* of Worksheets 9-12, most of the really doubtful spellings have been included. These pages will give further practice with the words that usually present most of the spelling problems. They will be met here *after* the use of the Word Charts. Then the pages of words and sentences in *Book 3* can be read.

The variety of ways of working, as well as the game-like activity involved in the whole approach, will remove the doubts that cause spelling to be difficult. The results of pupils' work on these Worksheets, which appear last in the sequence of exercises, will prove this point.

8   On *page 7* of these Worksheets, we begin Visual Dictation 2, in black and white. The words chosen are small words, indicating that we are no

longer concerned with spelling but with the education of inventiveness. The objective here is the understanding that *words are multivalent units* that can be used in a number of sentences carrying many meanings.

At the same time, pupils will learn (1) that sentences have structures; (2) that certain words must take certain places in sentences; (3) that clauses can be joined to make longer sentences; and (4) that meaning can be conveyed by different means, i.e., by fewer words, or more words, and so forth.

Page 8 takes the challenge one stage further: it asks pupils, first, to choose 25 words from among those already met in Word Charts and their books, and to make sentences with them. The first part of the exercise will bring out the pupils' capacity to discriminate between highly special words and usual ones, and between compatible words and words whose use excludes the use of others. The second part will be similar to the exercise on page 7. But since the responsibility for the choice of the words is left to the learners, the outcome of these combinations may be very different indeed, as a quick look at the completed Worksheets of different pupils should reveal. It may happen that, because of one pupil's particular choice of words, not a single sentence can be formed. Such results will sharpen the pupils' awareness of the function of words in sentences, and will pave the way for the study of structure and grammar that is to follow.

9   Pages 9 and 10 of Worksheets 8-12 relate the work done on words to the last tables of the *Word Building Book*. Since the study of spelling is still our concern, we ask questions here that relate the signs that form the words to the sounds they are supposed to convey. The main difference between pages 9 and 10 is obvious. On page 9, we leave it completely up to the pupils to see which signs are new and which they have already studied. On page 10, signs get lost in the words, and unless the words are known, it may be difficult to disentangle the signs from each other. For that reason, we make allowance for ignorance of some words on page 10. But the questions are really about the comparisons of two tables of signs and, therefore, require yet another ability. The extent of this ability is shown by the answers found on these pages.

Chapter III
Meeting of Spellings

10   Up to *page 10* of the Worksheets, we have restricted the study of words and sentences to those who have been following from the start.

We have stressed the importance of listening, of watching, of making images of words; as a result, we expect to develop more conscious spellers and more language users with greater awareness of words.

Although the development of such sensitivity is a valuable contribution to education, there are other aspects of communication through words which call for different gifts of the mind. Thus, the last six pages of the Worksheets are devoted to exercises that either develop or test these gifts.

11   On *page 11* of Worksheet 8, there is a sentence of twelve words, while on the same page of Worksheet 12, there is one of twenty-nine. The first question asks for a reduction of the number of words without altering the meaning. There may be a number of solutions to that problem, and pupils are encouraged to give as many as possible. The second question permits alteration of the meaning, but does not permit changing words.

By playing on the two variables of meaning and the vehicle of meaning (structure), we shall stress accuracy, economy of words, and adequacy of expression. From this stage of learning, we can make pupils aware of style, insofar as it is the outcome of a choice of a small number of words or a choice of many adjectives.

12   On *page 12* we embark on Visual Dictation 3, without giving it a name. The elements we now combine are sentences. The six sentences provided do not belong to the same story if read in just any order. But if some sentences are left out and the others reordered, something new appears: a joint meaning emerges from the sentences that seems to make a special sense of each and all, and at the same time.

Through this exercise, it is possible to discover something more about "words in time." Not only is time needed to utter words and, again, to convey the meaning that is the outcome of a sequence of words, but it serves also to make one feel something that neither each word nor each sentence can provide by itself. This cumulative meaning, which people already know very well in spoken speech, is now a special awareness that can be considered and worked upon.

13   On *page 13,* the study is of whether word sequences make sense or not. Words can, naturally, be said one after the other, but the sequence thus formed can (1) evoke a reality, (2) be in agreement with one's experience or contradict it, or (3) evoke puzzlement or even rejection. We ask the question in a way that may be elaborated by teachers. We want to know whether the pupils find in the sentence any one of the things above, but we ask only whether the sentences make sense or not. Of course, *her finger was looking* might make sense to someone whose imagination is wild, but to others, it does not. The lesson, therefore, cannot end with the "yes" or "no" answer requested. Elaboration seems required.

Teachers could begin in class by having one pupil write any sentence. Then, one word in it may be replaced so as to generate contradiction, or puzzlement, or rejection as nonsense.

Let us suppose that a pupil wrote

the snail moves slowly

A teacher could suggest replacing *moves* by *springs* or *jumps*. Those who have never seen a snail do anything other than crawl are likely to find the new sentence puzzling, but those who know nothing about snails may find it a possibility.

If, instead of replacing moves, the teacher replaces the word *snail* by *satellite,* then those who know that a satellite must move at great speeds will either find the statement absurd or see it as only part of another statement that may be true.

The statue moves slowly may generate feelings of awe or stimulate the imagination in a number of directions, while *the snail moves bulldozers* will generate feelings of disbelief and an affirmation of impossibility by the sheer comparison of sizes.

Any number of such statements can be looked at from this point of view, until the class realizes that there are very few cases in which everyone would say a given statement is nonsense.

What the pupils will acquire through this practice is the understanding that words as a *medium* of communication do not in themselves constitute the message, while feelings, for instance, may serve as both medium and message for each individual. One can be sad, and know it, and still say "I am happy." This important attribute of words, which is little pondered upon by their users, will be best understood in the statement of the French diplomat Talleyrand (around 1815): "Words have been given us so that we may disguise our thoughts."

It does not seem too early to introduce learners to this property of words just at the time they are again becoming aware, as they did while learning to talk, of words and their behavior.

"Truth" is to be known beyond words from the message they convey or fail to convey. That one can know oneself as capable (1) of reaching truth directly and knowing it through inner criteria, and (2) of testing whether or not the medium used carries it, without doubt an awareness whose implications should be seriously considered by all.

14 The exercise on *page 14* will test yet another power of the mind: the ability to be guided by a random set of words to produce a story of a certain length. What is given is a set of words to be included in the story. What is left variable are the images generated by *these* words in the mind of each pupil *and* the way in which imagery is translated into statements which communicate the pupil's thought fully.

Pupils will most likely provide a wide variety of solutions to the problems on page 14. These can be collected and kept by teachers, for use in stimulating further their own ability to follow the challenge put by such opportunities.

15 Now that we have shifted from reading to writing and made pupils more aware of their creative powers we are ready to look at the writing of

others. *Pages 15 and 16* of the Worksheets introduce the study of certain stories in the *Book of Stories.*

Each story in the *Book of Stories* contains a number of words that the pupils have not yet met; thus, each story helps to increase the pupils' vocabulary. Equally important, however, is that the pupils are able to recognize in each story a large number of words that they already understand.

Very often, they can infer the meaning of an unknown word from the meaning of the context in which it appears. This is everybody's right, and is to be made clear from the start of reading, since it has been used from the beginning of life to make spoken speech a possibility.

Page 16 of the Worksheets is designed to relate the pupils to the *Book of Stories* in another way. We can see that each story has a final paragraph. This is obviously the author's privilege but also in a way an arbitrary decision which can be open for examination. The author knew when writing these stories that they could be extended in many directions. This extension of the stories will be left to the pupils' own contributions so that they see the future as open as it really is. They can also note how their imagination is variously stirred by contact with one event or a relating of an event.

Naturally, since the *Stories* have a number of ideas to offer, various sensitivities will be struck by various aspects, and we hope the answers will reveal to teachers some of the more creative possibilities within children.

16   In this section, we have focused thus far more on the Worksheets than on *Book 3,* which is also part of our present study.

The major difference between *Book 3* and the Worksheets is that the book is a complete unit, designed to take pupils by the hand through some exercises, while the Worksheets are open-ended, and can be undertaken at different stages of the pupils' maturation. The book can be finished and put aside, but the Worksheets may always be restarted as the children's insights, into themselves and into the language, develop.

The book relates to teachers and to the language more than to the pupils, while the Worksheets relate to the specific pupils by testing the degree to which each can operate on his own.

Let us turn now to the last pages of *Book 3* (reproduced on the following pages). *Pages 36 and 37* are different from all we have done so far: they state what the program has achieved for the learners *(not* what a given group of learners have achieved for themselves). These statements reflect the experiences common to everyone who has taken the course as outlined.

—we can now read almost all the words of the english language

—many of them are not easy to spell because each sound may have so many forms and each form so many sounds

—we have met about three hundred and eighty forms for fifty-one sounds

—we can imagine the color for each special sound whatever the form, because we have met each sound associated with one color all along in our work with the charts

—in our word building book we have found how to put together the various forms that give one sound, we separated the vowels (which have sounds of their own) and the other signs that form syllables with the vowels, these last signs we call consonants because they need vowels to form sounds

—we found twenty-one sounds for the vowels and one hundred and eighty-eight forms for these vowels differing in shape or color

—we found one hundred and ninety consonants and thirty sound groups among them

—the english language which we speak makes use of all these signs that we found in these books, as well as in the charts and the word building book

—to write the english language as we should, we must practice reading aloud to see if we can give the right sound to the various shapes we look at

—the better we can do that the easier it will be for us when we want to write what we are thinking about

—the second visual dictation game we played showed us how many more sentences we could form than it seemed possible to begin with

—in this way we learned to write new things until we could write anything we wished

—when we can read and understand all texts and write whatever we think so that others know what we mean we say that we have a good knowledge of english

—this is what we have tried to achieve in this work

17 Finally, only some of the conventions of written English remain to be presented. Two of those conventions—capitalization and punctuation —are introduced on pages 38 and 39.

Study by the pupils of all the signs in the Phonic Code reveals that there are 26 constituent units (or letters) which can be collected in a sequence known historically as the *alphabet*. That is, there are 26 *letters* of the English alphabet that the 380 signs of the Phonic Code have reconstructed. The 26 letters, with their names, are given on page 38.

Once the alphabet has been introduced, its capital forms can easily be associated with its lower-case forms, which are by now very familiar having been used throughout the pupil materials. Each letter of English has a *capital* form and a *lower case* form. In a number of instances the capitals look exactly like the lower case we have used; (C, O, P, S, V, W, X, Z), in other instances (J, K, U, Y), they are similar enough to our lower case to be easily recognized. The remaining signs (A, B, D, E, F, G, H, L, M, N, Q, R,) will require introduction, but one lesson should suffice to familiarize the pupil with them. One (I) has already been introduced as a word.

We would suggest that the teacher introduce each of the unfamiliar capitals in conjunction with two already recognized. Here is one possible sequence among thousands, for such an introduction:

T	in	POT	G	in	EGG
A	in	CAT	H	in	HIS
B	in	TUB	M	in	MY
L	in	LOTS	N	in	MAN
E	in	TELL	R	in	RUN
F	in	OF	Q	in	QUICK
D	in	LID			

It is important to let learners know that the conventional rules for the use of capitals are varied:

- A capital is usually written for the first letter of the first word in a sentence.

- Names of people, days, months, seasons, countries, geographical entities, mountains, rivers, etc., begin with capitals.

- Some adjectives (e.g., the English language, the Swiss nation, a Wagnerian opera) begin with capitals.

Each of these conventions can be pointed out as the capitals are introduced and need not be given as a set of rules. Every look at a text can now be regarded as an opportunity to note which words have capitals and to determine which of the rules above applies.

Just as it seems important to teachers to make sure that pupils master the uses of capitals in English, it is important to pupils that teachers do not continue to repeat questions which are no longer challenging. Hence, teachers who watch their pupils assimilate the easy rules of capitalization through observation of case after case will know how to eliminate unnecessary testing.

18 *Book 3* ends with a text to be read continuously. It is a letter which shows all *the different marks of punctuation.* In it, all the conventions of written English are observed. The *Roman printing* typeface is introduced in the *Book of Stories* from Stories 36 to 40. By the time the pupils reach those stories, they will have completed *Book 3* and have the necessary experience to permit a shift to another typeface without any trouble.[8]

The qualitative difference between pages 36-37 of *Book 3* and the letter on *page 40* should be noted. The statements on pages 36 and 37 still remain separate statements, differing from previous ones mainly in the number of words they contain. The letter, on the other hand, is a narrative that

---

[8] Teachers find it very simple from now on to pick up two additional conventions in a few lessons: (1) *diacritical marks,* needed to use a dictionary, can be related to the Phonic Code (see Appendix 4), and (2) *rules for dividing words* when you "run out of space" on one line can be introduced. *The Webster's New World Dictionary of American Language* (New York, World Publishing Company, 1959) is easy for students to use. It is a paperback and has some background on word origins that students can also study. *Scholastic Dictionary of American English* (New York, Scholastic Magazines, Inc., 1962) is a paperback (TX 327) with slightly larger print for first graders, but little background on word origins. *A Concise Etymological Dictionary of the English Language* by the Rev. Walter W. Skeat of Cambridge University, England published in New York by Capricorn Books is a paperback with complete information on word origins to explain our unusual spellings in English.

conveys a message and requires that words be subordinated to the idea. The completeness of the letter is equivalent to the completeness of the transmission of an idea. A letter is not a story, and, though no question is asked in the Worksheets concerning this letter, teachers may want to use pages 40-41 to motivate their classes to write letters for a number of purposes: festivals (Christmas, New Year, special holidays, birthdays) and so forth. This part of the study of writing is left to the teacher to include or develop as he or she wishes.

Since this manuscript was written, a number of teachers have sent to the author some of the material produced by their pupils while learning to read and write. As an outstanding example let us name Sister Mary Leonore (Murphy) R.S.C. of Sydney, Australia who has communicated to her colleagues, through her book *Creative Writing*[9] all that her classes using *Words in Color* were able to achieve in a very short time. Mrs. Mary Fowles, principal of a public school in Reading, England, reports on the work of a whole elementary school.[10] We recommend these books to teachers.

Section 5
The Book of Stories and Worksheet 13

1 The *Book of Stories* was written specifically for this program. It contains 40 stories in 100 printed pages. Eleven illustrations have been inserted in the text, since they can contribute something words cannot convey: the uniform evocation of the seven characters of the stories, and elaboration of some other key aspects in them.

The stories cover subjects that could be of interest to learners of any age, though mostly to young ones.

Because the age of the readers is not used as a criterion for vocabulary limitation, it is possible to maintain in the stories a "way of talking" that is appropriate to the subject and the purpose of each story. Thus, these

---

9 See p. 97.
10 See Bibliography, p. 238.

stories may also be for the reader an enriching experience, a description of a complex situation, or a form of poetic expression.

2   The first "story" is really not a story at all. Its six sentences, very similar to those in *Book 2,* do not seem to be linked until *Story 2* recalls, in its first sentences, the names of the people mentioned in *Story 1,* and suddenly provides the links that did not previously exist. *Stories 2* and *3* are related in the same way. These early stories can be read as we read pages of the primers. In fact, all the stories can be read sentence by sentence. The images each sentence evokes in the reader's mind, however, form a pattern which is different from a simple collection of unrelated images, and it is this interweaving of images to which we apply the word "story."[11]

It should be clear in reading these stories that a writer and a reader do opposite things. The first looks for words that render a thought he has and the reader from these words draws a thought which may be akin to the one the writer had to begin with.

We therefore insist from the beginning upon the need for naturalness in reading to help learners reach meaning more readily, and hence to permit enjoyment of the experience left by that reading.

As we move from story to story, the characters are more precisely delineated. There has been an effort at maintaining consistency between the short passages. There is a kind of common background to the forty stories, but they are also independent entities and can be read in almost any order.

3   The stories provide for the learners an enormous increase in the written vocabulary; some of them have been deliberately written with this purpose in mind. The new vocabulary, however, is introduced naturally in the course of the story.

---

[11] For text and fuller discussion of the first three stories see pp. 102-103.

In *Story 14,* for example, two statements refer to the kitchen and food; the words they introduce are presented not as a vocabulary list, but as the appropriate words to create this story.

- *"well, may I prepare them?"*

- *"do you know how to do it?"*

- <u>*"I put water in the saucepan and place it on the stove, turn the knob round to light the gas, and when the water boils I put the eggs in it and let them stay for a while."*</u>

- *"good boy," said mother, "go ahead and prepare the eggs."*

- *while sam was doing that, mother asked him, "do you know how to prepare a french dressing for the salad?"*

- <u>*sam said, "I know that you put in oil and vinegar, salt and pepper, but I do not know how much of each nor in what order."*</u>

- *"well, we shall do it together when we have finished what we are doing."*

Story 18 introduces a number of words that refer to appliances and home furnishings in much the same way:

- **the other day a truck stopped at the door, and a big cardboard box was brought in.**

- *the man asked mom to sign a paper and then he left.*

- *"what is there in this box?" asked pat and tom at the same time.*

- *mom said, "I do not know, daddy ordered it and did not tell me."*

- *"can't you open it and let us see?"*

- *"no" said mother, "it is dad's order and he must be here to open it and see if he wants it."*

- *mom left the entrance hall and went to the kitchen.*

- the five children stood in front of the closed box and were very curious.

- sam pushed it a little and saw how light it was.

- "such a big box and so light, what can be inside?"

<u>*- they all started guessing: "not a washing machine," said pam, "not a refrigerator," said sam, "not a stove," said pat,*</u> *as all of them remembered that these arrived in crates of the same size as this carton.*

- "could it be a rug?" asked tim.

- they all stopped talking, thinking whether it was possible.

-sam said "let us roll up the rug in the front room and see if it is as light as this carton."

- they rolled the rug, but the five of them could barely lift it.

- they unrolled the rug, and put everything as it was.

- tom said, "let us go around the house and see everything we have and think of it as put into a cardboard box."

- "good idea," said sam, "let us go."

<u>**- they looked at chairs, armchairs, cupboards, blankets, sheets, curtains, and most of the things around, but none would fit the two things they knew about the box, its size and its weight.**</u>

- while they were still studying the items in the house, dad came in and said, "oh! this wretched thing has at last arrived."

- they all ran to him and asked together, "what is that wretched thing?"

- "it is a surprise for you: a flamingo like the one you saw at the zoo the other day, but this one is stuffed with foam rubber."

4 A study of the words used in this book will show that:

- all prepositions and conjunctions are introduced naturally, in the context of the stories

- verbs have been used in all moods and tenses; irregular and regular verbs have been given equal status

- adverbs, pronouns, adjectives, and nouns—along with the prepositions, conjunctions, and verbs-form the 1000-1500 words spelled in the forty contexts of the stories so that many areas of experience may be opened up to expression

If we total the number of different words used in the pupil books of this program, we find more than 2000.

Let us say a word here about spelling. Since exercises have been suggested to fortify the closer examination of words, teachers should expect that, by this point in the program, their pupils' spelling (i.e., the writing down of the word, not necessarily the naming of its component letters) will more often than not be accurate. There are, of course, more chances now to provide a good background for spelling, because we can separate reading comprehension from looking at the singular shapes of words in isolation and evoking them individually. The vocabulary met in the stories may already form part of the spoken speech of the reader. If so, then he has now to concentrate on the "physiognomy" of words so he is able to put them down spontaneously as they should be—that is, in perfect conformity to the models provided by conventional English.

But if some of the words are new, reading the stories will produce an increase in the spoken as well as the written vocabulary of the learners. The pupils can often infer the meanings of these new words from the context of the stories. Some pupils, however, may need to look at objects, drawings, or pictures to understand clearly their meanings. But the first attempt to get assistance is more advantageously made through teachers or pupils asking for explanations of this kind from classmates who may already know the set of meanings covered by the word. Teachers may be able to learn from some of their pupils how to reach others. They may also need to remove some general misunderstandings of some words, but such misunderstanding offers them insights into their pupils' minds.

5   In addition to exposing learners to a large number of words related within a specific situation (as tested on page 15 of Worksheets 8-12), each story deepens the learner's experience. What we mean by depth is a variable awareness of situations in which one is involved with other people, in mystery, in social conventions, with right and wrong, with imagination and aesthetic experience.

Involvement with other people: This is a theme of most of the stories, but some stories stress interpersonal relations in order to raise issues for discussion in class. *Stories 6, 12, 14, 15, 29, 31,* and *40* can all be treated as opportunities to learn from the pupils their individual views about the matter debated in each story.

By inviting pupils to express themselves, the teachers, if they restrain themselves from judging or taking sides, will learn much that they need to know about the ethical sense of their pupils. The author believes that the issues raised are real and important ones that need thrashing out among young as well as older learners, so as to develop the sense of "the other" or to stress distinctions sometimes neglected in certain environments.

Involvement in mystery: Some of the situations in the stories have been designed to foster reverence for what is still unfathomed in the universe. *Stories 11, 16, 21, 33,* and *37* are examples of such situations and appear to the author to have a perennial appeal.

Involvement in social conventions: Social conventions are not discussed as much. They are the subject of several stories, though, and the readers will feel the significance and value of some of these conventions by reading about them. *Stories 9, 12, 17, 22, 28, 30, 36,* and *38* are examples in which the expressions of socialized people are used naturally and lead to better understanding.

Cultivation of the imagination: Such situations are found in *Stories 8, 10, 13, 18, 19, 24, 26, 38,* and *39*, which also involve aesthetic components. These could lead pupils to attempt to communicate their own version of their own experience in some medium other than words.

6   The purpose of reading is to permit one *to gain experience by proxy,* that is, to experience something which one has not personally lived through, but which someone else has gone through and which is offered to us through the medium of words, films, or some other artistic production.

Most of us would be very poor if not enriched by experience-by-proxy. The proportion of direct experience to experience-by-proxy diminishes quickly as we read more and more, but the validity of the experience read about can only come from our direct experience. The author of the stories has, therefore, attempted to find "cores of direct experience" around which the expanded experience could be provided. Dreams are part of direct experience, as much as are mishaps, or joys, or adventures.

By reading the stories, teachers will see that no restriction except decency has been put upon the choice of topics. They will find that a story can be created "out of nothing" by simply analyzing happenings, feelings, wishes, and moods so that by successive approximations a more precise experience emerges. This is one of the vital contributions of the reading of the stories, and the author took care to cover a sufficient spectrum of experience without making the text too heavy, so that when the reader finishes the book he may want to go back to it for the abundance of life it contains.

7   However, the author had to keep in mind that these stories might be read during school time. At school, we study so as to become (1) clearer in our minds about our environment, (2) more aware of ourselves functioning in relationship, which means also (3) more aware of the language heritage of our group or society.

8   Up to this point in the program, the Worksheets have referred to the *Book of Stories* for vocabulary and to stimulate the learners to think of endings to the stories. Now, *Worksheet 13* asks the learners to look at a selection of sixteen stories out of the forty in the *Book of Stories* from the point of view of analyzing content, human beings, and feelings.

Naturally, one may have experienced much of what is covered by a story, and yet not be able to express it in words. There are different types of questions on each page, so that teachers may observe how each individual attacks each set of questions. Teachers may note (1) who prefers matter-of-fact questions; (2) who is disturbed by certain experiences, and by which ones; (3) who needs time to formulate in a way satisfactory to him what has been evoked in his mind; and (4) who is stimulated by what, and to what extent.

Teachers may feel that questions other than these should be asked about the content of these stories, or that other stories should have been selected. But if pupils find exercises such as these in Worksheet 13 profitable and enjoyable, they will wish to do more of them. It then becomes possible for the teacher to propose others. She can, for instance:

- add her own questions to the six the author has proposed for each of the sixteen stories

- ask for questions from her class and select those which evoke the most interest

- suggest that each pupil prepare six or more questions on the story or stories he likes best

Classwork can follow this individual work, since the various answers to the same questions can be read aloud for all.

Much more work could be done on this text, which has already served as

- a continuous reader for practicing reading at the speed of speech

- a source of enjoyment in varying degrees according to the content

- a source of experience-by-proxy

- a challenge relative to the expression of feelings, to the analysis of impressions, and so forth

- a contributor to vocabulary-building

- a source of word images leading to correct spellings

- a source of ethical, social, and personal issues which involve one at both theoretical and practical levels

9   In the next chapter, the same texts will become a source of structural and grammatical awareness, to which *Worksheet 14* is mainly devoted. In that chapter, we shall consider, in addition to the *Book of Stories,* the use of the Word Cards.

10   This present chapter is titled *The Meeting of Spellings.* But obviously we have met much more than spelling. Specifically, we have attempted to involve pupils in activities from which a deeper awareness of relationship can emerge.

It follows that the program is concerned with educating the person in every learner, while obtaining mastery of spelling as a by-product. This we deem very important in the world of today, where we are asked to conceive of a complex reality and to work in harmony with it, while acting on it to change it and ourselves.

Chapter IV
A Study of Structures

In the previous chapters we have explored the use of *Words in Color* to overcome the difficulties of learners who must move from spoken speech to written speech. We can now confidently assume that our pupils can make sense of every page of written English which uses words and expressions within their hearing and speaking vocabulary.

Still, the language they are using is more than a vehicle for communication. As an "object" developed over the course of centuries, it has a number of interesting characteristics which have deserved the attention of linguists over the generations. The modes of thought of a group of people find their way into a language and mold it. In turn, language users mold their own thought using their own language. The result is that one finds it natural to express one's thought in one's own language but far less so in "foreign" languages.

We have, therefore, a number of tasks left for us after making the techniques of reading and writing available to our pupils. Among them is developing an understanding in our learners of how our language behaves when it renders our thought. This includes grammar as one of the awarenesses reached ultimately in the process of becoming conscious of oneself talking or writing.

Since writing is more tangible than spoken speech, one being in space and the other in time, we shall naturally undertake these tasks on the written material and later on notice that our observations apply to both.

In this chapter we shall still remain within the material created for this program when it was first initiated. In particular, we shall use the pack of Word Cards and Worksheet 14. But before we get to this material, we shall briefly consider the role of dictation and writing in the study of the structures of English.

Section 1
Dictation and Writing

1 We have been using visual and oral dictation to promote flexibility in the study of words and sentences. Still we can now consider more closely what it can do for our pupils if we ourselves are aware that in oral dictation for instance, the pupil's memory is called in to perform a special job.

Indeed, considering our proposal of saying a sentence once only, with intonation and at the actual speed of the speech related to the content, we can see that when the teacher embarks upon such a dictation, she is calling the pupils' attention to the meaning involved and recognizing that this particular meaning is rendered by *this* set of words, in *this* order, and with *this* intonation and no other.

Hence, dictation is a tool which permits, on the one hand, an entry into this study and, on the other hand, a certainty that both pupils and teacher have material available in any amount needed for working as equals.

2 Dictation can be used in a number of ways:

- The teacher can utter a sentence once and ask the pupils to indicate that they have received it as uttered either (1) by saying it; (2) by finding it with the pointer among the words on the Word Chart[11](or, later, on the Word Card

---

1 See pp. 48-49.

sheets on the wall) or on the Phonic Code;[2] or (3) by writing it down. In the first two cases, only one pupil at a time can give the indication; in the third, the number of pupils participating is immaterial—a good reason for choosing the third alternative.

- The teacher can first read a succession of sentences which are linked by a meaning so that the whole is meaningful to the pupils. Then she can utter the sentences one by one—but as complete units with the intonation and speed required by the meaning-leaving no time between the sentences beyond what is needed to write them down. This approach links writing with whole statements which are retained because of their meaning and because a particular language has been chosen to render that meaning.

- The teacher can also start with an existing text recognized by the pupils as something they can read and understand. (This could be given through Visual Dictation on the Word Charts, or, later, on the Word Card sheets, as well as read by the pupils from a printed page.) To commit such a text to memory is to be able, after looking at it, to utter it again or to write it down. Hence the mental activity preceding writing is not very different from that preceding speaking.[3]

When one is aware of holding in mind the words rather than the meaning, he is relying on memory; but when one is aware of holding in mind the meaning rather than the words, he is only involved in understanding. *Both memory and understanding reinforce each other and can be cultivated by dictation.*

3   Statements used in dictation for the purpose of making learners aware of structure and the way in which it supports memory and understanding will naturally vary a great deal from simple phrases to quite long sentences. Teachers who already know their pupils' competence can short-cut the simple-to-complex sequence and start at a point that adequately challenges them. Here are graded samples to illustrate the movement from the simple to the complex structure:

---

2 See pp. 50 and 151.
3 See pp. 51-52.

- the man met his death by drowning

- the return trip was very sad, as they had to get his body back to his native town

- in the convoy there were his widow and his two children, his friends, and also their dog, feeling grief more than anyone

- it all happened during the holiday, the family had undertaken a long trip to reach a warm and quiet beach where for two weeks they would be really away from their strenuous occupations

- the place they found was ideal from every point of view; everyone was as happy as could be, running on the soft sand, rolling in the shallow water, feeling cool in the sea breeze after a dip

- one day they were tempted to move to a new point on the beach, in order to embrace the surf that was so inviting there, but no one except the little dog suspected that the ocean at this spot was treacherous and the incline at the bottom, steep

- the dog barked, scratched the mother and the daughter, making a nuisance of himself, refusing to get into the water or let anyone in, leaving the ball to float away rather than go to fetch it as he did the previous days

- when the man, his friend, and his son got into the water, they were happily singing and calling everyone to join them, pushing ahead to meet the waves with their chests and being thrown off their feet each time

- but their luck stopped suddenly, and all three felt the ground sliding under their feet, the son, who was svelte and not so far out as his father, managed to struggle against the current and reach a safer spot, the friend, a grown-up man, fought and fought for his life, unable to see his way to help the other man, drowning in spite of all his efforts

- it took a team three quarters of an hour to bring his dead body ashore[4]

Chapter IV
A Study of Structures

4 The sequence of sentences above makes a story, and can therefore be remembered as a whole because of the feelings and experiences it evokes. But to remember each word and each sentence exactly as it is, one has to concentrate *not* on the feelings or the events, but on each of the expressions used by the author. To achieve this purpose we have to break down the text into short statements and allow pupils to receive them as specific sequences of sounds as well as to receive them as feelings. Because the purpose of this exercise is to cause pupils to note words and their relationships and put them down as they are found in correct English, the teacher needs to insist upon conformity in this type of work because flexibility and freedom would not achieve this purpose. Discipline, then, is the requirement.

5 The discipline of a language is its grammar. To study grammar, one analyzes what one writes or says, or what others write or say. One interesting way of engaging pupils in such analyses is described in detail in the next section.

For most beginners, speech is an automatic function of the mind, and to learn to watch oneself using speech is not an automatic activity for most people. Writing is also automatic for those who have mastered it and know their language. But because signs must be put on paper, it takes longer to write than to talk. Hence, one has a little more time left to consider what one is doing. It is, therefore, sounder to look at written forms for a study of grammar than to examine the forms of oral speech in spite of their close correspondence.

**Section 2
Games with Word Cards**

1 The Word Cards are a set of 1227 words printed in black on various colors of cardboard. Each color cardboard is identified with one of the major classes of words in English (or "parts of speech," as they are frequently called), according to the following key:[5]

---

[5] The colors of the sets of Word Cards differ from those previously in circulation which were: green, *nouns;* salmon, *verbs;* yellow, *adjectives;* blue, *adverbs;* ivory, *conjunctions;* gold, *interjections* ; gray, *pronouns;* pink, *prepositions.*

red	*nouns*
yellow	*verbs*
blue	*adjectives*
green	*adverbs*
ivory	*conjunctions*
lavender	*interjections*
orange	*pronouns*
brown	*prepositions*

A complete list of the words on each color of cardboard—alphabetized within each color grouping—is given in Appendix 5.

2   The cardboard sheets on which the Word Cards are printed have been perforated to permit the change of sheets into packs.

We would suggest that one set of Word Cards be kept in the form of sheets for use on the wall in the games which involve most or all of the pupils, and that another set be broken into as many packs as are necessary for small-group work.[6]

3   When sheets rather than packs are used they are to be introduced ail at once. Since it was not possible, because of the varying length of words having the same initial, to preserve on each sheet an alphabetic ordering of words, to assist the teacher in learning them and their locations and since she will not be able to learn these a few at a time with the pupils as she did on the Word Charts, she must take some time in advance to become familiar with all of them. For some time, the teacher will need to have the Word Card sheets hanging where she can look at them frequently to take in their content, study the location of words on the sheets, and learn to distinguish sheets of the same color by the words printed on them.

We would suggest placing all the sheets on a wall and arranging those of the same color in columns, so that they display their content by length of the words from left to right. If there are more sheets than can fit in one column, the remainder should be in an adjoining column. The small but useful sets of conjunctions, prepositions, interjections, and pronouns can be placed together in an accessible area-perhaps between the nouns and the verbs or between the nouns and the adjectives, or as in the following arrangement.

---

[6] Since only one set of Word Cards is included in the classroom set of materials, teachers will probably wish to obtain a second set.

4   For the teacher who will be leading at the outset the games described below, it will be an easy task to select words that form a sentence. These words will be, of necessity, on a number of different Charts, and most frequently on Charts of different colors, since many sentences do not use more than one word with a given function.

The pointer may now be used to touch the chosen words in an order which creates a sentence (as in Visual Dictation 2, used earlier on the Word Charts)[7]—for example, *it is* or *it is my father* or *who was this man?* The teacher should find it increasingly easy to locate the words she wants as practice with the game familiarizes her with the Word Card sheets. It will profit both the teacher and pupils to use as wide a variety of different words as possible in composing visual sentences. Naturally, some words

---

[7] See p. 31 ff.

will be used with far greater frequency than others, and so will be found more quickly simply because they appear more frequently in normal usage. The following sentences illustrate a pattern of dictation which uses both keywords needed for many sentences and unusual words:

> *it is us*
>
> *it is not me*
>
> *it is not my dog*
>
> *it is a cat*
>
> *it is dark*
>
> *it is a black cat moving*
>
> *oh, it is a black cat moving in the dark*
>
> *oh, it is a black cat moving quickly in the dark because he is cunning*

The last sentence draws words from each of the eight categories of functions so that, at one stage or another in the evolution of this series, the pupils will have made some observations about the use of the various functions. From then on, it is these deeper insights that will organize the bulk of the material so that the pupils can move immediately from one function to another as the sentences are formed one after the other.

It may be of help to write down the sentences produced each day, and to try, the following day, to find them again with the pointer on the sheets on the wall. Since the positions of the words on the sheets are arbitrary, the pupils will need much practice to retain them.

5 Once familiar with the words, the teacher will be able to use these materials with her class. With classes who have been following the complete *Words in Color* program, the games described below are to be introduced last. With other classes—say between ages 8 and 10—these games can be used at any time, if the children are able to read the words.

Game 1 As the teacher points to selected words on the Word Card sheets, the class utters the sentence indicated. The rules here are the same as for Visual Dictation 2, met with the Word Charts. That is, the teacher points, at first slowly—and even word by word if necessary —to what is to be decoded, and increases the speed of pointing as the class's competence permits. The pupils are not told the meaning of the color of the background, and should never be. It is the goal of these games to bring to students' awareness the structure of English; to tell them anything about the color will remove most of the fun and most of the value of the exercises.

This game can go on for as long as it is useful. It is advisable to increase the challenge slowly, by gradually extending the sentences to include all the colored areas and more words in each color-group, thus making longer and longer sentences which demand all the attention of the pupils. Naturally, all this is done silently, and the pupils are left to judge whether or not the volunteer performers are right.

Game 2 The teacher dictates a sentence orally, and the pupils must point to the matching words on the sheets in the correct order.

Here the difficulties are greater than with Visual Dictation 2 because the same words may appear on a number of Charts of different colors. Thus, we may have to reject a solution volunteered because the color of the cardboard of some words has not been taken into account.

Pupils may not accept that they have chosen the wrong word, if they do not as yet consider the color. If the teacher points to the same word on another color chart, the reason for his doing so may still not be clear to the pupil still unaware of grammatical function. In order to assist pupils in developing an awareness of function, it is profitable to include, when playing Game 1, a sequence of example sentences which require that the same word be found among words in a different color-grouping because the function is different. Additional example sequences may also be taken up in Game 2. Some examples are:

let us form a line	and	*what is the form of this line*
people like him	and	*people like him are odd*
I said that that man was dead	and	*he had a two-inch escape*
this cup is full now	and	*he paid in full*
do not cross this line	and	*this cross is of gold*
	or	*it is cross-stitched*

Chapter IV
A Study of Structures

The number of such exercises is left to each teacher, who will find from the feedback in each group of pupils how many will be needed.

Game 3 One pupil points in silence to one sentence of his own, and the class writes it down. Then, if there are no objections to what he has done, the teacher asks that each pupil extend this sentence on his paper (using words available on the sheets) and then take his turn in showing his extended sentence, using the pointer on the sheets, while the class writes down each proposal so they can discuss the results later on. Obviously, Game 3 is both a mixture and a new extension of Games 1 and 2. The teacher will get confirmation of pupils' improved familiarity with the materials as well as of the extent of their developing imagination. The class as a whole, by pooling experience, will make greater progress in this extension of sentence power than if individual children work alone.

Examples from the author of this text will not help since classes behave very differently, and all experience teaches us that pupils enjoy this game once they have enough knowledge of the new materials and are not in doubt about the rules of the game.

6 Now, let us consider the packs of Cards formed by separating the words on the sheets and classifying them according to color and length. A small number of pupils can use one full pack, kept in a box.

Game 4[8] One pupil, after thinking of (not saying) a sentence, places any one word from it on the table or in a slot on the board (as in the following illustration.)

---

[8] The numbering suggests that this game comes after those just given, (pp. 185-186) which use the Word Cards on the wall, but this is not a firm rule. Teachers can learn something new if, with some pupils, they start with packs of Cards rather than with the sheets.

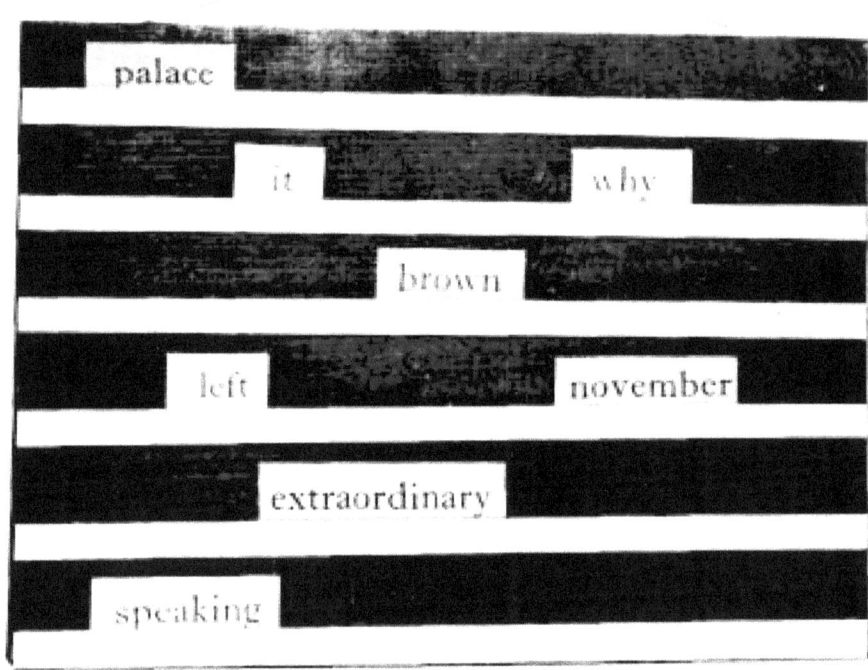

Someone else in the group places another word that is linked to the first in some way within a sentence he has in his mind. This is continued by a third student, a fourth, and so on—each placing a word that is linked in his mind with the words already placed by others.

It is natural to say "pass" when no sentence comes to one's mind and to give up one's turn. The game is over when no one can extend the set of words into yet another sentence.

After this game is played a few times, a new rule is added: only sentences totally new in this game can be used by members of the team. Then the teacher asks each pupil to put down the sentence he is thinking of before he adds his Word Card to the set. When the game is over, each pupil in turn reads his sentence or sentences so that the whole fabric of the game is clear to all.

Chapter IV
A Study of Structures

Here, except in the case of the pupil starting the round of games, no one is totally free to compose anything that comes to mind; the restrictions increase steadily, and the game stimulates the imagination by demanding that pupils integrate what is offered by others with additions of their own.

The colors of the Cards add further constraints to the game, since no Card can be added until the pupil knows in what part of the pack to look for it. If pupils are having too much difficulty in locating the Cards they want, the game will die, and the teacher will have to intervene either by suggesting that the pack be reduced in quantity or that some Cards showing words used very frequently be placed face up on the table for quick reference.

Another variation on this game is to give each pupil a certain number of words to form his pack, while there is a group pack open to all. There are enough nouns, verbs, and adjectives in the complete pack to permit, even at random, a sufficiently even distribution of Word Cards to create a feeling of fair competition, to challenge players, and to nourish the game for a little while.

This game forces the players to notice the place of words in a sentence, and to put each additional word in a special location, so that whatever the pupils are seeing at any instant does not clash with their intuitive feeling of what is "right" in their language. As the sentence becomes more and more complex, this intuitive feeling becomes more precise, to the point that rules for sentence structure can be formulated. With the help of the cardboard colors, these rules can be seen and, at the same time, be expressed—for example, the green Cards are always in a certain relation to the yellow Cards; the ivory ones are never found at the beginning or end of a sentence; the blue ones always precede the red if they come together; and so forth.

After a few such observations are made, and if the game continues to hold some interest, we recommend that the class be told the customary words that grammar books have used over the centuries for the color names we have been using. The teacher might say, for example,

"Name a word that is on a red Card." (Example: "island")

"This is called a . . ." (The teacher may say "noun" or point to it on the red sheet of words.)

"Can you give me three nouns that are among your Cards?"

A similar procedure can be followed for giving the conventional names for all the other parts of speech.

An obvious transfer could be obtained by taking any one of the sentences in the *Book of Stories* and asking pupils to tell (1) on which color cardboard each word would be found (if it were in the pack); or (2) which of the newly met conventional names would be given to each word in the sentence.

For example: *sam had vaguely heard tim cry and the next morning he asked him if he had* can be analyzed as "red yellow green yellow red yellow ivory blue blue red orange yellow orange ivory orange yellow" or "noun verb adverb verb noun verb conjunction adjective adjective noun pronoun verb pronoun conjunction pronoun verb."

7   Of course, this is only a beginning of the study of the language. All we are doing is classifying words according to some attribute that seems to belong to them. But words have functions with respect to each other: nouns seem to determine the order in which verbs appear in a sentence or to be ordered by them. For example, *sam heard* and *someone touched mom* give different impressions. In the first sentence, *sam* is the subject, that is, he initiates the action, while *mom* is called the object because *someone* initiated the action.

Hence, this new sensitivity to the function of words in relation to one another opens up a whole new field of experience to the learner. It is not possible in a course for beginning readers to explore the whole area of grammar. We have attempted simply to provide an entry point, leaving the boundaries of this new field to be set by the learners themselves.

8   **Game 5** Game 4 was designed to give pupils practice in expanding sentences; Game 5 provides the opportunity for practice in contracting sentences. Here, we begin with a long sentence and try to reduce it, a word at a time, to its basic structure.

Chapter IV
A Study of Structures

We discussed this game earlier when we described page 11 in Worksheets 8-12.[9] Now, we play it using the Word Cards, in order to reach a different awareness. Earlier, we were concerned with the alteration or preservation of meaning by the removal of some words. Now, we want to find which functions are the key ones, which carry the essential meaning. Obviously, the degree of consistency with which a colored Card appears in the colored image of the sentence will reflect the degree to which that function is essential in basic sentence structures.

Pupils will soon see that there is a hierarchy of importance among the functions of words—that some only qualify others, adding precision upon precision, while others are absolutely essential to the communication of the thought.

9   What we have learned with these games can be summed up as follows: in speech, and so in writing (which is written speech), we are mainly concerned with communication. We talk to convey meaning.

In the preceding games we left this in the background and worked upon words and their various links with each other as they carry out the job of conveying meaning—maintaining either the sense of a sentence or just some meaning which has grown with the habits of speech. We have inquired about how this was done, even when we could only get superficial answers. In every case, we have at least recognized that there exist certain dynamics behind speech that can be described, yet we have seen that transformations of these dynamics are possible that are compatible with meaning.

The transformations we have studied are:

1   expansions and contractions of sentences;

2   alterations of meaning by changes in the order of words or by removal of key ones;

3   maintenance of meaning by some change in the order of groups of words.

---

9 See p. 161.

We have indeed reached *structure* as a reality as easily manipulated intellectually as are sounds to create words. At least children will know that they are as free to use their imaginations in working with structure as they have been in working with words.

10 The Word Cards can generate other insights into structure we have not yet considered. For example, there are sometimes two, or even three or four, yellow Cards following each other in a sentence. This tells something about the structure of verbs, and how speakers render their consciousness of time in English. Events referred to in speech either have happened, are happening, or will happen. Mood and tense are the principal devices in English for communicating such *time* meanings. Use of the tenses is obviously still more subtle than this, and yet five-year-olds can already convey in their speech shaded meanings by *using different sets of words,* just as adults do. The Cards are useful for bringing time signals to the pupils' awareness, since pupils will ask themselves or the teacher why certain of the yellow Cards always seem to go together.

We would suggest that the teacher answer such questions with other questions, such as:

> "Why do you think the words *will* or *shall* (or *would* or *should)* have been used?"
>
> "When do *you* use each?"
>
> "How do you know that you are talking about something in the past?"
>
> "Would it sound right to you if I said,
>
>> *'yesterday I will go on vacation'*
>>
>> *'tomorrow I left with him'*
>>
>> *'went now'* (as an order)
>>
>> *'yesterday I have come walking from his shop'*
>>
>> *'they are coming from Mexico last week'?"*

Chapter IV
A Study of Structures

Appropriateness of sound goes with correctness of form, and they translate each other in spoken and written speech in the form of the grammar of the language. Between the gross, and sometimes incorrect, distinctions made by foreigners and the subtle discriminations made by cultured native speakers of a language, there is a whole spectrum of different usages which communicate, with varying precision, different capabilities. Teachers may find it useful to inquire more closely into their pupils' sensitivity to the shades of meaning verbs can effect. They can best do this by refraining from correcting and by challenging pupils with questions such as, "How does the meaning shift in the following sentences?"

I say goodbye
I come to say goodbye
I have come to say goodbye
I have had to come to say goodbye

OR

I said goodbye
I came to say goodbye
I had to come to say goodbye
I had had to come to say goodbye

OR

I will say goodbye
I will come to say goodbye
I will have to come to say goodbye
I will have had to come to say goodbye

OR

I would say goodbye if...
I would come to say goodbye if...
I would have to come to say goodbye if...
I would have had to come to say goodbye if...

Section 3
Worksheet 14

1   Although each of the Worksheets used so far has a contribution to make to the study of English as a language in contrast to knowing how to use it correctly, it is Worksheet 14 that provides an opportunity for testing the pupils' awareness of structures and of word functions within these.

The preceding lessons in structure will have sensitized the learners to grammar and interested them in looking at sentences in order to find something to justify the use of the particular words to communicate a meaning in mind.

2   *Page 1*

This is a test to determine whether the pupils have internalized the criteria for distinguishing the present tense from the others. Six sentences are given here, though a number from the *Book of Stories* could serve the purpose equally well. Some are straightforward and should not create a problem for learners. But one is more subtle. It says:

> *when it is warm we may sleep in the tent*

Since the problems on this page require only a "yes" or "no" answer, the pupils may take only a few moments to complete this page and the following two. If pupils are already beyond this stage, sentences using tenses which may be called present, past, and future, though not so immediately recognizable, could be proposed by the teacher. The example above shows this type of subtlety.

3   *Pages 2 and 3*

These follow the same pattern as page 1, and can also be treated as tests. When it is clear that learners are beyond this stage, new challenges should be offered by their teacher.

Chapter IV
A Study of Structures

4   *Pages 4, 5, 6*

If these are applied as tests without prior preparation, they will not prove much. Teachers must see to it that before giving the test, the words *conditional, negative, affirmative,* and *interrogative* are fully understood and can be used freely by their pupils. These terms can be introduced by generating a situation actually involving objects, and using speech naturally with it. Then, someone can be asked to repeat what was said, and to relate the words to the meaning. The teacher will get the point across more easily if she uses wrong tenses or wrong forms to generate the shock which will move consciousness to note what *is* relevant in the situation. Only after an adequate number of examples have been given will the teacher put into circulation the labels "conditional," and so forth. Then, exercises can be introduced which give opportunities to the teacher or the pupils to ask whether or not the statement is about some condition, question, negation, or affirmation. If the Worksheet pages are given a few days later, they can be used to test the pupils' familiarity with these new ideas and with the translation of meaning into moods or forms that will convey that meaning.

5   *Page 7*

In the previous section, we mentioned that words printed on the same color cardboard can still be distinguished by a secondary attribute. For example, nouns can be a *subject* or an *object*. When pupils understand this distinction, it is possible to introduce additional perceptible clues on the Cards by taking, for example, two of the packs of Cards and marking nouns with a special sign that from now on refers to this second attribute. But even objects can be differentiated according to whether they are *direct* or *indirect,* for example:

every living man has a body
    body is the direct object of *has*
this woman asked her child a serious question,

child is the indirect object of *asked,* since question is the direct object.

Now, additional marks can be added to those noun cards already marked as objects to make this third attribute clear.

Again, if pupils are quickly sure of these distinctions, teachers can challenge them further by continuing to give examples which will extend their capacity to observe words and find in them distinctive attributes.

6   *Page 8*

This test is concerned with the concept of a clause in a sentence. The awareness of a clause is developed very readily if one considers sentences as they are uttered. Good reading does not usually break the flow of words just to allow breathing. Instead, the pauses are linked with clauses, which one recognizes are the real units of meaning in written material.

Only the scrutiny of the number of verbs (or compound verbs) in a sentence will give the final count of clauses, if one takes into account that sometimes a verb is dropped because its meaning is understood without its being there.

7   *Pages 9* and *10*

These pages are self-explanatory and should not present any problem for those who know the meaning of the words "plural" and "present tense."

The inclusion of such material in the tests will serve as a smooth transition between the types of games we have played all through the program and the traditional grammar course which proposes mainly exercises of this kind.

8. *Page 11*

This page goes back to the *Book of Stories* and tests the pupils' maturity and self-confidence, more than their achievement. In fact, it requires that the *Book of Stories* be viewed as a whole and the stories classified according to four criteria. Though the criteria are by now familiar, it is a new exercise to use them as tools for classification. Any pupil who can complete this task as quickly as the teacher certainly deserves recognition of his progress.

9   *Page 12*

This page demands even more of the student than the preceding page. Can he recast a story from one type of presentation into another? He has knowledge of the existence of the types of presentation and can recognize them when he meets them. But can he perform such a transformation? Can he do it from beginning to end, consistently and correctly?

His success here is certainly another proof that he has been made aware of subtle and often hidden attributes of the written language, and that he is beginning to act beyond linguistic boundaries and is reaching new dimensions in written communication.

10   *Pages 13* and *14*

These pages take this entry into creative writing a little further. The questions are wholly unstructured and concern judgments of taste, of introspection, and of feelings, which on the whole in traditional teaching are left to take care of themselves because teachers believe that young children do not look at themselves enough to reach them. Observers of young children disagree on these matters. The tests are included here because the whole program can reveal that children are unknown to those who teach them and that they are much more competent than anyone ever suspected.

Thus, in a way, the tests are also testing the preconceptions of adults as well as the capabilities of children.

11 *Page 15*

The simple exercise on this page has been added in order to communicate to teachers that there may be many additional opportunities for learning that can be developed from the content of some of the stories.

On page 15 of Worksheet 14, stamp collecting has been used to show the relationship between what has been done with the study of English and the study of the social sciences.

Clearly, if words differ, they may somehow refer to different experiences, notions, and entities. Their consideration from a certain angle may suggest, for example, that our world has an existence of its own where among other things continents can be noticed. The subdivision of the land into countries, states, and counties is only one of the possibilities that may follow because now we are taking meaning from particular social experiences. The rest is the opening we talk about. We only ask for examples as definitions to start us off. Much more may follow and perhaps should.

12 *Page 16*

This page sums up the progress of the program. Though this page may represent weeks of work, its presence is a sign that students can retain all their experiences related to the development of their skills. And, because of the law of the cumulative effect of learning, a return to consideration of each of the Worksheets will give, at once, the evidence of the mastery which has been the constant aim of the program and, with it, the extension of what one can do with oneself. It should not be forgotten that we have considered reading as a skill. But it is a complex skill based on a number of others, awakening new powers of the mind and new possibilities for learning.

Because of our viewpoint, we have challenged and challenged the learners, always taking them to a higher level of competence through the exercises they are confronting and, hopefully, performing with greater and greater effectiveness.

13 We have used the Worksheets as tests of the program, hence of everybody involved in it—the author and the teachers as well as the learners. Since the learners are the recipients of the program, the fact that they (rather than the teacher or the author) take the tests, is merely a convenience, and not an indication that we believe we are testing only them, their qualities, and their achievements. Some teachers will start with the thought that we have placed the hurdles too high, and that very few pupils will achieve anything like the results we seem to expect. Experience will teach them, as it has taught us, that whoever has been able to mobilize the needed intellectual powers demanded by the learning of one's own family's spoken speech has far more power available than even these supposedly hard tests can test. We can say that we have learned to work with children only when we are certain of avoiding the confusions we may create, and so are always in contact with their mental powers. The tests, then, are a method of getting a feedback that our vision of these powers is not too inaccurate. In addition, these tests are merely samples of what could be done, so that the relationship of the teacher-program-student is continuously reviewed so as to become more and more the process by which each student reaches autonomy and independence with respect to language, while he becomes aware of his well-trained and smoothly working intellectual muscles.

Section 4
Conclusion—Self and Speech

This program started with the claim that it is easy for most people to learn to read and ended with another claim: that it is possible to make people aware of many dimensions of spoken and written speech which are traditionally considered a specialist's preoccupation.

Many teachers who have used this program in the past five years have not only reported that children learn to read much better and much faster than anyone before believed possible, but also have reported amazement at children's ability to show interest in aspects of language that had always remained beyond them until the teachers gave this program a fair and full trial. Now, we are usually amazed when we meet the extraordinary in life, and, in this case, our own ignorance of the challenges the language poses even to linguists makes us believe that what we find extraordinary in the performance of children is, indeed, outside the ordinary. The familiar, on the contrary, always escapes us until we become sensitive to what *is*. What linguists try to study, we all do most naturally, i.e., we use some language— our native tongue—competently and automatically very early in our lives. We must have made the proper observations of how language behaves in order to use it as the culture does. We must have been equipped with all the mental tools in order to make sense of speech so early in our life.

Does anyone know what equipment is required for such a task? Linguists are passionately seeking to understand and describe it.

What we can learn from the success of this program is that if anyone challenges young children (four years of age and older) with problems that require the same tools as the decoding of the spoken speech used in the environment, they respond by showing equal competence in making sense of the new challenges. For instance, they learn to read with as much understanding as they talk. But we have gone beyond this, and made them play games of transformations which look incredibly difficult to teachers and psychologists.

It may be that one of our most important findings involved in this approach is that no one can really do anything of value for oneself unless one notices the transformations compatible with what one is doing.

We obviously consume time in living; we obviously have learned from the start that everything has an infinity of appearances linked together by transformations that integrate change and produce permanence. Without any number of samples to represent it, no noun can exist as a noun. Nouns are concepts and, as such, cover classes. The link between the elements of the class is their equivalence through one or more attributes in common, even when many other attributes quite different can belong to some of the elements. Pronouns replace nouns and provide one of the transformations without which no one can talk. A change of system of reference from one speaker to another is needed in order to make sense of the fact that "my nose" can be described by another person as "your nose," and by another as "his nose," and so on. This sense of relativity with respect to many systems of reference is a prerequisite to speaking any language. This is another set of transformations we all have had to acquire around the age of two, though we may have been prepared for it much earlier.

It is, therefore, felt that we are nearer truth and reality, that we show more insight into what happens, if we can present any challenge as related to some transformation or several transformations, and refuse to fragment and distort it supposedly for the sake of simplicity.

What may be simple for children may be what is as complex as reality.

To learn to do in every direction what we propose here for reading is, to our mind, the challenge of education for the future. To be correct in any educational situation consists in taking reality into account, not just one's preconceptions. Our self is capable of generating the components of speech and specializing its production to finally show ownership of speech as it is used in the environment. But our self does more than talk or produce speech. We may find some clues for the understanding of speech and how we practice as speakers in some other study of the functioning of the self. Conversely, if we have made a true observation concerning the speaker in us, we may find that it helps us throw light on some other of our functionings.

Our program can now claim to have helped to make current among educators the idea that we must consider much larger chunks of reality than have been suggested by Descartes (1637) in order to get out of the many muddles our specialized and fragmented views have created. Because of the complexity we have learned to encounter and work on, we can on the one hand eliminate a number of pseudo-problems clogging education—among them that reading is hard—and on the other hand open up huge vistas which renew our hopes about the future while showing us how to begin an attack on apparently insurmountable obstacles.

The day is not far off when we shall see adults who have kept intact the zest for learning and life they had as small children, behaving with respect to reality as people who know what it is or can be.

We started with people and their powers and led them to their solving their problem of reading. We finish with people more conscious of their powers and their functioning

Appendix 1

Examples of a six-year old pupil's writing

pat met tom

tim met pat

papa met tim

tom is up

papa is not up

ma

tim pat met tom

papa met me tom

p p p p p p p

p p p p p p p p p

pat is up

auieo papa papa
tttttt pot   pet
tip kip kap pot pet

pot top it up
papa m meme

m m m
         met pat
pat met tom

pat pat up

tom pat up

tl m pat up

pat met tom
tim met
pat
papa met
tim
tom is
up
papa is not up

pat is up
papa is not u
p

Appendix 2

A Description of the Materials

For the teacher

Words in Color: Background and Principles (1962)
Teaching Reading with Words in Color—A Scientific Study of the Problems of Reading (1967)

For the class

21 *Word Charts* in color
Phonic Code (a set of 8 Charts)
Word Cards (sheets and packs)

For the pupil

3 basic books:

Book 1 — the first certificate of reading
Book 2 — all the sounds of English
Book 3 — all the spellings of English
Word Building Book (the last table corresponds to the Phonic Code used in the classroom—see above)

Book of Stories (a continuous narrative of 40 stories)

14 *booklets of Worksheets* (16 pages in each) used with the *Word Building Book*

Worksheets 1-7 (complementary to *Books 1* and *2*)

Worksheets 8-14 (complementary to *Book 3* and *Book of Stories*)

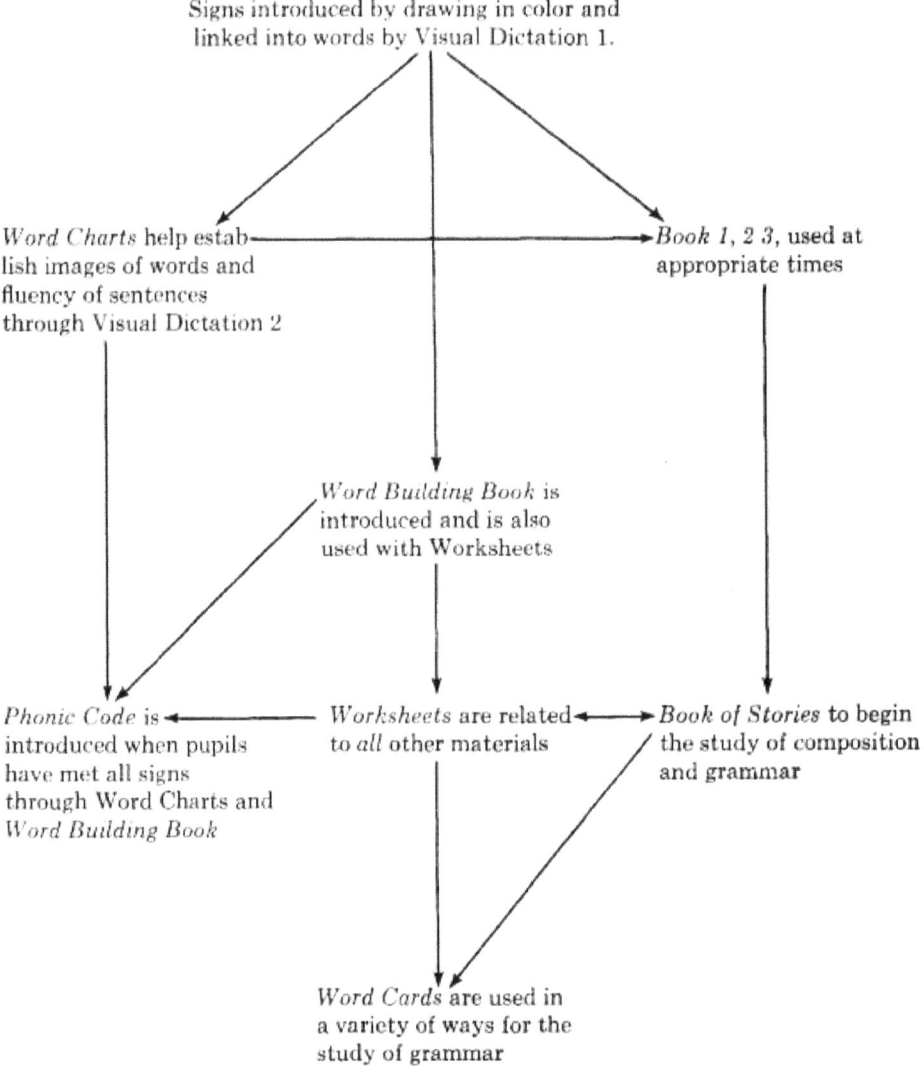

B Alternative Sequences for the Use of the Materials

(Note: This first teaching sequence is the one developed in detail in this book.)

Appendix 2

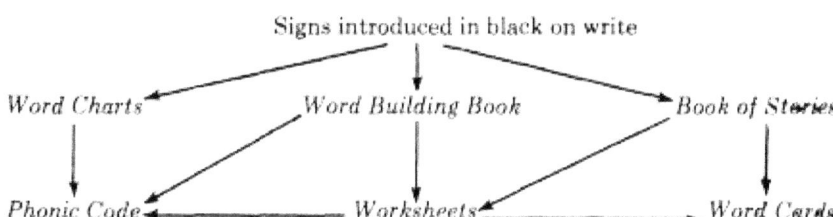

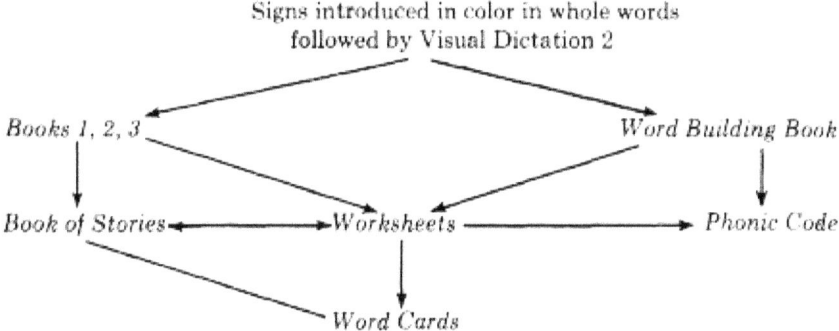

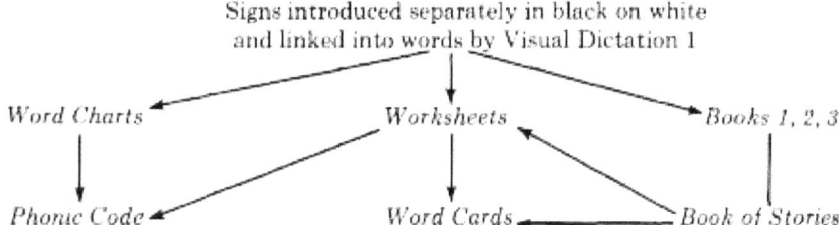

Appendix 3

Analysis of Links-by-Transformation Between Words on Word Charts 3, 4, 5, and 6

We have put this section in an Appendix so that teachers new to the program can choose *not* to look into it if it is not helpful to them when they begin.

Our experience, however, is that teachers who continue to work with *Words in Color* are newly fascinated each day through the discovery of many varied ways of introducing each new Chart: that is, the links (by substitution, reversal, addition, and insertion) its words have with those on preceding Charts and with one another. Some of these are indicated in the following diagrams, for the study of teachers.

Teachers may also find these diagrams helpful in alerting them to the numerous solutions for the Game of Transformations. The diagram relating to Word Chart 6 particularly shows a number of interesting things:

1. the introduction on this Chart of the *l* sign that adds the 'schwa' sound to the usual sound of that sign, and
2. the introduction of three spellings for one sound at one time *(k, ck, ke)*, two new spellings for another *(I, y, i)*, and a second sound for the sign *i*

require that the rules relating to equivalences (see p. 110 ff.) be used fully for the first time in analyzing transformations.

For example:

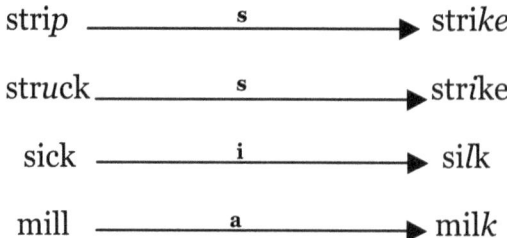

For Word Chart 3

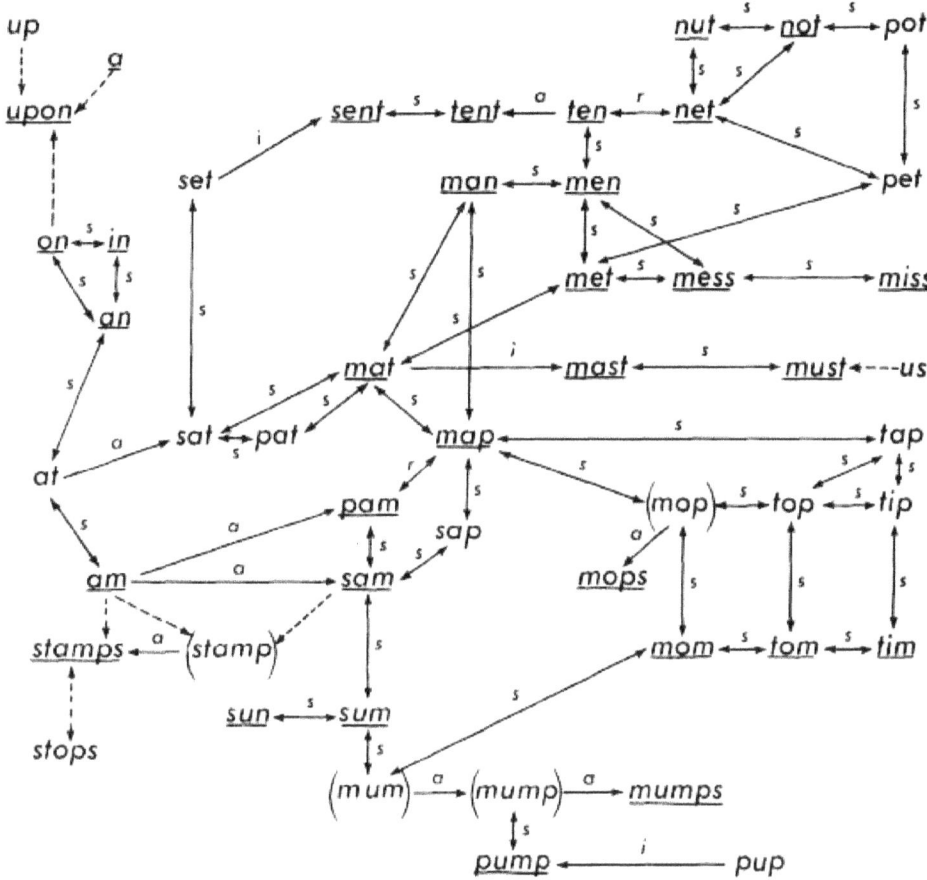

Underlined words appear on Word Chart 3.

Other words appear on Word Chart 2, except those in parentheses that are not on any Chart.

For Word Chart 4

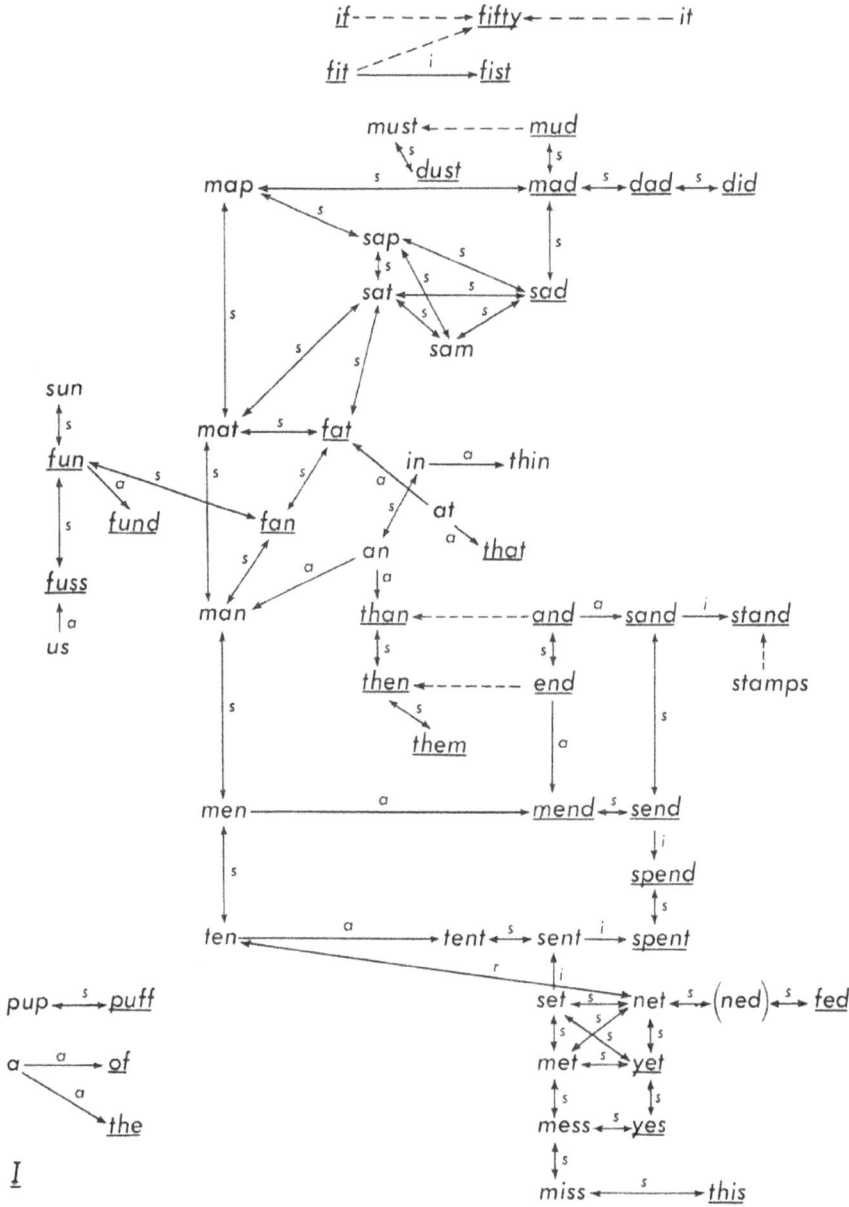

Only the underlined words appear on Word Chart 4, the others are on the preceding Charts.

For Word Chart 5

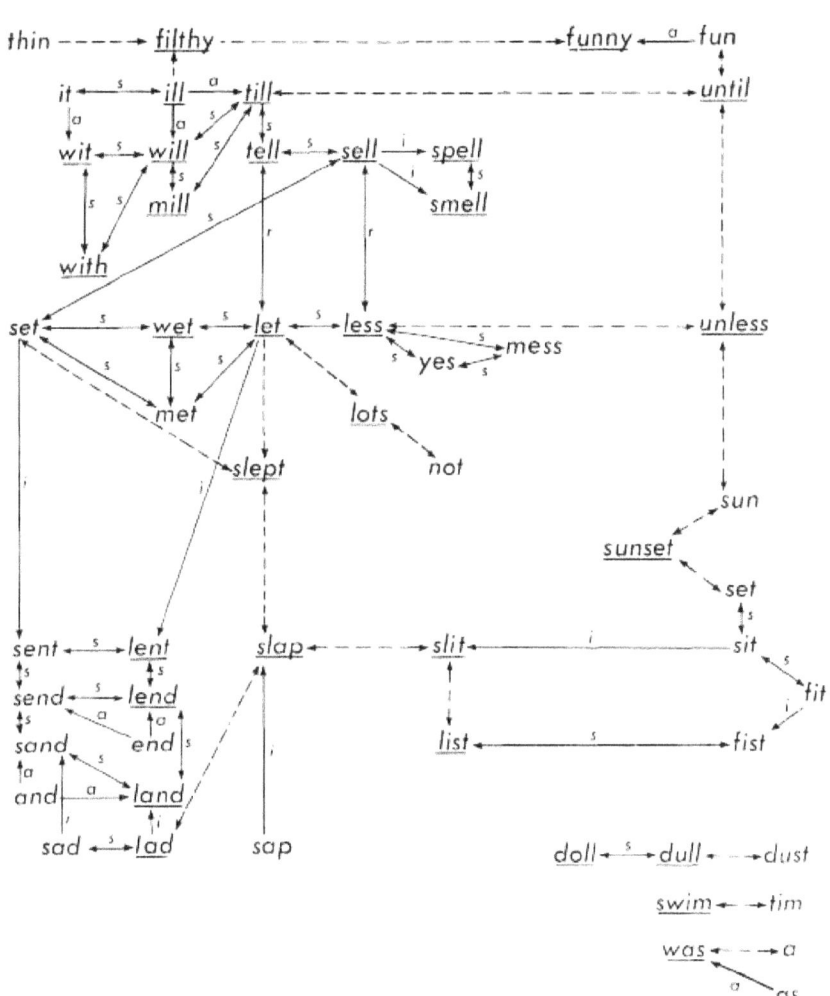

Only the underlined words appear on Word chart 5.

For Word Chart 6

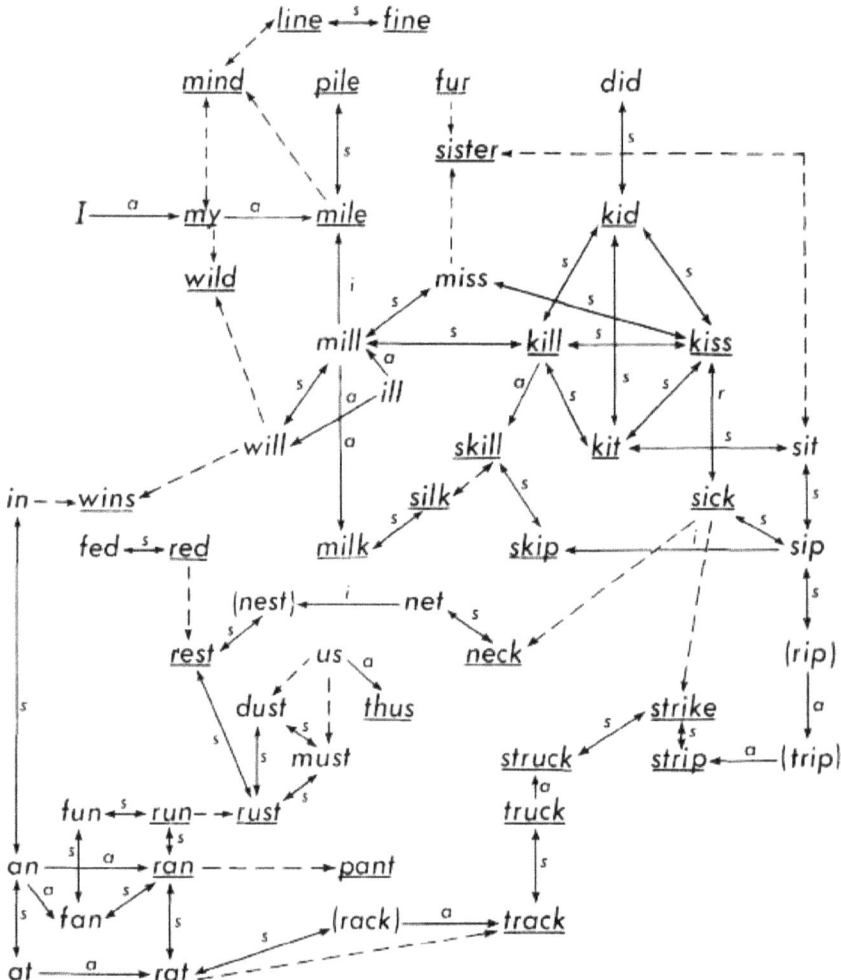

Only the underlined words appear on Word Chart 6.

Appendix 4

One word exemplifying each spelling on the Phonic Code.

As a reference *for teachers* new to the approach we are giving in this Appendix:

1. One word exemplifying each spelling on the Phonic Code. Teachers find that students on their own find for their log books *several* words using each spelling on the code of which the one given here is only an example.

    The list can also serve to assist the teacher on checking her own objective understanding of the sound intended for the column.

2. As a secondary reference for the sounds for the teacher, we have included one set of the standard dictionary diacritical markings.

    Once students have completed *Book 3* they can easily work out with little assistance from the teacher the markings dictionaries use to indicate the sounds of the various columns.

3. We have listed the *names* of colors used in this text, but we suggest that students not be burdened with this since in working with the Charts they need see differences only, not name them.

Appendix 5

List of words on Word Card sheets (alphabetized within categories)

NOUNS   *red cards*

action	black	chest	coward
age	blessed	choir	cross
aim	blood	chop	crown
answer	blue	circle	cunning
ant	body	climate	curb
apple	book	cloth	curtain
April	box	clothes	cut
area	brake	cloud	
arm	brain	clue	dance
art	breakfast	coal	dark
Asia	bright	coat	date
axe	brow	coffee	day
		color	dead
baby	carol	comma	dear
back	case	common	deep
bandit	castle	compass	deer
bank	cat	concern	degree
basin	chance	contrary	difference
bear	change	count	difficulty
beat	character	couple	distinction
bed	charm	court	

NOUNS – *cont'd*

doctor	farm	gas	hurry
dog	father	general	
dot	fault	girl	ice
double	feast	globe	idea
doubt	February	glue	image
dozen	fellow	god	Indian
draft	ferry	gold	invalid
dream	field	grace	invention
drink	fifteen	grammar	iron
drop	figure	green	island
duty	find	guest	
dwarf	fine	guide	jacket
dye	finger	gulf	jail
	finish	gymnasium	jam
ear	fire	gypsy	job
earth	fit		journey
east	floor	hail	
echo	flour	hair	key
edge	flow	hall	kid
education	flower	hallelujah	kiln
effect	flute	hand	kind
eight	fly	harbor	king
election	foam	hat	knee
elevator	focus	hate	knife
end	folk	head	knock
engine	force	heap	know
England	forecast	heart	knowledge
english	foot	help	
enough	form	hem	lad
equal	four	hen	lady
es (3)	fox	hero	land
Europe	french	hiccup	lass
eve	friend	home	laugh
eye	front	honor	laughter
fact	fuel	hope	layer
	fullness	horse	lead
fair	fun	hose	leap
faith	fuse	hospital	length
fall		hour	lid
fancy	garage	house	lie
fantasy	garden	hundred	life

NOUNS – *cont'd*

light	noun	point	salt
lightning	November	police	sand
list	nurse	post	sap
lord		potato	sauce
lot	object	present	saw
love	ocean	pupil	scene
	October	pussy	school
man	offer		science
mark	officer	quantity	score
market	one	quarrel	scot
marriage	order	quarter	scream
may		queen	screw
measure	pain	queue	sea
metal	paint	question	season
middle	pair		second (2)
mill	palace	rabbit	self
million	past	rage	sense
mine	path	rain	sentence
minute	patient	rash	sergeant
miss	pay	rat	set
Monday	peace	ray	seven
money	pen	reason	shade
monkey	pencil	record	shadow
month	penny	red	shame
moon	period	region	shape
mother	person	reply	sheep
mountain	photo	restaurant	shelf
mud	physician	rhythm	shoe
mule	pianist	ride	shop
	piano	ridge	shot
nail	picture	ring	shoulder
name	piece	roast	show
nature	Pig	rod	shred
navy	pill	roof	sick
need	pilot	root	side
news	plane	rope	sieve
night	plate	rule	sign
no	play		signal
nose	pleasure	s (4)	silk
note	plenty	sail	silo
nought	pocket	sake	silver

NOUNS – *cont'd*

sister	stalk	tea	umbrella
six	stamp	teacher	unit
size	stand	team	up
skill	star	tear	use
skin	station	teeth	
skull	steam	ten	valve
sky	step	tense	verb
slack	stomach	tent	view
slate	stone	thanks	villain
slave	stop	thing	visit
sleep	store	thirty	vocabulary
slice	storm	three	
slide	story (2)	throat	war
slip	strain	throw	water
snail	straw	Thursday	wave
snake	strike	time	way
soccer	stroke	tip	Wednesday
sock	study	tire	week
soldier	subject	tomato	wind
solid	sugar	ton	wine
son	suit	tool	winter
sorrow	Sunday	tooth	wood
sort	sunset	top	work
soul	surprise	total	worth
south	sweat	town	wrist
space	sweet	toy	
spade	swing	trade	year
speed	syllable	traffic	yes
sphere	syrup	transport	yesterday
spirit		treasure	youth
spoon	table	true	
spring	tailor	tube	zero
spy	tan	Tuesday	zoo
square	taste	tunnel	
stable	tax	turn	
staff	taxi	two	

VERBS – *yellow cards*

accept	born	die	fire
act	brave	differ	fit
aim	break	dim	fix
am	bring	direct	floor
answer	brought	discuss	flow
are	burn	do	flower
arise	burned	does	fly
arrive	bury	done	focus
ask		dot	follow
avail	came	double	foot
avoid	can	doubt	forbid
awake	carry	draft	force
back	cease	dream	forecast
bank	chance	drink	forget
be	change	drop	forgot
bear	charm	drunk	form
beat	chose	dry	found
become	close	dye	fox
been	cloud		fulfill
begin	coat	eat	
Wednesday	color	echo	gauge
week	comb	ed (3)	gave
wind	come	educate	get
wine	compass	eliminate	give
winter	complete	empty	given
wood	concern	end	go
work	conquer	endeavor	goes (2)
worth	could	equal	going (3)
wrist	couple	except	gone
year	cross		got
yes	crown	fail	grow
yesterday	cut	faint	guide
youth		fall (2)	
zero	d (3)	farm	had
zoo	dare	fancy	hail
begun	date	fasten	halve
being	deal	feast	happen
better	defy	figure	has
bless	deny	find	hasten
book	depend	fine	hate
	did	finish	have

VERBS — *cont'd*

head	lost	raise	set
hear	love	ran	sew
heard		read (2)	shake
held	made	reason	shall
help	make	receive	shave
hold	man	record	shoot
hope	mark	refill	shop
house	market	reflect	shot
hurry	may	refrigerate	should
	mean	regard	show
imagine	meant	remain	shown
ing (3)	might	remember	shrink
invent	miss	remove	shut
iron	move	reply	sing
is	must	request	sit
		respect	sleep
keep	name	rid	slice
kept	need	ride	slide
knew	nurse	ring	slow
knock		rise	smell
know	object	roast	soften
lake	obtain	run	spare
	occupy	rush	speak
last	offer		spell
lead	open	s (4)	spin
leap	order	said	spoke
learn	own	sail	squeeze
learned		sat	stamp
leave	paint	save	stand
led	pass	saw	star
left	pay	say	step
let	pick	scare	stood
lie	play	score	stop
light	pocket	scream	stride
like	point	screw	strike
list	pray	second	study
listen	present	see	subtract
live	purr	seek	succeed
long	put	seem	swim
look		seen	swing
lose	quarter	seize	

VERBS — *cont'd*

take	threw		went
taken	throw	use	were
takes	time	used	will
talk	tire	visit	win
taste	told		work
tear	took	wait	worry
tell	top	was	would
tend	toss	wash	write
thank	touch	waste	
think	turn	wear	

ADJECTIVES *blue cards*

a	close	each (2)	few (2)
able	common	easy	fifteen
all (2)	complete	effective	final
alone	considerable	eight	fine
American	contrary	eighteen	first
an	coward	either (2)	fit
another	cunning	elder	five
anxious		eldest	foreign
any	dark	eleven	foremost
	dead	empty	former
back	dear	english	forty
bad	decent	enormous	forward
basic	deep	enough	four
best	different	equal (2)	fourteen
better	difficult	even	fourth
big	definite	every	frank
bigger	dim	excellent	free
black	direct	extraordinary	french
blessed	dirty		full
blue	discreet	faint	funny
both	disgraceful	fair	furious
brave	double	faithful	
broad	drunk	false	general
brown	dry	fancy	good
busy	due	far	gray
	dumb	farther	great
clever		fast	green

ADJECTIVES — *cont'd*

half	mean	real	superior
happy	middle	red	sure
hard	more (2)	regardless	sweet
heavier	most	regular	
heavy	much	remarkable	tall
her		remote	tender
high	near	rich	tense
his	neither	right	tenth
holy	new	rough	that
honest	next (2)	rude	the
horrible	nice		their
huge	nine	sad	these
human	nineteen	same	tidy
hundred	no	scarce	thin
impossible	none	scotch	third
Indian	north	second	thirteen
intelligent	number	self (2)	thirty
invalid	numerous	seven	this
jolly		sharp	those
just	off	sheer	three (2)
keen	old	short	top
kind	one (2)	shy	twelve
large	only	sick	twentieth
last	open	silly	twenty
late	opposite	simple	two
latter	orange	singular	
least (2)	other	six	ugly
left	our	sixteen	unequal
less (2)	out	slack	unique
light	owing	slow (2)	upper
like (2)	own	small	upright
little		smooth	useful
long	pale	soft	usual
longest	plenty	solid	vain
lost	plural	some	various
loud	poor	sore	vast
low	possible	sorry	very
lower		special	visual
	quiet	stupid	weak
		such	well
mad	ready	sudden	what
many			

ADJECTIVES — *cont'd*

which	wide	yellow
white	wise	young
whole	wrong	your

ADVERBS — *green cards*

about	by	hard	none
above		hardly	nor
across	close	here	not
after		high	now
again	dear	highly	
ago	deep	how	off
all (2)	direct	however	often
almost	down	huge	on
alone	due		once
aloud		just	only
also (2)	easy		opposite
already	either	late	otherwise
altogether	else	last (2)	out (2)
always	enough	least (2)	
any (2)	equally	less	perhaps
apart	especially	little	
around	even	long	quickly
as	ever	low	quite
aside	exactly	ly (5)	rather
away			
	fair	more	ready
back	far	most (2)	
because	farther	mostly	same
before	fast	much (2)	seldom
behind	fine		since
below	first (2)	near (2)	slow (2)
beneath	foremost	nearby	slowly
best	forth	neither	small
better	forward (2)	never	so
between	from	next (2)	suddenly
but	full	no	sure

ADVERBS — *cont'd*

that	today	underneath	where
then	together	up (2)	while
there	tomorrow		why
thereby	tonight	vastly	without
therefore	too	very	yet
though	twice		
through		well	
to	under (2)	when	

CONJUNCTIONS *ivory cards*

after		or	
although	for		unless
and (4)		since	when
as	if	so	where
			whether
because	neither	than (2)	while
before	nor	that	
but	now	then	yet
		therefore	
either	once	though	
except	only	till	

INTERJECTIONS *lavender cards*

ah!	oh!	so!

PRONOUNS *orange cards*

another	I	ours	
any	it		us
as		same	
	me	she	we
both	mine	so	what
	more	some	whatever
each	most	such	where
either (2)	much		which
every	my	that	who
		their	whom
former	neither (2)	theirs	whose
	none	them	
he		these	you
her	one	they	your
him	other	this	yours
	our	those	

PREPOSITIONS *brown cards*

a	below	in	
about	beneath	into	since
above	beside (2)		
across	between	less (2)	than
after	but	like	through
all	by		till
along		near (2)	to
amid	down	next (2)	
among			under
an	except	of	underneath
around		off	up
at	for	on	upon
	forth	opposite	until
before	from	or	with
behind		out	without

Appendix 6

Complete array of 21 Word Charts

```
a a aa aaa
u u uu uuu
i i ii iii
aiu uia uiu iau
e e ee eee
aei eua eaiu
o o oo ooo
aaeeoo ieoii
oaa aoie oou
                1
```

The arrangement of the following pages is meant to assist teachers in planning their Visual Dictations 2 and 3 when they are not working directly with their set of Charts.

pat pit pet pot at it up tap tip top pep pup pop tot as us is sat sit set stop step pass stops steps past sap sips test pest <div align="right">2</div>	mat tim met tom mom must mumps miss mast mess map am stamps a mops pump sum sam pam not nut net ten men man an sun in on tent upon sent <div align="right">3</div>
fan fun fist fit if of fat puff fuss spend spent dad I sad mad fed and send mend sand mud fund stand end dust did that this them then than the thin yes yet fifty <div align="right">4</div>	let lad sell tell lots smell spell slap list slit doll dull mill ill until till lend lent land less unless filthy funny wet wit with swim was will sunset slept <div align="right">5</div>

Appendix 6

---

pant wins thus rat ran red fur strip my sister wild mind rest kid kit kill neck milk skill silk kiss pile mile skip sick line fine truck track struck run rust strike 6	her his has hat him hot bat but brick promise flat simple impossible suddenly horror worry word work world there burden back black sorry brother son from little 7
hate same late male more fatal home bone woke he me we date egg use unite fuse girl first go got get leg globe make made nose any like fire nine ninety 8	sold thirty no gone dirty off hundred seven april usable five give tiger thanks hose thirsty hungry dog gold bankrupt front firm duty loss so horse robe big gum bigger 9

shop she ship china church chin shall shred michigan chicken wish cherry for or nor chorus child children hotel far shut channel charm shell shot done does chips goes chill have **10**	cat crime blood cry quickly question call all by watch small false clutch next orchestra capable criminal character garden phrase catch fantastic box match are were such air **11**
father mother able animal family ate to do too potato two tooth look fool took tomorrow school education soldier generation gem john judge joan jack adjective **12**	elephant physics photograph foot be see sleep feet been why where when who whom whose these between you youth our your soup hour young sing house courageous **13**

Appendix 6

14.
eyes day may
high thigh night
they saturday
gray greyhound
money honey prey
prayers wood would
should cool field
aged finished
conceived conceit

15.
stopped rolled told
talk walk sigh lie
listen lesson push
fast fasten door
sugar sure busy
business heir one
once england lamb
ocean dumb put
good better well the

16.
write right written
wrong sword sworn
know new knew
knowledge knee tea
news great pear
tear pearl tear
lead bread lead
people hear here there
ear weird heart buy

17.
measure leisure
either treaure
plateau beauty paul
lawn because said
mail maintain paid
doubt laugh taught
bury daughter water
paw poor pour pore
raw therefore quiet

flown flowers boy sew sow sow buoy fruit suit suite sweet moist isle zip zoo zero oil eight eighty height freight board bored boar soar sore saw cloak broke 18	tough cough though thought through bough examination thorough anxiety half mix exist thursday woman true women wednesday halves calves loaf hiccup taxi cramp loaves borrow swamp 19
guard calm shoes guarantee scissors scythe ghost adieu service diaphragm hymn yatch aisle science indict prosaic sieve friend yield debt straight seize siege reservoire receipt 20	pneumatic cage scheme schist rhythm jewel righteous hallelujah tissue amoeba psalm azure bathe vulture trekked pension quay blithe clothes awkward cube queue clique vision region mayor 21

Bibliography

Armington, David, Sally Kirsdale and Lee Switz. Right to Read: A Pilot Program in Adult Literacy. Cleveland, Ohio: PACE (Program for Action by Citizens in Education), 1965. (Out of print.)

Armington, David. *The Words in Color Remedial Reading Project Central Junior High School,* (September 16 - October 27, 1965). Mimeographed report. Cleveland, Ohio: Cleveland Board of Education, 1965.

Baily, Carolyn. *A Comparison of the Effectiveness of Two Reading Programs and a Language Development Program with Culturally Disadvantaged Children.* Unpublished doctoral dissertation. Nashville, Tennessee: George Peabody College for Teachers, 1966.

Bentley, Harriet. "Words in Color," *Elementary English.* Champaign, Illinois: National Council of Teachers of English, May, 1966.

—— "Words in Color A Reading Program?!!," *Issues and Innovations in the Teaching of Reading,* ed. Joe L. Frost. Glenview, Illinois: Scott, Foresman and Company, 1967.

Curtis, Olga. "The Rainbow Road to Reading," *Empire Magazine,* (April 4, 1965). Digested for the *Catholic Digest.* Denver, Colorado: *The Denver Post,* 1965.

Defner, Hilda and Lee Temkin. *A Unique and Exciting Action Program.*

Adult Literacy Program, Report of the Fourth District of Wisconsin Congress of Parents and Teachers. Milwaukee, Wisconsin: Annual Meeting of National Congress of Parents and Teachers, 1966.

Dodds, William J. A Longitudinal Study of Two Beginning Reading Programs: Words in Color and Traditional Basal Readers. Unpublished doctoral dissertation. Cleveland, Ohio: Western Reserve University, School of Education, 1966.

Dulcina, Sister M., C.PP.S. "Words in Color: Excerpts from a First Grade Teacher's Diary," *The Community Post,* (September 29 - December 23). Minster, Ohio: 1965, ten articles.

Fowles, Mary. *Elementary Education Enhanced,* a third monograph in a series on *Words in Color in the Classroom.* Copies available in this country from Schools for the Future, P.O. Box 349, Cooper Station, New York, New York 10003. Reading, England: Educational Explorers Limited, 1968.

Gallagher, Joan. *With the Five Year Olds,* a fourth monograph in a series on *Words in Color in the Classroom.* Copies available in this country from Schools for the Future, P.O. Box 349, Cooper Station, New York, New York 10003. Reading, England: Educational Explorers Limited, 1968.

Gattegno, C. *La Lecture en Couleurs: Guide du Maître.* Neuchâtel, Switzerland: Delachaux and Nièstle, 1966.

—— *Metodo Morfologico-Algebraico,* Segunda edicion, completamente revisada. Madrid, Spain: Cuisenaire de España, 1961.

—— *The Morphologico-Algebraic Approach to Reading and Writing,* ed. D. Hinman. Mimeographed by the Student Government of the San Francisco State College Center. Santa Rosa, California: 1959.

—— *Notes on Words in Color,* Pamphlet. Reading, England: Educational Explorers Limited, 11 Crown Street, 1963.

—— *Report on One Month Experiment in Public School 113 in New York City.* Mimeographed. New York, New York: Schools for the Future, P.O. Box 349, Cooper Station, 1966.

—— "Short Passages." Part of the *Silent Way for Teaching English As a Second Language.* Reading, England: Educational Explorers Limited, 1968.

—— "The Subordination of Teaching to Learning," *Teaching Foreign Languages in Schools.* Reading, England: Educational Explorers Limited, 1963, Ch. 1.

—— "Teaching Reading: An Indefinitely Renewable Problem," *Spelling Progress Bulletin.* North Hollywood, California: 5848 Alcove Avenue, 1964.

—— *What Does Words in Color Demand of Us?* New York, New York: Schools for the Future, 1966.

—— *Words in Color — Background and Principles,* revised edition of *The Morphologico-Algebraic Approach to Reading and Writing.*

New York, New York: Learning Materials, Inc., Xerox Education Division, 600 Madison Avenue, 1962.

—— *Words in Color — Classroom and Pupil Materials,* revised edition. New York, New York: Learning Materials, Inc., Xerox Education Division, 1962-63.

—— *Words in Color: Further Reading.* 3 vols.: (1. The Eastern Beam, 2. The White Canary, 3. The Magic Forest and Other Tales.) Reading, England: Educational Explorers Limited, 1968.

—— "Words in Color—The Morphologico-Algebraic Approach to Teaching Reading," *The Disabled Reader: Education of the Dyslexic Child,* ed. John Money. Baltimore, Maryland: The Johns Hopkins Press, 1966, Chap. 11.

—— *Words in Color—Teacher's Guide,* revised edition, New York, New York: Learning Materials, Inc., Xerox Education Division, 1962.

Hinds, Lillian R. *An Evaluation of Words in Color or Morphologico-Algebraic Approach to Teaching Reading to Functionally Illiterate Adults.* Unpublished doctoral dissertation. Cleveland, Ohio: Western Reserve University, School of Education, 1966.

Hinman, D.: "The Current Status of Words in Color in the United States," *The Disabled Reader: Education of the Dyslexic Child,* ed. John Money. Baltimore, Maryland: The Johns Hopkins Press, 1966, Addendum to Ch. 11.

—— *Questions Frequently Asked About Words in Color,* pamphlet. New York, New York: Learning Materials, Inc., Xerox Education Division, 1962-63.

—— "Words in Color," *Current Approaches to Teaching Reading,* ed. Helen K. Mackintosh. Elementary Instructional Service Leaflet. Washington, D.C.: Chief Elementary School Organization Section, U. S. Office of Education, EKNE Department, National Educational Association, 1965.

Holland, Allan R. *A Comparative Study of First Grade Reading Programs: Initial Teaching Alphabet, Words in Color, and a Traditional Basic Reading Approach.* Unpublished doctoral dissertation. Cleveland, Ohio: Western Reserve University, School of Education, 1967.

Holland, Merry. *My Experience Teaching Words in Color in a First Grade.* Unpublished master's research project. San Francisco, California: San Francisco State College, 1966.

Hopkin, Brenda. "Eight Hours to Literacy," *School and College Journal*. England: 1964. Jones, Gretchen H. *An Experiment Evaluating the Words in Color Method of Teaching Reading to Fourth and Fifth Grade Pupils*. Unpublished master's research project. Deland, Florida: Stetson University, 1965.

Lee, Terrence. *Writing the Talking*. Report by County Borough of Rotherham Education Committee. England: Schools Psychological Service, 1967.

Leonore (Murphy), Sister Mary, R.S.C. *Beginning to Read: A Report on Teaching of Reading, Writing and Spelling in the Infant School*. Reading, England: Educational Explorers Limited, 1964.

—— *Creative Writing*, a first monograph in a series on *Words in Color in the Classroom*. Copies available in this country from Schools for the Future, P.O. Box 349, Cooper Station, New York, New York, 10003. Reading, England: Educational Explorers Limited, 1966.

—— *Douglas Can't Read*, a second monograph in a series on *Words in Color in the Classroom*. Copies available in this country from Schools for the Future, P.O. Box 349, Cooper Station, New York, New York 10003. Reading, England: Educational Explorers Limited, 1968.

—— *To Perceive and to Write*, a fifth monograph in a series on *Words in Color in the Classroom*. Copies available in this country from Schools for the Future, P.O. Box 349, Cooper Station, New York, New York 10003. Reading, England: Educational Explorers Limited, 1968.

"Reading by the Rainbow," *Friends*, (October, 1966). Detroit, Michigan: Ceco Publishing Company (Chevrolet), 1966.

"Reading by Rainbow," *Time*, Vol. 83, No. 24, (June 12, 1964). Report on Dr. Gattegno's demonstration at the U.S. Office of Education, (May 26-28, 1964). New York, New York: Time-Life, Inc., 1964.

Spaulding, Robert L. *Report of the Durham Educational Improvement Program—A Project of the Ford Foundation*. Durham, North Carolina: Duke University, 1966.

Steele, Jeremy. *A Solution for Secondary School Non-Readers*. Reading, England: Educational Explorers Limited, 1965.

"Words in Color," *Current Approaches to Teaching Reading*. Washington, D.C.: National Education Association Journal, December 1965.

Films and Filmstrips

Gattegno, C. *Words in Color*. Training film, color, 16mm, 39 min. Copies available in this country from Schools for the Future, P.O. Box 349, Cooper Station, New York, New York, 10003. Reading, England: Educational Explorers Limited, 1965.

Words in Color. 32mm filmstrip of 29 frames showing each of the 21 Word Charts and the 8 Phonic Code Charts. New York, New York: Learning Materials, Inc., Xerox Education Division, 1963.

Index

Addition, 34, 36, 37, 44, 54, 60-63, 77, 79, 80, 89, 110, 112, 113, 139, 143, 211

Algebraic operations, 120

insertion, 36, 37, 50, 60, 62, 63, 77, 79, 80, 89, 110, 112, 139, 211
repetition, 13, 15, 16, 17, 41, 122, 125, 157
reversal, 15, 18, 34, 36, 37, 44, 45, 50, 56, 60, 61, 63, 77, 79, 80, 85, 85, 110, 113, 211
substitution, 34, 36, 37, 44, 60, 63, 77, 79, 80, 85, 110, 111, 113
subtraction, 37, 60, 63, 110, 111, 113
susbtitution, 60

Alphabet, 14, 107, 151, 166

Appendix, 81

Blending

syllables, 18, 20, 21, 23, 26, 28, 43, 44
words, 20, 23, 44

Books

Book 1, 12, 16, 15, 22, 23, 25- 27, 29, 31, 32, 39, 41, 42, 48, 60, 67, 196, 207
Book 2, 9, 36, 75, 76, 80, 86-93, 96, 98, 99, 103, 117, 151, 163, 201
Book 3, 123, 127, 128, 135, 140, 144, 145, 156, 157, 158, 159, 164, 165, 168, 207, 217
Book of Stories, 102, 103, 104, 127, 156, 164, 168, 169, 175, 176, 190, 194, 196, 07

Capitals, 156, 166, 167

Codification, 42

Color

color-blind, 70
correspondence with function, 184
correspondence with color, 71
correspondence with grammatical function, 165, 181, 183, 186
correspondence with grammatical functions, 186, 189
correspondence with sound, 171, 186, 190

Combination, 15, 17, 18, 41, 43, 74, 84, 105, 107, 122, 134, 145

Completion games, 58, 60, 108

Comprehension, 33, 52, 54, 172

Consonants, 6, 13, 17, 23, 26, 28, 34, 44, 73, 83, 98, 122, 123, 140, 145, 165

Continuous feedback, 82

Conventions of the written code, 6

Correct, 7, 33, 36, 48, 50, 51, 56, 57, 58, 66, 106, 120, 144, 152, 153, 154, 176, 181, 186, 201

Correction
self, 108

Criteria, 49, 51, 105, 106, 119, 121, 155, 158, 159, 194, 196
inner, 16, 105, 154, 163

Cumulative effect of learning, 3, 74, 95, 97, 123, 138, 143, 198

Decoding, 8, 14, 92, 200

Diacritical marks, 168

Diphthong, 15, 71, 141, 143

Equivalence, 89, 110, 111, 113, 200, 211
horizontal, 110, 112, 139
vertical, 110-113

Experience
by proxy, 9, 174
spectrum of, 164
vicarious, 9

First Certificate of Reading, 2, 11, 207

Functioning, 7, 18, 29, 154, 175, 201

Game of Transformations, 8, 43, 43, 59, 65, 81, 85, 86, 98, 109, 111, 114, 119, 150, 211

Games, 40, 41, 55, 58, 59, 60, 65, 67, 82, 85, 94, 109, 111, 114, 144, 150, 151, 157, 159, 182, 184, 185, 186, 189, 191, 196, 200

Grammar, 3, 9, 160, 177, 181, 189, 190, 193, 194, 196, 220

Graphemes, 27, 55, 107, 121, 122, 123, 124, 127

Horizontal equivalence, 110 112, 113, 139

Imagery, 22, 35, 40, 48, 60, 87, 153, 154, 163

Images, 55, 58, 98, 106, 108, 122, 124, 138, 153, 154, 161, 163, 169, 176

Imagination, 19, 30, 39, 40, 41, 42, 57, 59, 86, 87, 97, 102, 106, 108, 120, 162, 164, 173, 174, 187, 189

Inner criteria, 16, 105, 154, 163

Insertion, 36, 37, 50, 60, 62, 63, 77, 79, 80, 89, 110, 112, 139, 211

Intonation, 4, 9, 25, 28, 29, 33, 153, 154, 178, 179
proper, 6, 29, 68

Language
phonetic, 5

Languages, 2, 3, 5, 6, 12, 15, 104, 122, 125, 177

Linguistic
awareness, 8, 9
growth, 109
powers, 2, 9, 17, 53

Meaning, 4-7, 8, 20, 33, 46, 48, 52, 57, 59, 102, 106, 122, 124, 131, 133, 142, 150-156, 157, 160, 161, 164, 170, 178, 179, 186, 191, 193-196, 198, **See** *also Comprehension, Understanding*

Memorization, 38, 73, 125

Memory, 18, 25, 27, 34, 35, 125, 148, 178, 179

Mental transformations, 46, 80, 130

Mistakes, 125, 154

Motivation, 18

Object (gr.), 190, 195, 196

Oral dictation, 14, 15, 48, 49, 50, 51, 52, 82, 102, 103, 127, 150, 151, 153, 154, 155, 178

Parts of speech (gr.), 181, 190

Permutation, 17, 56, 57, 105, 122

Phonemes, 27, 55, 107, 121, 122, 124

Phonetic clue, 7, 72, 96

Phonic Code, 31, 41, 72, 98, 110, 111, 119, 128, 140, 142, 143, 145, 147, 148, 149, 150, 151, 152, 153, 156, 166, 168, 179, 207, 217, 241

Pointer, 6, 11-33, 39, 42, 49, 50, 51, 52, 56, 75, 77, 80, 82, 84, 87, 122, 143, 148, 150, 151, 153, 157, 178, 184, 185, 187

Punctuation marks, 156, 166, 186

Reading
as-talking, 6
first certificate of, 2, 11, 207
fluency, 142
fluent, 55, 68
second certificate of, 125

Recognition, 9, 18, 31, 57, 84, 105, 106, 107, 133, 197

Remedial, 12, 15, 42, 76, 130, 145, 150, 237

Repetition, 13, 15, 16, 17, 41, 122, 125, 127

Restricted language, 2, 3, 9, 15, 27, 38, 39, 42, 52, 54, 55, 58, 67, 68, 72, 105, 97, 102, 103, 123, 154
vocabulary, 39, 72, 95, 103

Reversal, 15, 18, 34, 36, 37, 44, 45, 50, 56, 60, 61, 63, 77, 79, 80, 85, 89, 110, 113, 211

Reward, 8, 18

Roman type, 156

Schwa, 73, 74, 76, 88, 123, 131, 145, 211

Second Certificate of Reading, 125

Self-correction, 108

Sentence
structure, 78, 164, 189, 191
study, 31, 43, 78, 82

Sequence for use of the materials, 179, 207

Silence, 17, 20, 187

Slow learners, 130, 143

Sound, 4, 5, 6, 12, 13, 15, 16, 18, 19, 20, 21, 22, 23, 25, 29, 30, 34, 35, 36, 55, 57, 59, 69-75, 77, 81, 83, 84, 85, 88, 89, 90, 91, 93, 94, 97, 98, 106, 107, 110, 111, 112, 122, 123, 124, 128, 130-142, 144, 145, 150-154, 156-159, 165, 192, 193, 211, 217
correspondence with color, 24, 69, 70, 71, 73, 75, 77, 83, 84, 88, 89, 90, 91, 110, 128, 133, 135, 136, 138, 139, 141, 147

Speech
parts of (gr.), 181, 190
speed of, 50, 176
spoken, 4, 42, 44, 67, 162, 164, 172, 177, 178, 199, 200
written, 5, 153, 177, 191, 193, 199

Spelling, 3, 6, 7, 14, 24-26, 37, 85, 88, 92, 98, 107, 110, 122, 125, 128, 135, 136, 137, 138, 140, 142, 144, 145, 147, 150, 151, 152, 153, 154, 155, 156, 159, 160, 172, 176, 217
correct, 7

Spoken speech, 4, 42, 44, 67, 145, 162, 164, 172, 177, 178, 199, 200

Stress, 4, 20, 48, 96, 98, 132, 161, 173

Structure (gr.)
analysis of sentence, 78, 134

basic sentence, 191
rules for sentence, 189
Subject (gr.), 190, 195
Subordinating teaching to learning, 68
Substitution, 34, 36, 37, 44, 60, 63, 77, 79, 80, 85, 89, 110, 111, 139, 211
Subtraction, 37, 60, 63, 110, 111, 113, 118
Syllables, 6, 17, 18, 19, 20, 21, 22, 23, 24, 27, 28, 43, 44, 91, 131, 134, 165, 222
Table, 26, 41, 55, 56, 92, 102, 107, 120, 122, 123, 144, 145, 147, 148, 187, 189, 207, 222
Temporal sequence, 5, 6, 7, 31, 122, 142
Tests, 57, 104, 120, 157, 194, 195, 196, 197, 198, 199
Time, 1, 5-7, 13, 16, 17, 25, 33, 51, 94, 108, 122, 161, 175, 178, 192, 200
consciousness of, 192
Transfer, 18, 20, 21, 33, 34, 190
Transformation, 34, 37, 38, 39, 40, 43, 52, 60, 63, 64, 65, 77, 79, 80, 84, 85, 110, 111, 114, 119, 139, 150, 197, 201
Triphthongs, 15
Understanding, 9, 11, 29, 38, 55, 57, 63, 72, 93, 105, 106, 110, 121, 125, 143, 145, 147, 153, 155, 160, 163, 173, 174, 177, 179, 217
Unstressed vowels, 18
Vertical equivalence, 110, 111, 112
Visual Dictation, 13, 16

Visual Dictation 1, 17, 25, 27, 28, 29, 31, 32, 36, 38, 40, 41, 42, 43, 46, 52, 54, 59, 75, 76, 92, 96, 122, 143, 148, 149
Visual Dictation 2, 25, 29, 31, 32, 33, 39, 42, 43, 46, 49, 51, 52, 54, 76, 78, 79, 86, 92, 102, 129, 157, 159, 184, 185, 186
Visual Dictation 3, 48, 54, 102, 103, 161
Vocabulary, 9, 14, 41, 42, 44, 72, 95, 103, 142, 164, 169, 170, 172, 173, 175, 176, 177, 222
Voice, 4, 153, 108
Vowels, 6, 7, 18, 23, 26, 27, 73, 165
"long" and "short", 15, 74, 97, 123
unstressed, 18
Word Building Book, 11, 26, 27, 29, 30, 40, 41, 42, 52, 56, 58, 65, 67, 76, 92, 93, 98, 100, 102, 105, 101, 110, 120, 121, 122, 123, 127, 140, 143, 144, 145, 147, 148, 157, 160, 207
Word Cards, 176, 178, 181, 182, 183, 187, 189, 191, 192, 207
Word Charts, 78
Word Chart 1, 15, 31, 73
Word Chart 2, 12, 13, 31, 32, 33, 36, 37, 38, 41, 42, 43, 48, 49, 53, 60, 75, 76, 78, 79, 85, 213
Word Chart 3, 30, 55, 73, 74, 75, 76, 79, 81, 82, 83, 89, 93, 96, 213
Word Chart 4, 13, 31, 55, 71, 76, 79, 83, 84, 89, 95, 97, 145, 214, 215
Word Chart 5, 85, 86, 89, 215
Word Chart 6, 85, 89, 211, 216
Word Chart 7, 71, 76, 88
Word Chart 8, 75, 89
Word Chart 9, 89, 131, 135
Word Chart 10, 89, 90, 98
Word Chart 11, 89, 90, 98
Word Chart 12, 85, 88, 90

Word Chart 13, 89, 128
Word Chart 14, 130
Word Chart 15, 96, 132
Word Chart 16, 134
Word Chart 17, 135
Word Chart 18, 136
Word Chart 19, 138
Word Chart 20, 141
Word Chart 21, 141, 145

Words
as a medium, 163
function of, 160, 193
origins, 121, 168
study of, 8, 92, 161, 178

Worksheets
worksheet 1, 12, 26, 55, 56, 57, 58, 65, 73, 104, 114
worksheets 1-7, 104, 105, 207
worksheets 8-12, 157, 160, 173, 191
worksheet 13, 169, 175
worksheet 14, 176, 178, 194, 198

Writing
compositions, 42
creative, 67
free, 120
stories, 54, 102

www.ingramcontent.com/pod-product-compliance
Lightning Source LLC
Chambersburg PA
CBHW080535170426
43195CB00016B/2575